MW01102014

Department of ... English,
University of
Paul-Elizabeth.
27. vii. 92

THE REVELS PLAYS

ANTONIO AND MELLIDA

THE REVELS PLAYS

★available in paperback

THE REVELS PLAYS

ANTONIO AND MELLIDA

JOHN MARSTON

edited by W. Reavley Gair

MANCHESTER
UNIVERSITY PRESS
Manchester and New York

*Distributed exclusively in the USA and Canada
by* St. Martin's Press

Introduction, critical apparatus, etc.,
© W. Reavley Gair 1991

Published by Manchester University Press
Oxford Road, Manchester M13 9PL, UK
and Room 400, 175 Fifth Avenue,
New York, NY 10010, USA
Distributed exclusively in the USA and Canada
by St. Martin's Press, Inc.,
175 Fifth Avenue, New York, NY 10010, USA

ISBN 0 7190 1547 2 CASED

British Library Cataloguing in Publication Data
Marston, John 1575?–1634
    Antonio and Mellida.—(The Revels plays).
    I. Title
    822.3

Library of Congress Cataloging in Publication Data
Marston, John, 1575–1634.
    Antonio and Mellida/John Marston.
        p.   cm.—(The Revels plays)
    Includes index.
    ISBN 0-7190-1547-2
    I. Title.   II. Series.
    PR2694.A52   1991
    B22'.3—dc20   90-13557   CIP

Typeset in Hong Kong
by Best-Set Typesetter Ltd
Printed in Great Britain
by Bell and Bain Ltd., Glasgow

Contents

TO KATHRYN AND RONALD

General Editors' Preface

The series known as the Revels Plays was conceived by Clifford
Leech. The idea for the series emerged in his mind, as he explained in
his preface to the first of the Revels Plays in 1958, from the success of
the New Arden Shakespeare. The aim of the new group of texts was
'to apply to Shakespeare's predecessors, contemporaries and success-
ors the methods that are now used in Shakespeare editing'. The plays
chosen were to include well known works from the early Tudor period
to about 1700, as well as others less familiar but of literary and
theatrical merit: 'the plays included,' Leech wrote, 'should be such as
to deserve and indeed demand performance.' We owe it to Clifford
Leech that the idea became reality. He set the high standards of the
series, ensuring that editors of individual volumes produced work of
lasting merit, equally useful for teachers and students, theatre
directors and actors. Clifford Leech remained General Editor until
1971, and was succeeded by F. David Hoeniger, who retired in 1985.

The Revels Plays are now under the direction of four General
Editors, E. A. J. Honigmann, J. R. Mulryne, David Bevington and
E. M. Waith. The publishers, originally Methuen, are now Manchester University Press. Despite these changes, the format and essential
character of the series will continue, and it is hoped that its editorial
standards will be maintained. Except for some work in progress, the
General Editors intend, in expanding the series, to concentrate for the
immediate future on plays from the period 1558–1642, and may
include a small number of non-dramatic works of interest to students
of drama. Some slight changes have been forced by considerations of
cost. For example, in editions from 1978, notes to the introduction are
placed together at the end, not at the foot of the page. Collation and
commentary notes will continue, however, to appear on the relevant
pages.

The text of each Revels play, in accordance with established
practice in the series, is edited afresh from the original text of best
authority (in a few instances, texts), but spelling and punctuation are
modernised and speech headings are silently made consistent. Elisions
in the original are also silently regularised, except where metre would
be affected by the change; since 1968 the '-ed' form is used for

non-syllabic terminations in past tenses and past participles ('-'d' earlier), and '-èd' for syllabic ('-ed' earlier). The editor emends, as distinct from modernises, his original only in instances where error is patent, or at least very probable, and correction persuasive. Act divisions are given only if they appear in the original or if the structure of the play clearly points to them. Those act and scene divisions not found in the original are provided unobtrusively in small type and in square brackets. Square brackets are also used for any other additions to or changes in the stage directions of the original.

Revels Plays do not provide a variorum collation, but only those variants which require the critical attention of serious textual students. All departures of substance from 'copy-text' are listed, including any relineation and those changes in punctuation which involve to any degree a decision between alternative interpretations; but not such accidentals as turned letters, nor necessarily additions to stage directions whose editorial nature is already made clear by the use of brackets. Press corrections in the 'copy-text' are likewise included. Of later emendations of the text, only those are given which as alternative readings still deserve attention.

One of the hallmarks of the Revels Plays is the thoroughness of their annotations. Besides explaining the meaning of difficult words and passages, the editor provides comments on customs or usage, text or stage-business—indeed, on anything he judges pertinent and helpful. Each volume contains a Glossarial Index to the Commentary, in which particular attention is drawn to meanings for words not listed in *O.E.D.*

The Introduction to a Revels play assesses the authority of the 'copy-text' on which it is based, and discusses the editorial methods employed in dealing with it; the editor also considers his play's date and (where relevant) sources, together with its place in the work of the author and in the theatre of its time. Stage history is offered, and in the case of a play by an author not previously represented in the series a brief biography is given.

It is our hope that plays edited in this fashion will promote further scholarly and theatrical investigation of one of the richest periods in theatrical history.

E. A. J. HONIGMANN
J. R. MULRYNE
DAVID BEVINGTON
E. M. WAITH

Preface

In the preparation of this edition, my primary debt is to David Bevington, of the University of Chicago, general editor of the Revels series. He made many valuable suggestions for the introduction, text, and commentary to this play. My thanks are extended to Michael Mills of the University of New Brunswick for advice on a number of thorny matters of classical interpretation, and to David Crowther of Memorial University (Newfoundland) for much laborious proof-correction. My wife has constantly assisted in a variety of ways in the preparation of this work, and has always gladly assisted with the time-consuming details of its preparation.

Without the generous financial assistance of the Social Sciences and Humanities Research Council of Canada, the work on this text would have been much more difficult and would have taken much longer.

W. R. G.

Abbreviations

A.R.   *Antonio's Revenge.*
Bond   R. W. Bond, *The Complete Works of John Lyly*, Oxford: Clarendon
Press, 3 vols., 1902.
Bullen   A. H. Bullen, *The Works of John Marston*, London: J. C. Nimmo,
vol. 1, 1887 (reprinted Hildesheim: Georg Olms, 1970).
Dent   R. W. Dent, *Proverbial Language in English Drama Exclusive of
Shakespeare 1495–1616*, Berkeley: U. of California Press, 1984.
Dilke   C. W. Dilke, *Old English Plays: Being a Selection from the Early
Dramatic Writers*, London: Whittingham and Rowland, vol. 2, 1814.
E.E.T.S.   Early English Texts Society.
Feuillerat   A. Feuillerat, *The Complete Works of Sir Philip Sidney*, Cam-
bridge: C.U.P., 4 vols., 1912–26.
Halliwell   J. O. Halliwell, *The Works of John Marston*, London: J. R. Smith,
vol. 1, 1856.
H.L.Q.   *Huntington Library Quarterly.*
Hunter   G. K. Hunter, The Regents Renaissance Drama Texts, *The History
of Antonio and Mellida*, London: Edward Arnold, 1965.
J & N   Macdonald P. Jackson and Michael Neil, *The Selected Plays of John
Marston*, Cambridge: C.U.P., 1986.
Jack Drum   *Jack Drum's Entertainment or The Comedy of Pasquil and
Katherine.*
Keltie   J. S. Keltie, *The Works of the British Dramatists*, Edinburgh: W. P.
Nimmo, 1870.
McKerrow   R. B. McKerrow, *The Works of Thomas Nashe*, London:
Sidgwick and Jackson, 5 vols., 1910.
M.L.N.   *Modern Language Notes.*
M.L.R.   *Modern Language Review.*
N. & Q.   *Notes and Queries.*
O.E.D.   *Oxford English Dictionary.*
Paul's   Reavley Gair, *The Children of Paul's: the Story of a Theatre Company,
1553–1608*, Cambridge: C.U.P., 1982.
P.M.L.A.   *Publications of the Modern Language Association of America.*
Q   Quarto.
R.E.S.   *Review of English Studies.*
S. of V.   *Scourge of Villainy.*
Schoonover   Katherine Schoonover, 'An Edition of John Marston's *Antonio
and Mellida*', Ph.D. diss., Toronto, 1976.
Sh. Q.   *Shakespeare Quarterly.*
St. Phil.   *Studies in Philology.*
1633   W. Sheares, *The Works of John Marston*, London, 1633.
U. P.   University Press.
Wood   H. H. Wood, *The Plays of John Marston*, Edinburgh: Oliver and
Boyd, vol. 1, 1934.

All quotations from the plays of Shakespeare are taken from *The Complete Works*, ed. P. Alexander, London: Collins, 1951. Quotations from the plays of Ben Jonson are derived from the Herford and Simpson edition (Oxford: Clarendon Press, 1925–52) and citations from the works of Seneca are taken from the editions in the Loeb series. The translations from the plays of Seneca, unless otherwise indicated, are also taken from the Loeb volumes. Marston's poems are cited from the edition of A. Davenport, Liverpool: Liverpool U. P., 1961. These citations, however, along with all other citations from Elizabethan authors, have been modernised.

THE
HISTORY OF
Antonio and
Mellida.

The firſt part.

As it hath beene ſundry times aɛted,
by the children of Paules.

Written by *I.* *M.*

LONDON.
¶Printed for *Mathewe Lownes,* and *Thomas Fiſher,* and
are to be ſoulde in Saint Dunſtans Church-yarde.
1602.

Title-page of the 1602 quarto

Introduction

(a) The Quarto

Antonio and Mellida was entered in the Stationers' Register on 24
October 1601 by Mathew Lownes and Thomas Fisher. The Register
describes it as 'a booke called The ffyrst and second partes of the play
called Anthonio and melida' and, of course, the second part is
Antonio's Revenge. Both plays were published in quarto in 1602. The
title-page of *Antonio and Mellida* affirms that 'it hath beene sundry
times acted, by the children of Paules'; it is 'Written by I. M.' and it is
to be sold 'in Saint Dunstans Church-yarde'. On the title-page there is
a halcyon device which belongs to Thomas Fisher; the printer was
Richard Bradock.[1]

The quarto is, on the whole, well printed and the five acts, with all
their introductory apparatus, are neatly fitted into nine full gather-
ings. Bradock did, however, use a set of very badly cast punctuation
marks: colons lean to the right; in semi-colons, colons, and question
marks the upper portion of the point often fails to print; full points
appear on, above, and below the line; some marks are indeterminate,
either commas, periods, or slurs. No real attempt has been made to
indicate the many interrupted speeches in the play, and there are
some instances of mislineation. On the other hand, proof reading is,
spasmodically, in evidence.

The Lownes and Fisher quarto of *Antonio and Mellida* exists in
seven states. There are eleven copies of the quarto known to me. Six
of them, one of those in the British Library (643.c.78), and the copies
in the Victoria and Albert Museum, the Bodleian Library, the Folger
Shakespeare Library, Princeton University Library, and the Henry
E. Huntington library all conform, in every respect, to each other.
The second of the three copies in the British Library (C.131.c.16) is
also, essentially, to be included in this group, for it conforms in all
respects to the other six with the single exception of the reading at
Induction 130 which reads 'censure', whereas in the other quartos (on
B) there is a slur over the first 'e' and the 'n' is, therefore, omitted.

The consistent running title of these seven copies is 'Antonio and
Mellida.' and 'The first part of' or 'The first Parte of', but the copy in

the Boston Public Library has variant running titles at B2v (Prologue), where it reads, 'The first Part of' (no 'e' on 'Parte'), and on B4v (I.i.) is found, 'The first booke of' (a change from 'parte' to 'booke'). Otherwise the text conforms, in every particular, to the other seven.

The third copy in the British Library, Ashley 1099, which was formerly owned by T. J. Wise, contains two variant readings. At C3 (II.i.33) is found, '. . . for feare of being then of marke', whereas the other copies of the Quarto read '. . . for feare of being men of marke'. In addition at E3v (III.ii.49) there is 'That creature faire; but prout; him rich, but so:', whereas the general reading is, 'That creature faire; but proud; him rich, but sot:'. In both cases it is, I suggest, self-evident that these are alterations made to correct misplaced or omitted type.

The copy in the Harvard University Library also varies on E3v, where it reads, 'That creature faire; but proud; him rich, but so:'; in this case it is the final 't' of the last word in the line which has had to be replaced. The situation is similar in the case of the Texas copy (formerly in the Pforzheimer), where E3v reads, 'That creature faire; but prout; him rich, but so:'. In this case not merely is the final 't' omitted, but the error previously seen in Ashley, 'prout' for 'proud', is also present.

These corrections in proof would suggest that the Ashley, Harvard, and Texas copies of the quarto contain one (in Ashley's case two) early sheets which had not yet been corrected in the printing house. The Boston copy, with its variant running headings, is unique, but has no bearing on the establishment of the text of the present edition; the case is similar with the British Library copy C.131.c.16. All the variants in proof are of the same kind: obvious corrections noticed at the time when the sheets were being printed and altered in the printing house. They do not amount to alternative possibilities for the text itself.[2] I have, therefore, based the text of this edition on a full collation of all copies of the quarto known to me, using as my copy text the eight essentially identical copies of the edition previously enumerated.

The manuscript used to set the play in type gives the impression overall of being a literary autograph rather than a prompt book, but it does contain some clearly theatrical elements. At IV.i.28.1 (F4v), occurs the direction, 'Enter Andrugio, Lucio, Cole, and Norwod'; the list of choristers at Paul's in 1598 included a Robert Coles and a John Norwood.[3] This stage direction, then, preserves the names of two of the original actors of the play. Further evidence of this kind is supplied by the text of *Antonio's Revenge*, where on E3 (III.i.1–2), the quarto reads:

> *An.* The black iades of swart night trot foggy rings
> Bout heavens browe. (12) Tis now starke deade night.

The number in parentheses, which directs the sounding of the chimes of midnight, is a note to the prompter for the sound effect to be inserted. All of these theatrical notes could, however, have been made by Marston in his autograph manuscript.

The literary quality of the text is clearly established by a number of other features. One sign of this origin for the text is the presence in the quarto of numerous italicised *sententiae*, or 'scholarly' citations, from Seneca as *Dimitto superos, summa votorum attigi*, B3 (1.i.60); *O me Celitum excelsissimum!*, B3*v* (1.i.78); *O lares, misereri lares*, G*v* (IV.i.87), and from Virgil, Sinequeo flectere superos, Acheronta mouebo, A2 (Dedication); *Sic, sic iuuat ire sub umbras*, 14 (V.ii.238). This use of highlighting in the text is likely to have been a device to confer academic weight upon 'the worthless present of my slighter idleness' (Dedication, 7–8). Similarly, some phraseology in the stage directions sounds latinate in form, e.g., '*Beeing entred, they make a stand in diuided foyles*', B2*v* (1.i.34.4–5), where the influence of the ablative absolute construction is apparent. There are, also, several speech headings missing in the quarto, A3 (Ind.1), E (III.i.12), FI*v* (III.ii.149), G4 (IV.i.217), and H3*v* (V.ii.4), as well as many omissions of necessary exits. These missing directives may well be the result of the author's concern with the continuity of the action, rather than the details of the staging of the play.

Further evidence of literary autograph origin for the quarto is found at B3 (1.i.75–7), which reads:

> *Fel.* Confusion to these limber Sycophants.
> No sooner mischief's borne in regenty,
> But flattery christens it with pollicy. *tacitè*.

This marginal annotation uses the Latin for 'silently' or 'secretly' to indicate an aside or soliloquy.

The majority of the evidence about the nature of the manuscript used to set the Lownes and Fisher quarto would suggest that it was Marston's original autograph to which some details had been added as a result of the performance of the play. William Percy, who, at the turn of the seventeenth century, wrote plays designed for the Children

4 ANTONIO AND MELLIDA

of Paul's, also appears to have added notes and details to autograph copies of his plays, as a result of performances.[4]

The text of the quarto, as it has been received, represents the first whole dramatic composition by John Marston, who in 1599 was twenty-three years old. It is, as might be expected, heavily literary in its dependence upon other authors for most of its plot and its characters. It also displays signs of haste; no scenes are marked in *Antonio and Mellida*, whereas in *Antonio's Revenge*, the acts are carefully divided into scenes. There is also some evidence of carelessness in composition, e.g., at v.ii.54, where Galeazzo is called 'Prince of Milan', whereas in fact he is 'Prince of Florence'. On a number of occasions the metre is uneven, with syllables either omitted or unnecessarily included in the line, and a half-state between prose and verse is not uncommon, e.g., v.ii.81−94 (and see v.ii.39−40n). In addition, at iv.i.77−9, there appear to be first and second versions of the manuscript text printed in the Quarto side by side. These are all, however, features which we might expect to find in a young man's first composition for a new stage. When *Antonio and Mellida* was first presented at Paul's, its text was somewhat hesitant and uneven. The object of this edition has been to attempt to provide for the reader a text of the play as nearly as possible like that first performed in late 1599.

(b) Later editions

In 1633 William Sheares, 'at the Harrowe in *Britaines Bursse*', published a collected edition of six of Marston's plays: *Antonio and Mellida*, *Antonio's Revenge*, *Sophonisba*, *What You Will*, *The Fawn*, and *The Dutch Courtesan*. *Antonio and Mellida* occupied signatures B to E6 in this octavo edition. Sheares edited *Antonio and Mellida* independently from a copy of the 1602 quarto, modified various textual obscurities, improved the lineation, and reduced the printer's errors, but, in so doing, he also removed many of Marston's verbal coinages by substituting more familiar, current forms, as with 'heavy' for 'heathy' (Prol. 17), and 'sudden' for 'sodden' (iv.ii.11). There are two issues of Sheares's 1633 edition: the first describes it as *The Workes of Mr. John Marston*, whereas the second declares it to be, merely, *Tragedies and Comedies collected into one volume*. As the Malone editor remarks, Sheares's edition was 'an unintelligent stationer's reprint produced ... during the author's absence and apparently contrary to his wishes, for his name was later removed from the remaining portion of the stock'.[5]

The only other seventeenth-century issue of Marston's plays was by Henry Mortlock. In his *Remains of Sr. Walter Raleigh,* 1675, Mortlock advertises '*Mr. John Marston's six Playes, in 8vo.*' The only known example of this collection has been broken up by the Huntington Library, and its plays sold off as separate units.

The first modern edition of the play appeared in 1814; edited by C. W. Dilke, it formed one of his *Old English Plays: Being a Selection from the Early Dramatic Writers,* London: Whittingham and Rowland, 2:99–193. While Dilke's work mainly followed Sheares's edition of 1633 rather than the quarto of 1602, it did much invaluable pioneering work on the text. Dilke expanded contractions, corrected the Italian dialogue, made changes to the prose/verse lineation, and translated Latin stage directions. Many of his textual corrections have been accepted in the present edition.

Dilke was followed by J. O. Halliwell in 1856, *The Works of John Marston,* London: J. R. Smith, I:1–68, who declares that his edition presents the plays 'reprinted absolutely from the early editions, which were placed in the hands of our printers, who thus had the advantage of following them without the intervention of a transcriber. They are given as nearly as possible in their original state, the only modernization consisting in the alterations of the letters *i* and *j* and *u* and *v*' (I:xxii). In fact, however, while based on the 1602 quarto, this edition is no facsimile, for Halliwell makes many 'silent' adjustments to the text, mainly derived from Sheares's edition. J. S. Keltie was next after Halliwell. In *The Works of the British Dramatists,* Edinburgh: W. P. Nimmo, 1870, pp. 347–64, Keltie, on the whole, adopted Dilke's methods, but based his text mainly on the 1602 quarto. As with Halliwell, Keltie declared that his text was 'printed as it stands in the original editions, except that the spelling is modernized' (p. 347); he, in fact, made a number of unacknowledged grammatical and verbal 'modernizations'.

The most influential of the modern editions and one still fairly readily available, is that by A. H. Bullen, *The Works of John Marston,* London: J. C. Nimmo, 2 or 3 vols., 1887, and reprinted Hildesheim: Georg Olms, 1970. *Antonio and Mellida* is to be found in vol. 1:1–93. Bullen began the process of supplying the text with the modern *apparatus criticus,* with notes on variant readings, and explanatory and illustrative commentary taken from earlier editors. Bullen based much of his commentary on Dilke, but added many notes of his own. His text was based on the 1602 quarto with adjustments from the 1633 edition. Bullen divided Act III into two scenes, whereas previous editors had left all the acts undivided, as in the quarto. Next to appear was a facsimile reprint (no. 46) in the Malone series, *Antonio and Mellida and Antonio's Revenge*, London and Oxford: Oxford U.P., 1921, edited by W. W. Greg. This edition began the process of the collation of the quarto copies of the text; it was based on British Library copies C.131.c.16, and 643.c.78, and on the copies in the Dyce collection and the Bodleian.

In 1934 *Antonio and Mellida* appeared in the most recent complete edition of Marston's plays, by H. H. Wood, *The Plays of John Marston*, Edinburgh: Oliver and Boyd, 1934, I:1–63. This edition aroused much critical acrimony. It purported to be an accurate rendition of the 1602 quarto in old spelling, but, in fact, it is inconsistent in almost all respects; punctuation and spelling changes are varied and often arbitrary; emendations have been adopted haphazardly from earlier editors; stage directions are often changed, and the commentary ranges from the most austere of act, scene, and line references to speculative suggestions as to origins for the plot. Wood's edition suffers from an inconsistency of editorial philosophy; it fails to be either a modern edition or a diplomatic reprint.

A later edition of *Antonio and Mellida* is that by G. K. Hunter for the Regents Renaissance Drama Texts (*The History of Antonio and Mellida*, London: Edward Arnold, 1965). This edition is in modern spelling and is mainly based upon the 1602 quarto and the editorial work of Bullen but, because of economies of space, its collation and commentary are severely limited. Hunter accepted Bullen's division of Act III into two scenes and further divided Acts IV and V into two scenes each.

The most recent edition of a selection of Marston's plays (*Antonio and Mellida, Antonio's Revenge, The Malcontent, The Dutch Courtesan, Sophonisba*) is in a series published by Cambridge University Press: *Plays by Renaissance and Restoration Dramatists*. The Marston volume is edited by Macdonald P. Jackson and Michael Neil, 1986, and *Antonio and Mellida* occupies pages 7–91. The text is in modern spelling (with the exception of the names of the characters), and the series declares that its texts are 'fully annotated', with notes to 'gloss the text or enlarge upon its literary, historical or social allusions' (Preface). While the text is edited from a copy of the 1602 Quarto, the editors rely upon previous editions for all collations; they make, however, many emendations to the Lownes and Fisher quarto. The notes, which are limited by restrictions of space, do not always supply the literary references to the quotations embedded in the text and are, more often than not, explanatory rather than amplificatory. The introduction is limited to an outline biography and a bibliography.

There have been two editions as doctoral dissertations. The first is by Conrad Stolzenbach, 'A Critical Acting Edition of *Antonio and Mellida*', University of Michigan, 1963. This edition is in modern spelling, with the text and notes based largely upon Bullen. The second, a much more substantial contribution to the editorial work on this play, is by Katherine Schoonover (University of Toronto, 1976). The text is in modern spelling, and there is a wide selection of comparative usages of words and phrases in the commentary. Some of Ms Schoonover's notes have been utilised in the present edition.

(c) This edition

The present text is based upon the copy of the Lownes and Fisher quarto in the Folger Shakespeare Library; against this, all other extant copies of the quarto have been collated. There are no divisions into scenes in any of the quartos; Bullen was the first to divide up the text in this way and he was followed by Hunter. There is no reason to reject their precedent.

All departures from the quarto are recorded in the collation, and a conservative attitude has been adoped towards emendations. While no attempt has been made to provide a variorum collation, emendations of the quarto are collated when and if they suggest a substantial verbal or sense change in the copy text. If there exists a choice of possibilities of more or less equal probability, all are recorded in the collation. Minor variations in spelling and punctuation are ignored, and foul case and turned letters are silently corrected. Whenever the quarto text made some sense it has been retained, since Marston was often deliberately striving for meaning by new and radical syntactical devices; sometimes these were explicit, sometimes they remained obscure. Whether clear or cloudy, however, these often tortuous statements are likely to be Marston's original words.

In accordance with the practice of this series, the spelling in the text, commentary, and introduction has been modernised. This process has also been applied to the names of the characters. Where the original form of the spelling of words, as they appear in the quarto, seems to indicate an attempt by Marston to combine two or more senses into one word, these forms are commented upon in detail in the commentary.

The punctuation has been adjusted to conform to modern practice. The punctuation of this edition is generally lighter than that of the

quarto, and the many run-on and interrupted speeches have been
punctuated by the use of the dash, to interfere as little as possible with
the freedom of the flow of the rhetoric. There are a number of
instances where one character cites the precise words of another, or an
identifiable word or phrase which is intentionally highlighted in a
speech. These have been shown by the use of single quotation marks.

While the quarto is relatively rich in precise stage directions for the
larger movement of characters or groups about the playing areas, it is
often deficient in the more exact provision of 'exits' and 'asides', to
make the movement of the action explicit. These have been provided
and, in places, more elaborate, additional directions are supplied to
allow the reader some imaginative involvement with the action of the
play. These directions are given in accordance with the analysis of the
original performance of the play as given in the discussion on 'The
Play in its Theatre'.

2. JOHN MARSTON'S CONTEMPORARY REPUTATION[6]

According to contemporary satirists, there was in London at the turn
of the seventeenth century a poet who had distinctive red, curly hair,
and a beard, and was 'a man born upon little legs' (*Poetaster*, II.i.92).
He was also chronically in debt. In *The Gull's Hornbook*, of 1609,[7]
Thomas Dekker speaks further of these distinguishing features: '. . .
if the writer [of the play you are viewing] be a fellow that hath either
epigrammed you, or hath had a flirt at your mistress, or hath brought
either your feather or your red beard, or your little legs etc. on the
stage, you shall disgrace him worse than by tossing him in a blanket,
or giving him the bastinado in a tavern . . .' (p. 31). The allusion to
the 'blanket' is reminiscent of Balurdo's phrase in *Antonio and
Mellida*, 'I'll toss love like a dog in a blanket' (IV.i.273), while the
'bastinado' could call to mind the admission by Felice that he
'bastinadoed' Castilio (III.ii.279).

In *Poetaster*, Jonson calls Marston, Rufus Laberius Crispinus,
meaning the red, curly-haired, maker of mimes, and has him arrested
for debt at the suit of an apothecary (III.iv); Crispinus admits that
he owes him 'money for sweetmeats' (III.i.152). Horace (Jonson)
declares that Crispinus looks foreign, perhaps 'continental' in
appearance, for he has 'much of the mother' (III.i.185) in him. Jonson
may be suggesting that not only Crispinus but also Marston reflected a
foreign heritage. Marston's mother came of Italian stock. These
allusions to red hair, short legs, and a 'foreign' appearance are,

however, general enough to apply to more than one individual and may indeed be garnered from the features of several poets. Both Dekker and Jonson, on the other hand, seem to agree on these characteristics in general terms, and Marston makes a number of allusions himself to short legs and red hair.

In *Antonio and Mellida* Felice protests, '. . . Methinks I am as like a man [as Castilio]. / Troth, I have a good head of hair, a cheek / Not as yet waned, a leg, faith, in the full. / I ha' not a red beard' (III.ii.71–4). In *What You Will* (1600) Meletza speaks of her ex-lover Fabius as having a 'beard . . . directly brick colour and perfectly fashioned like the husk of a chestnut' (F2); similarly Brabant Junior of *Jack Drum* (1601) is described by Winifred as, 'a proper man, / And yet his legs are somewhat of the least' (B2v). In *The Malcontent* (1604?) Marshal Make-room is described as 'a proper gentleman in reversion as — and, indeed, as fine a man as may be, having a red beard and a pair of warped legs' (V.v.34–6). These numerous references may be ironic comments by Marston upon himself or, at least, upon the caricature that had been thrust upon him, and could indicate that he had a lively sense of humour, since he could cheerfully indulge in self-parody. In the absence, however, of an authenticated portrait of John Marston, these personal characteristics must remain conjectural.

The same caveat must apply to Jonson's portrait of Crispinus/ Marston in *Poetaster*, for while Marston and Dekker certainly recognised themselves in Crispinus and Demetrius, Jonson might well have blurred the portraits to avoid the direct accusation of invective. It seems reasonable, nevertheless, to assume that at least some of the characteristics given to Crispinus were features of John Marston. In *Poetaster*, Crispinus has an excellent singing voice. In the second scene of the second act he performs the song, 'If I freely may discover' (162–72), and Ovid's response is to declare, 'If there were a praise above excellence, the gentleman highly deserves it' (174–5). Similarly, according to Cytheris (IV.iii.54), he was an accomplished player on the viol, and he himself boasts of his talent for dancing (III.i). In addition he claims to be interested in Stoicism (III.i.28), possibly an allusion to the Stoicism of Andrugio in *Antonio and Mellida* and that of Pandulpho Felice in *Antonio's Revenge*. The characters of *Poetaster* freely admit that Crispinus has a claim to gentility and, when he is arrested for debt, he defends himself on the grounds that he is 'a gentleman' (III.iv.62). Crispinus is made to claim that he has 'new turned poet' (III.i.23–4) and that he is anxious to write 'odes' or 'sermons' or 'anything indeed' (26),[8] and that, recently, he has 'been a

reveller and at my cloth of silver suit and my long stocking in my time'
(175–6). It is true that Jonson is hostile to Crispinus in *Poetaster* but
the primary object of his criticism is not specifically Marston nor
Antonio and Mellida but the linguistic style of *Antonio's Revenge*; only
one of the words vomited by Crispinus, 'glibbery' (v.iii.), is from
Antonio and Mellida, where it occurs three times: I.i.109, II.i.6, and
IV.i.69.[9] While there is obviously exaggeration in Jonson's jibes
against Crispinus, they may indicate that contemporary opinion saw
Marston as a versatile writer, given to a rather riotous life.

his father's will Since June 1597, John Marston had been living in the Middle
Temple sharing his father's chambers. By 1599 the arrangement had
become a distinctly unhappy one. While he was in the process of
composing *Antonio and Mellida*, Marston was badly estranged from
his father. In addition he was in serious financial difficulty. His father
was so upset with his behaviour that he almost decided on a bitter,
death-bed castigation of his son's conduct, and planned that his will
should read:

> my law books being a double course thereof, I bequeath them [to him that
> deserveth them not, that is my willful disobedient son, who I think will sell
> them rather than use them, although I took pains and had delight therein.
> God bless him and give him true knowledge of himself, and to forgo his
> delight in plays, vain studies, and fooleries.]

Before he died, however, his father became more able to accept the
distress his son was causing him, leaving his law books to:

> my son. Wherein I have taken great pains with delight, and hoped that my
> son would have profited in the study of the law, wherein I bestowed my
> uttermost endeavour. But man purposeth and God disposeth; His will be
> done, and send him His grace to fear and serve Him.[10]

Apart from the 'law books', and 'the bedding and furniture in my
chamber in the Middle Temple, and my apparel there and elsewhere',
the only legacy that Marston received immediately was a 'black
trotting gelding'. Aside from a few small bequests to friends and
servants, Marston senior's estate either went directly to his 'well
beloved wife Mary', or was entailed to her for a period of some years,
before Marston junior could have possession of any part of it. Marston
receives some meadowland called the Overeys in Wardington,
Oxfordshire, but is required to pay his mother 'ten pounds by year
during her life' for the use of them; and, if he defaulted, his father
required that Mary should 'distrain for the sum'. In addition, while he

leaves one half of his 'plate and household stuff' to his son John, Mary is to retain it for six years, 'without spoiling, altering or changing the same, other than by reasonable wearing'. This half share is to be carefully inventoried, 'without concealment or undervaluing thereof'. Only after Mary's death is John to take possession of the mansion house in Coventry with all its furniture and fittings.

John Marston senior clearly continued to hope that his son would grow tired of his frivolous behaviour, but, at the time of his death, he seriously mistrusted him, for he appears to assume that his son might well seek to deprive his mother of her portion. Until his death, then, John Marston was convinced that his son was a reckless spendthrift who had to be protected from the consequences of his own prodigality.

The father's anger with his son was probably caused both by the irritation he felt that John junior did not share his fascination with the law as a career, and by his wholly unsuitable alternative choice of 'plays', and other 'fooleries'. John Marston senior appears to have prided himself upon his own genteel origins and on his suitable marriage. On his mother's side, John Marston the dramatist was descended from Balthazar Guarsi, who had been surgeon to Katharine of Aragon and Henry VIII. Balthazar had gained his qualifications at Cambridge in 1530 and became a Fellow of the College of Physicians in 1556; an Italian by birth, he remained resident in England. Marston's mother, Mary Guarsi, whom his father had married on 19 September 1575, was the daughter of Elizabeth Gray, of a London merchant family, and Andrew Guarsi, Balthazar's son.

The disagreement between Marston and his father had been growing for some time. It certainly existed as early as 27 May 1599 when *The Metamorphosis of Pygmalion's Image and Certain Satires* was entered in the Stationers' Register, and it would have been exacerbated by the second of his son's publications, which followed on 8 September in the same year, *The Scourge of Villainy*. John Marston senior may well have hoped that his son's book would fail to sell, but *The Scourge* was reprinted twice in 1599. There are already indications in this latter work as to the direction in which Marston's interests are moving:

> *Luscus.* What's played today? 'Faith now I know!
> I set thy lips abroach from whence doth flow
> Naught but pure Juliet and Romeo.
> Say who acts best Drusus, or Roscio?
> Now I have him, that ne'er of ought did speak

But when of plays or players he did treat.
H'ath made a commonplace book out of plays
And speaks in print, at least what e'er he says
Is warranted by curtain plaudities.
If ere you heard him courting Lesbia's eyes,
Say, courteous sir, speaks he not movingly
From out some new pathetic tragedy?
He writes, he rails, he jests, he courts, what not,
And all from out his huge long-scraped stock
Of well-penned plays. (XI:37–51.)

Already in 1598, Marston was a fervent admirer of Shakespeare's
Romeo and Juliet, and did not forget its details when he came to write
Antonio and Mellida. Even when his satires were a success, Marston
had a distinct interest in the theatre. An opportunity soon arose for
him to try his hand at drama, and it seems highly probable that he
created, largely by revising an older work, the Christmas Entertainment at the Middle Temple for 1598/9, *Histriomastix*.[11]

This Middle Temple entertainment is part allegory, part pageant;
its main function is to interest an audience of lawyers, and it satirises a
rascally troupe of common players, Sir Oliver Owlet's Men. Their
repertoire, '*Mother Gurton's Needle*, a tragedy; / *The Devil and Dives*,
a comedy; / *A Russet Coat and a Knave's Cap*, an infernal; / *A Proud
Heart and a Beggar's Purse*, a pastoral; / *The Widow's Apron-Strings*, a
nocturnal' (II.i) is as absurd as are their antics. They are condemned
by Chrisoganus, the moral censor of the play, because they have
devalued the high calling of poetry by their incompetence:

Write on, cry on, yawl to the common sort
Of thick-skinned auditors! Such rotten stuff's
More fit to fill the paunch of esquiline
Than feed the hearings of judicial ears.
Ye shades triumph, while foggy ignorance
Clouds bright Apollo's beauty. Time will clear
The misty dullness of spectators' eyes,
Then woeful hisses to your fopperies. (III.i)

Chrisoganus seems to be arguing that, while many plays are merely
insubstantial mass entertainment for the ignorant, there are some of a
much more refined artistic quality. These latter plays, yet to be
written, will prove a revelation to theatre audiences and eclipse the
tawdry performances of professionals like Sir Oliver Owlet's Men.

The first of Marston's books of satire had included an attack on a contemporary rival satirist, Joseph Hall and his *Virgidemiarum, Six Books*, of 31 March 1597. Marston seems to have assumed that Hall's violent attack on lascivious poets and poetry was designed to include his *Pygmalion's Image*.[12] Marston's second work attacks both Hall and also a certain E. G. (probably Everard Guilpin, the author of *Skialetheia*, 1598). Both Hall and Guilpin had attended Emmanuel College, Cambridge, and Guilpin was a member of Gray's Inn. Marston, like them, was seeking to establish himself as a new wit of the fashionable London literary scene.

Contemporary opinion seems to have been almost unanimous in accepting Marston as a literary success, and his fame as a satirist certainly went beyond mere notoriety. Charles Fitzgeoffrey in *Affaniae* (1601)[13] speaks of his two satires as equally glorious, and John Weever in *Epigrams* (1599) equated him with Horace.[14] Similarly Robert Allot's *England's Parnassus* (1600), a collection of quotations from 'The choicest flowers of our modern poets', cites *Pygmalion's Image* twice and *The Scourge of Villainy* fifteen times.[15] Francis Meres in *Palladis Tamia* (1598) lists 'the author of *Pygmalion's Image*, and *Certain Satires*' among 'the best for satire', in the same company as the author of *Piers Plowman* (p. 283v). Marston's poems are also cited on at least five occasions in Bodenham's *Belvedere* (1600),[16] another compilation from 'The Garden of the Muses'. In 1601 Marston was invited to contribute verses, along with Jonson, Shakespeare, and Chapman, to Robert Chester's volume *Love's Martyr* in honour of the awarding of a knighthood to Sir John Salusbury of Lleweni. His contribution suggests a personal acquaintance with the Salusbury family.[17]

He had enemies too. Among them was John Weever, who had at first been an admirer. In *The Whipping of the Satire* (1601),[18] an attack on contemporary satire and satirists, Weever assumes that the problem with modern social critics is that they are suffering from 'some strange disease' (375), and he decides to consult expert medical opinion:

I sought a famous Cantabrigian[19]
And brought a picture with me for a fee.
He hastily replied, 'Thou foolish man,
It is the flux of a luxurious tongue.
Give him a spoonful of some new cow's dung.' (410–14)

Immediately after this anecdote Weever cites the title and first line of Marston's 'Cynic Satire' (415–16), thus making the story a personal insult. For Weever, Marston is the epitome of bad contemporary satirists.

In *II Return From Parnassus* or *The Scourge of Simony* (c. 1601–3), Ingenio asks Judicio to comment on the achievements of Spenser, Constable, Lodge, Daniel, Watson, Drayton, Davies, Marston, and Marlowe.[20] Of Marston he says:

> Methinks he is a ruffian in his style.
> Withouten band's or garter's ornament,
> He quaffs a cup of Frenchman's Helicon.
> Then roister doister in his oily terms
> Cuts, thrusts, and foins at whomsoever he meets,
> And strews about Ram Ally meditations.
> Tut! What cares he for modest close-couched terms,
> Cleanly to gird our looser libertines?
> Give him plain naked words stripped from their shirts
> That might beseem plain-dealing Aretine.
> Ay, there is one that backs a paper steed
> And manageth a penknife gallantly,
> Strikes his poinado at a button's breadth,
> Brings the great battering-ram of terms to town,
> And at first volley of his cannon-shot
> Batters the walls of the old fusty world.

Marston's fame as a satirist, and, one surmises, his father's fury, probably reached their apogee at the same time. His two books of satire were condemned as offensive to public decency. On 4 June 1599, an 'Order of Conflagration' by Archbishop Whitgift of Canterbury and Bishop Bancroft of London commanded these two books, with eleven others, to be burnt by the common hangman in the Hall of the Company of Stationers. It was perhaps this incident that led to Marston's debts, and, within four months, he was trying to borrow money.

The fact that Marston was forced to seek a loan of £2 from Henslowe on 28 September 1599[21] probably indicates that his father had withdrawn his living allowance as he was failing to attend to his legal studies. On the evidence of his contempt for the professional theatre, as evinced in *Histriomastix*, this borrowing from the Admiral's Men may indicate that Marston was in dire financial straits. Since Henslowe speaks of 'Mr. Maxton' as a 'new poet', it looks as if this was Marston's first attempt to earn money by his pen. It may be that he seized on the opportunity, when it presented itself, to become involved with the Children of Paul's as a way out of his financial difficulties and, perhaps also, as a way of escaping the unpleasant necessity of being indebted to the professional actors, whom he had ridiculed as the incompetent Sir Oliver Owlet's Men.

Since he clearly had no money, before or after his father's death (the will was proved on 29 November 1599), whether or not he pawned the 'law books', he could not have contributed financially to the revival at Paul's. He may, however, have offered other kinds of help to Pearce and Stanley. In *Poetaster* Crispinus is full of admiration for the location where he finds Horace [Jonson]: 'By Phoebus, here's a most neat fine street, is't not? I protest to thee I am enamoured of this street now more than of half the streets of Rome. Again, 'tis so polite, and terse! There's the front of a building, now. I study architecture too. If ever I should build, I'd have a house just of that prospective' (III.i.26–9). There is no proof here, but a suggestion that Crispinus had a hand in some design work for a building, perhaps an allusion to the remodelling work probably undertaken at the Paul's playhouse before the reopening. The stage façade of the Paul's house had doors below and one or more windows above, and thus simulated a street.

As far as most contemporaries were concerned, whatever Jonson's opinion may have been, Marston was a leading and successful literary figure at the turn of the seventeenth century. William Camden, in the 1605 edition of his *Remains Concerning Britain*,[22] declares, after citing examples of ancient British poetry, '. . . if I would come to our time, what a world could I present to you out of Sir Philip Sidney, Edmund Spenser, John Owen, Samuel Daniel, Hugh Holland, Ben Jonson, Thomas Campion, Michael Drayton, George Chapman, John Marston, William Shakespeare, and other most pregnant wits of these our times, whom succeeding ages may justly admire.'

3. SOURCES[6]

In the seventh chapter of *Il principe* (*The Prince*), 1513, Niccolò Machiavelli deals with 'New principalities which are acquired either by the arms of others or by good fortune' and, as examples of these two 'methods of rising to be a prince by ability or fortune', he cites 'two examples within our own recollection, and these are Francesco Sforza and Cesare Borgia. Francesco, by proper means [later, he says 'through being martial' ('*per essere armato*')], and with great ability, from being a private person rose to be Duke of Milan, and that which he had acquired with a thousand anxieties he kept with little

trouble'.[23] Machiavelli, then, sees Francesco Sforza as the epitome of
the self-made governor. Francesco, whose career as a *condottiere*, a
mercenary captain, in Lombardy eventually made him, through
innate ability, the finest general in the north Italian plain, acquired
the Dukedom of Milan through a combination of political guile
and military ability. In late sixteenth-century England, the name
'Sforza' was to become synonymous with tyrannical, Machiavellian
opportunism.

In the *Induction* to *Antonio and Mellida*, Alberto advises the youth
who plays Piero Sforza to

> ... thus frame your exterior shape
> To haughty form of elate majesty,
> As if you held the palsy-shaking head
> Of reeling Chance under your fortune's belt,
> In strictest vassalage. Grow big in thought
> As swoll'n with glory of successful arms. (7–12)

Marston's imaginary Piero Sforza, as well as the historical Francesco
Sforza, followed this advice to the letter.

The most famous of the historical Sforzas, Francesco was employed
as a captain-general in a war between Milan and Venice. He was
fortunate enough, in July 1448, to trap the Venetian fleet in a narrow
branch of the Po at Casalmaggiore.[24] The Venetians had barred access
to their ships by a defence line of stakes, but Francesco forced them to
retreat from this position by an artillery bombardment. Unable to
manoeuvre in the narrow waters where only one vessel at a time was
able to pass, the Venetian ships attempted to escape singly but were
all destroyed in the narrow neck of the channel. On 18 July 1448 the
bells of Milan rang out to celebrate the great victory.

In the first scene of the first act of *Antonio and Mellida*, Antonio,
son of the recently defeated and deposed Andrugio, Duke of Genoa,
describes the sea fight in the Venetian gulf, which led to his losses:

> Antonio, hast thou seen a fight at sea,
> As horrid as the hideous day of doom,
> Betwixt thy father, Duke of Genoa,
> And proud Piero, the Venetian Prince,
> In which the sea hath swoll'n with Genoa's blood
> And made spring tides with the warm reeking gore
> That gushed from out our galley's scupper holes,
> In which thy father, poor Andrugio,
> Lies sunk ... (7–15)

Despite the glories of his victory over the Venetian fleet, the historical Francesco Sforza changed sides in the conflict and, by 18 October, was in the employ of Venice against the Milanese.[25] By a series of adroit military and diplomatic moves, however, Francesco was invited, on 26 February 1450, to become Duke of Milan. At this time he already had a son and heir named, on the recommendation of the previous noble house of Milan, the Visconti, Galeazzo Maria.[26] One of the main characters in *Antonio and Mellida* is Galeazzo, son to the Duke of Florence, and later in *Antonio's Revenge*, Maria appears first as widow of Andrugio and mother to Antonio, and then as wife to Piero Sforza.

Francesco's son, Galeazzo Maria Sforza, lacked his father's diplomatic, military, and personal qualities. After a short reign of luxury, lechery, and idleness, during which there were ascribed to him many lurid cruelties, he was assassinated by a trio of conspirators, Andrea Lampugnani, Carlo Visconti, and Girolamo Oligati, on the steps of the church of S. Stefano in 1476.[27] Andrea and Carlo were killed on the spot by the followers of Galeazzo Maria, but Oligati escaped for a while and became a legendary folk hero in popular ballads.[28] The assassination was later justified by cataloguing the sins of Galeazzo as typical of the worst kinds of tyranny; even his wife admitted that he was versed in 'wars, licit and illicit, sacks, robberies, and the like, extortions from subjects, neglect of justice, and at times deliberate acts of injustice, imposition of fresh taxes without exemption of clergy, carnal vices, notorious and scandalous simonies, and other innumerable sins'.[29] In *Antonio's Revenge*, Piero Sforza is assassinated by three conspirators, Antonio, Alberto, and Pandulpho, all of whom accuse him of crimes against humanity. Antonio delivers the judgement upon him:

> Thus charge we death at thee. Remember hell;
> And let the howling murmurs of black spirits,
> The horrid torments of the damned ghosts,
> Affright thy soul as it descendeth down
> Into the entrails of the ugly deep. (v.v.68–72)

After the execution, the conspirators declare their intention to 'live enclosed / In holy verge of some religious order, / Most constant votaries' (v.vi.34–6). They too are intent upon becoming the stuff of legend.

Galeazzo Maria was succeeded by his uncle Lodovico, known as Il Moro (The Moor), and he was outstanding in his patronage of the

B

arts.[30] Lodovico was fortunate enough to act as patron to Leonardo da Vinci,[31] who designed some of the costumes for a wedding masque in honour of the marriage of Lodovico and Beatrice d'Este.[32] Lodovico commissioned 'The Last Supper' in the Refectory of Sta. Maria delle Grazie, as well as a great equestrian statue (never cast) of Francesco. It was also during the last and most brilliant years of his reign as duke that Baldassare Castiglione, author of *Il Cortegiano*, lived and was educated in Milan. This, the most famous of the courtesy books in Renaissance England, was translated by Sir Thomas Hoby as *The Courtier* in 1561; Marston had read this translation.[33]

In *The Courtier*, Castiglione expressed his concern that 'you all knew not the Duchess [Beatrice of Milan] ... that you might never again wonder at a woman's wit (*per non aver mai piu a maravigliare di ingegno di donna*)' (Ff. iiiv). Earlier, in a letter written to Jacomo Boschetto da Gonzaga of 8 October 1499,[34] he spoke of the Castello of Milan, the fortress of Francesco Sforza, as a gathering place where there assembled 'del fior degli uomini del mondo'. For Castiglione, Duke Lodovico and his Duchess, Beatrice d'Este, were the 'flower of the world'. Castilio Balthazar is a member of the court of Piero Sforza in *Antonio and Mellida*.

The main plot, then, of *The History of Antonio and Mellida* and in particular the character of Piero Sforza, owe much both to the general notion of tyranny connected with the name 'Sforza', and also to the events in Italy that characterised the historical Sforza dynasty, in their rule of the Duchy of Milan between 1450 and 1535. While the closest similarity is with the first of the Sforza dukes, Francesco, there are some suggestions of details taken from the two subsequent reigns of Galeazzo Maria (particularly in *Antonio's Revenge*), and Lodovico (particularly in the final act of *Antonio and Mellida*). Marston's character Piero is a conscious fiction, for this first name does not occur in the historical Sforza family. The location of the play is also imaginary; the Sforzas were never Dukes of Venice. The plot is a historical fiction based on actual events in fifteenth-century Italy; it is an original and creative invention in which the persons are literary images evolved from the merging of actual historical people and events.

Marston's knowledge of these events in the history of Italy could have been derived, at least in part, from P. Giovio's *Vita di Sforza*, Venice, 1558, and perhaps also G. Capella's *Commentarii delle cose fatte per la restituzione di Francesco Sforza II*, Milan, 1539, but more likely his general knowledge of the period derives from his family. His mother's family, the Guarsis, were Italian emigrants to England in the reign of Henry VIII and, of course, Marston's knowledge of Italian was substantial, as this play bears witness.

Marston's contemporary audience at Paul's could hardly have been expected to be familiar with the details of Milanese history, although they might well have heard, in general terms, of the Sforza family. They would all, however, have recognised the reconciliation speech of Piero at the end of the fifth act, where he declares to Andrugio:

To solemnise our houses' unity.
My love be thine, the all I have be thine.
Fill us fresh wine. The form we'll take by this:
We'll drink a health while they two sip a kiss.
[*A health is drunk; ANTONIO and MELLIDA embrace.*]
Now there remains no discord that can sound
Harsh accents to the ear of our accord. (v.ii.261–6)

The love of Antonio of the house of Andrugio and Mellida of the Sforza dynasty has reconciled the enmity of the elder generation, of Andrugio and Piero; Marston offers a happy ending to the *Romeo and Juliet* story.

Marston seems to have simply assumed that his audience would recognise the similarity-in-difference of the ending of *Antonio and Mellida* and that of *Romeo and Juliet*. The evidence suggests he was right, for in *Antonio's Revenge*, written some eighteen months after *Antonio and Mellida*, the technique is repeated. Here he demands a much more detailed familiarity with the action of Shakespeare's *Richard III*, for in the dumb show that precedes Act III Piero copies the method of Richard's wooing of Anne in his suit to Maria. In the ensuing act, no further explanation is given of the results of his suit, and it is simply assumed that the audience is aware that Maria has agreed to marry him. The action can only be understood by spectators familiar with the plot of Shakespeare's play.

This technique of dramatic quotation, flattering his audience with his assumption of their intimate knowledge of contemporary theatre, occurs again in *Antonio and Mellida* at III.i.92, where Marston makes an oblique reference to the dream sequence of *Richard III* and later, in the last act, v.i.62–9, he glances, again indirectly, at Orlando's wooing of Rosalind from *As You Like It* (III.i.78–102). Similarly, in the confrontation between Piero and Mellida (IV.i.247–60), after she has attempted to elope with Antonio, Marston deliberately reminds his audience of the anger of Old Capulet with Juliet.

While the influence of Shakespeare's plays is evident, it is much less pervasive than that of the drama of Seneca. Marston cites the *Phoenissae*, III.ii.203; the *Hercules Oetaeus*, IV.i.87; the *Medea*, III.i.63 and IV.ii.29–32; the *Oedipus*, III.ii.53; and the *Thyestes*, I.i.60 and 78, III.i.116, IV.i.36–7, and he takes a substantial segment from the same play at IV.i.45–65, where Andrugio argues that true majesty does not consist in outward show but rather in inner Stoic virtue and integrity of moral character. This long citation from the *Thyestes* illustrates the other main source of this play: an eclectic borrowing of passages, some substantial, some only fragments, from a wide range of authors, both living and dead.

As G. K. Hunter has pointed out,[35] two important devices of the play are probably derived from Sidney's *Arcadia*. The disguise of Antonio as an Amazon mimics the Amazonian disguise of Pyrocles in his wooing (Ind., 73), and the denouement, with Andrugio presenting his own head to Piero and claiming the offered reward for his own capture, v.ii.160–2, is reminiscent of the similar offering by Plexirtus of himself to his enemy Leonatus, 'with a rope about his neck, barefooted'.

Marston has read Erasmus's dialogue on the nature of ghosts, II.i.234–41, and uses an elaborate simile from the same colloquy, 'Proci et Puellae' at IV.i.13–17; he knows of Montaigne's argument that nature creates nothing without a purpose, III.i.28–34; he is familiar with the exploits of the ballad heroine, Mary Ambree, I.i.105; he has taken a lively interest in the recent controversy between Richard Stanihurst, Gabriel Harvey, and Thomas Nashe over Stanihurst's translation of Virgil's *Aeneid* into English hexameters, II.i.31; he knows Aesop's fable of the Ass and the Lion, II.i.10–11; he has heard of, and perhaps has read, Margaret Tyler's *Mirror of Princely Deeds and Knighthood*, II.i.35; he borrows a metaphor from Sylvester's translation of Du Bartas's *Divine Weeks*, Ind. 59–61; he seems to know John Florio's *Second Fruits*, I.i.112; he repeats a contemporary tavern jest, probably as related by George Peele, II.i.251–2; he uses quotations from Virgil's *Aeneid*, Dedic. 11 and v.ii.238; he knows Kyd's *Spanish Tragedy*, Ind. 79, III.ii.53 and IV.i.217; he mines Nashe's *Summer's Last Will and Testament* for some stage business, v.ii.28–33; and he is, of course, familiar with various passages in the Bible, e.g., II.i.129, 282–3 and IV.i.217.[36]

This density of quotation from and allusion to contemporary works suggests that Marston is using his 'commonplace book' as an essential source for the construction of his play. This loose assemblage of

incidents and ideas is further enhanced by the strictly personal
allusions that Marston adds to the present text. Apart from showing
off his fluency in Italian, IV.i.189–206, he also has his own portrait
brought on stage in V.i.10–13, as well as a second portrait which may
be that of the theatre's current patron, George Stanley, V.i.8. As with
his casual use of the history of Milan under the Sforzas, so with his
quotations from his wide reading, Marston's play is a syncretic
construct upon an eclectic base. The plot is, therefore, highly flexible
and capable of being adapted to any situation. In the sequel, the
Piero/Andrugio conflict was absorbed into a new version of the
Hamlet story.

4. DATE

Antonio and Mellida was entered in the Stationers' Register on 24
October 1601. This provides an ultimate date limit for the play. The
play was 'sundry times acted by the Children of Paul's', but this
company was not operating until after the appointment of a new
Master for the Choristers of St Paul's Cathedral in mid 1599. This
choir formed the acting company who performed *Antonio and
Mellida*.[37] The children's theatre companies at Paul's and at the
Blackfriars, which had flourished in the 1580s, were repressed by
order of the Privy Council in late 1590 or early 1591. There was, then,
no regular public performance by child actors in London from this
date until the revival at Paul's at the close of the sixteenth century.[38]

It was on 22 May 1584 that Thomas Gyles had received his
appointment as Master of Choristers, as successor to Sebastian
Westcott, but, by early 1599, Gyles was so ill that he seems to have
been seriously neglecting his duties.[39] One of the results was that the
children were somewhat unkempt, for while they were 'well
instructed and fit for their places . . . they have not their gowns lined
as in former times were used, their surplice are commonly unclean,
and their apparel not in such sort as decency becometh'.[40] The result
was that the Dean and Chapter determined to appoint a successor
without dismissing Gyles from his office. The place was offered to
Edward Pearce, who already held a similar appointment at the Chapel
Royal.

On 11 May 1599, Edward Pearce 'of the city of London, gentleman'
was appointed as Gyles's successor and he was instructed to take up
his new duties in person, not later than 25 June 1599. While Gyles
lingered—he did not in fact die until 4 July 1600—Pearce was denied

some of the perquisites of his office, including the use of the
Almoner's house, usually assigned to the Master of the Choristers, for
the old Master continued to reside there. While Gyles lived, Pearce
clung to his appointment at the Chapel Royal, not resigning finally
until 15 August 1600.

Clearly, taking up a new appointment under such awkward
conditions, and still retaining responsibilities at the Chapel Royal,
would have made Pearce's first months at Paul's very busy and
harassing. It is, therefore, extremely unlikely that Pearce sought to
reorganise the Paul's Boys acting troupe until the late summer or early
autumn of 1599. Similarly, when *Antonio and Mellida* was registered
for publication, it was accompanied by its sequel, *Antonio's Revenge*,
and consequently it must predate that second part by some period of
time. The date limits for the play, then, may be narrowed, at least, to
between late 1599 and early 1601, for the Induction makes it clear that
Antonio's Revenge was only a tentative plan when *Antonio and Mellida*
was performed for, 'those persons ... that are but slightly drawn in
this comedy, should receive more exact accomplishment in a second
part which, if this obtain gracious acceptance, means to try his
fortune' (143–7).

A cryptic and possibly partially forged entry in Henslowe's diary
affords some evidence that Marston was involved with the professional stage rather than the Paul's troupe, as late as 28 September 1599.
Henslowe lent 'unto Wm. Borne ... to lend unto Mr. Maxton the
new poet (Mr. Mastone) in earnest of a book', the sum of 40s.[41] No
indication is made as to what this 'book' might be, but there is no
sound reason to suppose that 'Mr. Mastone' is not Marston. While,
therefore, the evidence of Henslowe's diary cannot be used to date
Antonio and Mellida, it does indicate that it was probably produced
later than the end of September 1599 after Marston had ended his
brief flirtation with the Admiral's Men.

In *Jack Drum's Entertainment or The Comedy of Pasquil and
Katherine* (F4–F4v), which may be dated about May 1600[42] and which
was 'sundry times played by the Children of Paul's', occurs what
seems to be the first mention of *Antonio and Mellida* in another literary
context:

Brabant Junior. Brother how like you of our modern wits?
　　How like you the new poet Mellidus?
Brabant Senior. A slight bubbling spirit, a cork, a husk.
Planet. How like you Musus' fashion in his carriage?
Brabant Senior. O filthily, he is as blunt as Paul's.

The identification of 'Mellidus', the masculine form of Mellida, 'honey-sweet' or 'darling', with *Antonio and Mellida* and thus with Marston has been challenged by Antony Caputi,[43] who argues that since 'Musus' and later 'Decius'—who are also mentioned in this context—are not plays or parts, then 'Mellidus' cannot be trusted as a specific reference either. The association of 'Mellidus', however, with 'Paul's' is absolutely specific, and Planet is inquiring whether or not Brabant Senior likes his style. Marston's style was the subject of an intense contemporary debate, the Poetomachia, which culminated in Jonson's attack upon him as Crispinus in *Poetaster*. The evidence is, therefore, extensive, and this reference, in my judgement, makes it clear that *Antonio and Mellida* is to be dated before *Jack Drum*; this limits the *terminus ad quem* to early 1600. This conclusion is supported by other evidence.

In the first scene of the fifth act of *Antonio and Mellida*, a painter enters with two portraits, and Balurdo describes them: ' "*Anno Domini 1599*". Believe me, Master Anno Domini was of a good settled age when you limned him—1599 years old! Let's see the other, "*Aetatis suae twenty-four*"—by'r Lady, he is somewhat younger. Belike *Master Aetatis suae* was *Anno Domini*'s son' (8–13). John Marston was christened on 7 October 1576,[44] and on 4 February 1591/2 he appears in the matriculation register of Brasnose, Oxford: 'John Marston War[wickshire] gen[tleman's] fil. [son] aet. [age] s. [his]—16.'[45] When he matriculated he was 15, but in his sixteenth year. The portrait *Aetatis suae twenty-four* has, therefore, usually been assumed to be a painting of Marston himself.

The ascription of this portrait to Marston was challenged by D. J. McGinn,[46] who argued that Marston was not yet 24 in 1599 and thus the portrait could not be of him, but G. Cross[47] pointed out that

'Etatis suae' in *Antonio and Mellida* has exactly the same significance as it has in the Matriculation Register—it means literally what it says—and the correct interpretation is not, as McGinn supposes, 'aged twenty-four' but 'in his twenty-fourth year.' Marston entered his twenty-fourth year on his twenty-third birthday, some time before October 7, 1599, and the inscriptions on the two pictures would thus have been biographically accurate any time from the beginning of October 1599 until March 24 1600.

With this conclusion I fully concur, and I have no hesitation in assuming that one of the portraits is indeed of Marston himself. This self-display is entirely in accord with the whole tone of the play.

P. J. Finkelpearl has suggested that the second of these portraits is of Marston's father, for he died in late 1599 and his will was proved on November 29.[48] Apart from the concern in the play that a father has lost a son, and a son a father (Antonio and Andrugio), it is difficult to see what possible connection a portrait of Marston's father had with this play, or its actors, or its audience. Moreover, Marston and his father were scarcely on speaking terms at this time; they were bitterly at odds over Marston's failure to pursue the law because of his burgeoning career as a dramatist. While it is true that the play is personal in tone, it could hardly be described as a memorial, and thus I find this ascription highly unlikely. The second portrait, of a man old enough to be Marston's father, is more likely to have been someone with a connection with the Paul's company. One possible candidate is Edward Pearce, but it is unlikely that he was old enough; perhaps more probable is the financier of the revival, William Stanley, sixth Earl of Derby.[49]

On the evidence of the portrait in the first scene of the fifth act, and the report in *Jack Drum*, the date limits for *Antonio and Mellida* may be confined to the period October 1599 to the end of March 1600. *Antonio's Revenge*, the second part of this 'history', was produced in the winter of 1600–1[50] and thus offers no help in formulating a more precise date for *Antonio and Mellida*.

Antonio and Mellida has a number of features suggesting that it was designed for the opening night of the newly revived Paul's company.[51] On the evidence of *Jack Drum*, it quickly became a sensation. By 13 November 1599, Rowland Whyte reported to Sir Robert Sidney that 'My Lord Derby [William Stanley] hath put up the plays of the Children in Paul's to his great pains and charge'.[52] If *Antonio and Mellida* was indeed the play for the opening night, it was first produced before mid-November. Late October or early November 1599 is, therefore, the most likely date for its first performance.

5. THE PLAY AND ITS PURPOSES

Antonio and Mellida is, in Polonius's definition, a 'tragical-comical-historical-pastoral' (*Ham.*, II.ii.395–6); all of these four elements blend to effect 'the comic crosses of true love', v.ii.279, and they are all, in turn, subject to satire and parody within the action. The plot is overlaid by other purposes that result in considerable convolution within its structure. Marston is using this play to project a particular image of himself and a detailed concept of the Paul's company to its audience. It is a play that is consciously intimate and personal, and sometimes this latter, extra-dramatic purpose takes over the action. *Antonio and Mellida* does not have a simple or single, integral design by which to unify plot, persons, and presentation; rather, it has several of these designs. Its purposes are as various as its dramatic kinds. The play is not organised as a linear progression but rather as a sequence of variations of mood, attitude, theme, and pageant-like displays that are interconnected by a common plot-line. The entertainment value of *Antonio and Mellida* is greatly enhanced by the sheer variety of its forms.

In the Induction, Prologue, and Epilogue, Marston subordinates the 'history' of the love affair of Antonio and Mellida to the more urgent purpose of advertising the Paul's actors and his own abilities as a dramatist. The play illustrates those acting and creative talents which he wishes to advertise. The *History of Antonio and Mellida*, then, is both a 'historical-comical' and an illustration of the kind of play Marston is capable of writing and of the type this new company, the Children of Paul's, is capable of performing. Often the fictional story of the love of Antonio and Mellida and the real-time struggle of the actors to attain competence in their new profession are used to create a blend where history and fiction merge into a new whole. Marston takes much delight in frequently, and often surprisingly, altering the perspective from which a character or an incident is viewed, a process which seeks to induce recognition with astonishment.

There are in *Antonio and Mellida* incidents that are clearly extra-dramatic, like the sudden breaking into Italian by Antonio and Mellida (iv.i.189–206), and the presentation of portraits by Balurdo of the author of the play and, possibly, the theatre's patron, William Stanley, in the first scene of the last act (7–13). The story of the love affair of Antonio and Mellida is the principal plot of the play, but the audience is also made conscious of the formation and training of the acting company performing the play. These elements often seem essentially independent and parallel, but they also deliberately overlap. The result of this multiple purpose is to leave the perception of the reader/audience blurred. The fictional action of the Antonio/Mellida plot and the introduction, in the Induction, of the actors and, in the last act, of the dramatist to the audience, become a blend of romantic fantasy and theatrical practice. Marston is seeking to create a vibrant illusion of verisimilitude by suggesting that his own life and those of his actors are co-extensive with the lives of his characters. As with the historical sources, where fact and fiction had become almost

indistinguishable—Piero is fancy, but the Sforzas are fact—so with
the play's elements: *Antonio and Mellida* is a love story acted by
children who, in life, are on the threshold of love themselves but who,
on the stage, are concerned with the plausibility of their dramatic
illusion as lovers. The lives of the actors and those of the characters
they personate are part of a greater whole which includes both
dramatist and audience. This sense of being dazzled by variety is an
essential part of the play's appeal.

The Induction serves, conventionally, to introduce the actors to the
audience as new players and to describe the roles they play, as well as
to outline the characters of the plot to the audience. Alberto defines
Piero's 'tragical-historical' part as requiring him to 'Grow big in
thought / As swoll'n with glory of successful arms' (11–12), but Piero
interprets his role satirically, where he will 'stroke up the hair and
strut' (14), and Alberto, anticipating Felice's mordant depiction of a
degenerate world, agrees that such 'rank custom is grown popular'
(15). Alberto must play both Andrugio and Alberto, the latter
characterised as a parody of the romantic, lovesick youth. Balurdo is
declared to be an example of the courtly servility that Felice is to
satirise; Felice himself is defined as a cancer in the breast of princes,
whereas Forobosco becomes a more or less harmless example of
'brainless gentility' (60–1). Antonio is 'an hermaphrodite' (70), for,
while disguised as an Amazon, he plays the son of the tragic, deposed
Duke of Genoa who is a romantic-pastoral lover. He does, however,
cast some doubt, albeit ironically, upon his ability to be convincing in
the role of Florizel: 'I a voice to play a lady!' (74–5). In Mazzagente,
the 'man queller', we are reminded of the historical origins of the
play; he is son to the Duke of Milan, a 'modern braggadoch' (93–4)
and will play his part like a 'tufty Tamburlaine' (91); he combines the
militaristic qualities of Francesco Sforza with the degenerate nature
of his son, Galeazzo Maria. It is Galeazzo who must display the most
extensive repertoire of personalities, for he is required to range
between 'a formal majesty' (127) and the opposite extreme of courtly
absurdity, when he will be as 'neat as a barber's casting bottle'
(133–4).

These multiple purposes and character types prepare the audience
for a constantly dichotomous sequence of experiences. The opening
note of the play is one of alienation, where man and society are
dislocated: Antonio and Andrugio are parted; Andrugio has lost his
dukedom and is alienated from his subjects, the Genoese; Antonio has
lost Mellida, and is so far sundered from his own nature that death

seems his only option, I.i.I; the usurpation of the Dukedom of Genoa
has dislocated life itself.[53] This sense of alienation is offset by other
purposes. While ostensibly Antonio is part of the tragic experience of
the play, he, in fact, acts as an anti-hero, for he is unheroic and
unromantic in almost everything he does. This anti-heroic stance is
also satiricial, for it criticises the behaviour at Piero's court and
therefore at courts in general. Antonio is unmanly and lovesick; he
appears as a woman (Florizel) and hides in the costume of a sailor; he
is hysterical, highly emotional, full of exaggeration and wishing only
to die, as in his opening remarks, 'Veins, sinews, arteries, why crack
ye not?' (I.i.3); he is, at times, extremely voluble (as in the opening
speech of the play) and, at others, inarticulate, afflicted by aposiopesis; he fails every test of valour, and even in death he is the opposite of
his purported kind, for the death is but feigned. Antonio is neither an
avenger nor a lover; his failure to articulate is paralleled by his failure
to act. Antonio's character constantly surprises the audience by its
changes of mood and attitude. Antonio is represented as lacking the
experience to portray a mature tragic figure, and therefore, as actor
and character, he is an outcast. Ironically he is also the mainstay of the
romance in the plot, and his love for Mellida is, later, presented
completely sincerely, as in the moving scene where he laments her
supposed death and calls to his page:

> I prithee sing, but sirrah, mark you me,
> Let each note breathe the heart of passion,
> The sad extracture of extremest grief.
> Make me a strain. Speak groaning like a bell
> That tolls departing souls....
> *The boy runs a note; ANTONIO breaks it.* (IV.i.138–42, 154.1)

In moments of emotional crisis, Antonio is able to act his role with a
sincerity that belies his preciosity. Once more, Marston shifts the
audience's perspective with a surprising change of focus from parody
to sincerity.

   In the same way as the audience's perception of the nature of the
characters suddenly and violently changes, so the background against
which the love affair of Antonio and Mellida is detailed will abruptly
shift its mode. This is clearly demonstrated in the first act. The play
proper opens on an impassioned, almost hysterical, tragic note with
Antonio's cry 'Heart, wilt not break?' (1). He longs for the passionless
response of the Stoic to calamity, so as to leave 'the slough of viperous
grief behind' (6). He is, from this opening moment, clearly prone to

exaggeration and hysteria. This 'tragical' beginning quickly merges
into the 'historical', with the gory details of Andrugio's defeat at sea
when 'warm reeking gore / . . . gushed from out our galley's scupper
holes' (12–13): as with the historical Venetian fleet at Casalmaggiore
in July 1448, so Andrugio's Genoan 'blood' (11) has been massacred
by a Sforza. At the same time this 'tragical-historical' context has
pastoral-romance overtones. Antonio is *disguised like an Amazon*',
I.i.0.1–2, and is in search of his 'beauteous Mellida' (19), forced,
however, to adopt a 'strange disguise' (28). The first speech of the
play has set the tone for the whole development of the main romance
plot, which interweaves tragic emotion, verging on the hysterical,
historical fictions, and romantic pastoral conventions.

The first glimpse of the villain of the piece, Piero Sforza, portrays
him in conventional tragic guise, with boastful overtones suggesting
an affinity with Marlowe's Tamburlaine. He glories in his victory with
self-evident tragic hubris: 'My fate is firmer than mischance can
shake' (41). He is deliberately characterised as a successful *condottiere*,
like Francesco Sforza at the height of his success after his great victory
over the Venetian Fleet. Omens of a future disastrous turning of the
wheel of fate are, however, already dominant, as Felice remarks that
'Pride' (48) will 'lift thee to improvidence' (49) and the result will be a
fall like that of Rome itself. This note of overconfidence is clearly
designed to recall Marlowe's overreachers. It also strongly reminds
the reader of the atmosphere of foreboding that dominates *Romeo and
Juliet*, as in the opening Chorus, which might, in fact, epitomise this
play of Marston's:

> From forth the fatal loins of these two foes
> A pair of star-crossed lovers take their life;
> Whose misadventured piteous overthrows
> Doth with their death bury their parents' strife. (5–8)

The only variation in this formula is the survival of the lovers, and it is
Piero who seems foreshadowed to suffer 'overthrow', rather than his
daughter and her paramour.

Suddenly the play's mood alters; the ladies 'above' (in a central
upper acting area) change the tragic-historical notes of the plot to a
pastoral romance, where the interest centres on the potential prowess
of the lover/soldiers who are being inspected 'below' (on the lower
stage). The assessment of the qualities of these suitors is interrupted
by the appearance of Antonio as Florizel the Amazon from Scythia
(172–3). Antonio re-enters the plot as a woman with a voice

'viragolike', Ind. 76. He links together the romance element of the plot and its historical-tragic aspect with his vivid recall of the wreck of the Venetian fleet:

> The issue of black fury strewed the sea
> With tattered carcasses of splitted ships,
> Half-sinking, burning, floating, topsy-turvy. (198–200)

This tragic atmosphere is continued in Antonio's description of the storm at sea, which is derived from the storm sequence in Seneca's *Agamemnon*. The description of how 'gusty flaws struck up the very heels / Of our mainmast' (216–17) and the ship broke its 'neck' (220) is, of course, a recounting by Antonio of his own death. As far as the characters of the plot are concerned this is a tragedy, but for the audience it is ironic comic exaggeration, for Florizel is Antonio. The point is re-emphasised by Rosaline's invitation to Florizel to be her 'bedfellow' (258).

In this first act of *The History of Antonio and Mellida* Marston has demonstrated a variety of talents as a dramatist, in history, tragedy, comedy, and romance. These elements are sometimes blended into each other, as with the tragic account of Antonio's death; sometimes they are merely juxtaposed to change abruptly the rhythms of the plot, as with the shift of mood between the boasting of Piero and the inspection of the lovers by the ladies. Indeed, this inspection in itself epitomises the various nature of the play: the soldiers are being inspected by the new Duke, since they form his guard, and are also being appraised, on a very different set of criteria, by the ladies as lovers. In a similar way, the audience would surely have been aware that the excess and hyperbole of Piero as a Marlovian overreacher was deliberately paralleled by the exaggerated bombast of Antonio as a lover; Marston, the satirist of literary convention, is also in evidence.

It is, in fact, a satire on the affectations and absurd exaggerations of lovers that constitutes the sub-plot for the Antonio and Mellida story. This satire on the lovers themselves and on the whole literary convention of romance at times spills over into an attack, in general terms, on the moral degeneracy of contemporary society. Dildo and Cazzo parody both the glorification of the martial arts and Piero's pride in his own victories; as Cazzo says, 'was't not rare sport at the sea battle . . . to view our masters pluck their plumes and drop their feathers for fear of being men of mark?' (II.i.30–3). Cazzo points out that all the pride in arms evaporates in the face of likely death and becomes indistinguishable from cowardice. Similarly, Dildo links the satire on soldiers to the parody of romance convention in *The Mirror of Knighthood* (II.i.35), where Rosicleer performs miraculous feats of arms and is always invulnerable.[54]

This parody, complete and consistent in itself, makes it clear that, at times, the behaviour of both Piero and Antonio is not to be taken seriously; both are intentionally exaggerated as examples of the kinds criticised. The characters do not, of course, intentionally parody themselves or the play's lovers; this parody effect is for the delight of the audience and it highlights Marston's satire on foolish excess. The main action of the plot, the love affair of Antonio and Mellida, comes in for more derisive treatment by both Cazzo and Flavia, and Rosaline and Balurdo, when both couples jest at each other's pretence of affection. The indignation against lovers and their hyperbole increases in intensity until it becomes, in Felice, an outpouring of moral righteousness against 'this queasy age' (II.i.92). While Felice is the principal mouthpiece of the social criticism of the play, which Marston aims at both courtly duplicity and amorous lasciviousness, he is himself subjected to satiric ridicule. In the second scene of the third act, Felice attacks the hypocrisy of women:

> I have put on good clothes and smudged my face,
> Struck a fair wench with a smart speaking eye,
> Courted in all sorts, blunt and passionate,
> Had opportunity, put them to the 'ah!',
> And, by this light, I find them wondrous chaste,
> Impregnable ... (84–9)

Already it is apparent that he is an unsuccessful lover, and this explains his satiric vein; he is jealous of the success of others. This revelation about Felice shows up the primary satiric mouthpiece of the play as, in some ways, socially inept. The frequency with which the apparent role of a character is inverted, as with Antonio and Felice, gives the impression that alienation has created a permanent state of identity crisis for all those involved. It also, of course, mocks the pretentiousness of satirists, for satire is itself subject to satiric ridicule.

In the second act of the play, Marston allows the social criticism in the plot to move from generic moral outrage to an attack upon specific social abuses. There he focuses on contemporary speech habits and the fashion for new and fanciful vocabulary. Balurdo relishes the new-coined word 'unpropitiously' (II.i.106–7), and in the next seven lines Marston uses three more 'new' words: 'applausive' (111), 'elocuty' (111) and 'groping' (114). While the tone of these speeches is clearly excessive, as in Forobosco's 'exquisite, illustrate, accomplished, pure, respected, adored, observed, precious, real, magnanimous, bounteous' (II.i.117–19), and intentionally becomes precious, Marston's delight in new verbal forms makes his attack on speech preciosity ambiguous. The satire itself becomes uncertain, for Marston is attracted by the very verbal forms he is condemning. In this play as a whole, out of a vocabulary of some 3,300 words, Marston uses about three per cent for the first time in a formal spoken or written context. He will often use these 'new' words more than once, as with 'unpropitiously' (II.i.106–7, 107, 108), or 'glibbery' (I.i.109, II.i.6, IV.i.69), or 'limn' (Ind. 141, v.i.6, 7, 10). More often than not, these words are used quite seriously.

Marston was fascinated with many forms of verbal expression and saw the newly-coined words of his own day as a source of infinite richness in the language. Similarly, he was intrigued by idiosyncrasies of speech as a means of reflecting both character and mood. In this play Antonio is sometimes afflicted by aposiopesis, which is designed for a twofold purpose. It reflects the inarticulateness of the young lover in moments of intense emotional stress and also, perhaps, suggests the awkwardness of the inexperienced youth who is performing the role. Antonio is often at a loss for words, usually when gazing at or thinking about Mellida, as 'She comes like—O, no simile / Is precious, choice, or elegant enough / To illustrate her descent' (I.i.152–4). Balurdo is similarly afflicted: 'I think I am as elegant a courtier as—' (III.ii.134), and 'I'll toss love like a prank— / "Prank it?"—a rhyme for "prank it"?' (IV.i.270–1). In Antonio's case the inability to verbalise is justified because Marston is seeking to create the suggestion that Antonio's love for Mellida is genuine and deep. A lover who can glibly articulate his feelings is, in comparison, as shallow as his affection. In Balurdo, aposiopesis functions differently; it is a device to satirise the absurd hyperbole of speech affected by courtiers.[55]

The visual equivalents of the instances of aposiopesis in the play are the sudden collapses of the principal characters. Andrugio casts himself to the ground to emphasise his despair at the pointlessness of life (III.i.40). Andrugio embraces the earth to emphasise his mortality, to choke his throat with 'dust' (44). His son takes to the earth no fewer than four times. On the first occasion (II.i.210.1), Antonio is still disguised as Florizel, and his sudden 'faint' is designed to interrupt the enforced dance to which Mellida is being subjected by command of Piero, but the action also reflects Antonio's inability to command his crises of emotional feeling. On the second occasion (III.ii.193.2), his collapse reveals his total despair at a threat to Mellida when she has lost his note arranging the details of their escape. The third and fourth prostrations (IV.i.27.1, 163.1) are both directly comparable to Andrugio's. Antonio establishes his kinship with death as did his father: 'Clod upon clod thus fall' (IV.i.27), and 'O trifling Nature, why inspir'dst thou breath?' (IV.i.165). The pressure of the circumstances surrounding the youth Antonio is such that both his tongue and his body become paralysed. Yet the serious intention is overlaid by a comical satiric purpose. Antonio is both inarticulate and unable to act when faced by an emotional crisis, and thus his love for Mellida is at once inexpressibly intense and absurd, for he is tongue-tied.

Prior to Antonio's fainting spell in the character of the Amazon, Florizel (II.i.210.1), Piero had entered the scene in the full dignity of his rank as Duke (160.1–4). This entry introduces a novel dramatic device: a pageant develops out of a dumb show. Piero sits honouring Florizel while mocking his daughter's grief for her lost lover, Antonio. There is a deliberate suggestion that Piero is physically attracted to this Amazon while his daughter is denied him/her. Mellida, being forced to dance with suitors whom her father is trying to force upon her while she mourns Antonio, is still suffering the ironic anguish of dancing unknowingly in the presence of her lost lover. The apparent love intrigue developing between Piero and the Amazon may be compared, ironically, to the equally mistaken but, in this case, not mismatched, affair suggested unknowingly by the amorous Rosaline to Antonio/Florizel at the end of the first act.

Antonio interrupts the set pageantry by the exaggerated jealousy of the lover. He casts himself upon the ground (II.i.210.1), but this gesture, which reflects the depths of his anguish, is promptly parodied by the pragmatic Rosaline who is willing to spend a night with anyone (227–9), and by Balurdo, who cannot find an epithet for love (232), and who goes on to an erudite discussion of the habits of ghosts. It is, of course, Antonio who is this ghost of himself, in the person of Florizel.

This sequence of events concludes with an opportunity for a disclosure between the lovers. The romantic note of the reunion of the principals suggests that they are to be taken more seriously than the previous action has indicated, for they determine to fly from a world which is 'wretched and miserable, / Banished, forlorn, despairing'

(280–1). In this they show more real sense than their literary ancestors, Romeo and Juliet. The conclusion to the second act, then, unexpectedly takes the lovers seriously as persons, and their emotions are portrayed as probable. These lovers have, at least momentarily, ceased to be parody; they are, for a moment, forgiven their absurdity, for they are human. Perhaps we are also intended to conclude that the actors playing the parts have underestimated their skills.

As the third act opens, there occurs another abrupt change of tone from romance to a mood uniformly 'tragical-historical'. The tone of the scene is philosophical, triggered by the proclamation by Piero of the reward for Andrugio and Antonio 'dead or alive'. Andrugio, reflecting a scepticism derived from Montaigne (28–34), questions the validity of a philosophy which argues that the cosmos is benevolent and purposeful. He is becoming convinced, by the pressure of his own sufferings, that life is a bitter jest in a malignant universe. He takes refuge in a passionless, stoical retreat within the self: 'There's nothing left / Unto Andrugio but Andrugio' (60–1), but, equally promptly, dismisses it as useless, replacing it with a call to 'a fair cause of arms' (86). He begins to see himself in a historic mould, charged with a sacred mission—the text is packed with lines half-cited from the conclusion to Shakespeare's *Richard III*—where his role becomes that of fulfilling a destiny conferred upon him by a higher power, for 'Legions of angels' (92) will fight upon his side. For a moment, Andrugio sees himself as the founder of the Tudor dynasty. The scene concludes with a defiant assertion of intent: 'ere yon sun set, I'll show myself myself' (114). Andrugio here is a study in the psychology of the Stoic, but he, like Pandulpho Felice of *Antonio's Revenge*, ultimately rejects the Stoic creed as incompatible with man's emotional nature.

The resolute determination of Andrugio within the structure of the 'tragical-historical' plot is not allowed to dominate the action, for his behaviour is satirised and undermined by the criticism of Felice, Castilio, Cazzo, and Balurdo directed against courts and courtiers. Felice bitterly condemns the lying self-centredness of courtly butterflies (III.ii.17–18), and Castilio and Cazzo parody the affectation of the perfumed courtier. Similarly, in Balurdo, there is a visual satiric attack on empty ornament, for his gold teeth (III.ii.129) and outrageous costume, 'a yellow taffeta doublet cut upon carnation velour, a green hat, a blue pair of velvet hose, a gilt rapier, and an orange-tawny pair of worsted silk stockings' (V.i.81–4), create a focus for both laughter at absurdity and indignation at his flaunting of excess. Castilio too, who represents both the court and the ideals of courtesy, is shown to be a hypocrite and a liar, for his supposed love-note from Rosaline is, in fact, an unpaid tailor's bill. Piero also is often shown in a satiric guise, as with his exaggerated, hysterical reaction to his chance discovery of Mellida's letter of assignation. These false values constantly remind the audience of the real insubstantiality of the vows and resolute protestations, however genuinely meant, that occur within the tragic-historic frame of the play's action.

Antonio and Piero are often paralleled: the one as a foolish lover, the other as a gross and improbable tyrant. Just as the resolution of Andrugio is questioned by the courtly satire of the play, so Antonio's commitment to Mellida, at the end of the second act, is undermined by his inability to adjust to the malignancy of fate. When, in the next act (III.ii), Piero discovers the lovers' plan to elope, Antonio at once despairs, crying 'curse thy birth / And die' (III.ii.211–12), and he wishes only to 'fill a seat / In the dark cave of dusky Misery' (219–20). Antonio does, however, recover sufficiently to defy fate and live in hope (231). Antonio's extreme reaction to misfortune is similar to Piero's overreaction to his chance for revenge. He vows he will 'drink carouse ... / ... in Antonio's skull' (237–8). This, the reaction of the Marlovian overreacher, is in keeping with the dominating satirical mood of the third act, for it continues the attack on courts and courtiers as it is tantamount to a denunciation of tyranny: Piero has become a caricature, and the Renaissance despot is, thus, a supreme example of the foolish self-infatuation of courtiers.

The action of the fourth act is strongly reminiscent of Shakespeare's *Romeo and Juliet*, for Piero, discovering that Mellida has deceived him and escaped, reacts with an extreme outburst like that of Old Capulet when Juliet rejects the proffered marriage to Paris: 'Light and unduteous! Kneel not, peevish elf, / Speak not; entreat not. Shame unto my house, / Curse to my honour!' (IV.i.247–9). Mellida's response is to plead 'Good father——' (252), but Piero cuts her off: 'Good me no goods' (253), just as Old Capulet shouted at Juliet: 'Thank me no thankings, nor proud me no prouds' (*Romeo and Juliet*, III.v.152).[56] Within this Romeo and Juliet framework there is a blend of the tragic, romantic, and philosophical themes with which the audience is already familiar.

The fourth act opens on a tragic note with Antonio again in the bleak misery of utter despair, 'Antonio's lost' (2), but Andrugio introduces a more rational explanation—the world is 'infected with a general plague' (38) and, thus, no honourable man can respect it. It is at this point that the 'tragical' and philosophical themes of the play reach their climax with Andrugio's self-discovery, derived from the *Thyestes*, that 'not the barèd pate, ... / Tyrian purple, chairs of state / ... confirm a prince / ... he's a king, / ... that dares do aught save wrong' (46–9, 52–3). This is not simply a reaffirmation of the Stoic creed but rather a moral humanist viewpoint which is reinforced by Stoicism. Andrugio relates the decay of the moral fibre of the world to the historical aspect of the play by again decrying the fickleness of his former Genoese subjects: 'Was never prince with more despite cast out, / Left shipwrecked, banished, on more guiltless ground' (74–5).

The second recognition scene of the play is that between Antonio and Andrugio; the first was the reuniting of Mellida with the presumed drowned Antonio. Andrugio, having discovered himself and the true nature of rule, urges Antonio similarly to attain self-knowledge by a return to the simplicities of nature. He invites his son into a hovel where they will 'sit weeping, blind with passion's tears' (IV.i.132) and where Antonio may 'rip / The inwards of [his] fortunes' (130–1). Andrugio has already indicated that he sees his dynasty subject to some great 'scalding vengeance' (120). While he was Duke of Genoa, his house was selected by nemesis for destruction for some 'black sin' (118)—once again a half-memory of the pattern of nemesis at the conclusion to Shakespeare's first tetralogy of history plays.

The recognition of Andrugio and Antonio is immediately followed by another rediscovery: Antonio finds Mellida again, although initially she replays the irony of Antonio as Florizel, for she overhears him lamenting her loss while she, Mellida, is a transvestite as a page. Despite Antonio's hyperbole of compliment, the lovers are presented here as seriously committed to each other. Just as Shakespeare showed that Romeo's love for Juliet was no mere infatuation by having them converse in a formal sonnet at their first meeting (I.v.90–104), so Marston seeks to show the enduring nature of the Antonio and Mellida bond by their interchange of vows in Italian: 'O, the heart dissolves in a gentle kiss. / The senses die in the object of desire ... Grant me rule over your most welcome love, / Which blesses me, with an everlasting honour; / Thus, in this way, it is fitting that I die' (197–8, 204–6). The difference in the tone of the relationship between Antonio and Mellida is created by the formal change of language, from the idiomatic English to the literary Italian couched in the extravagant phraseology of the *commedia dell'arte*. Just as the tragic plot culminated with Andrugio's self-discovery, so the romance plot culminates here with this avowal. Marston is seeking to produce an ideal blend of the personal (he is Italian) and the historical-fictional (the scene is Italy, the lovers speak Italian). Unfortunately, the effect of this commitment scene becomes somewhat diffused because, firstly, the page explains it as a personal aberration of the author and, secondly, Balurdo makes a joke of his discovery of Mellida to Piero.

The dual restorations, of Andrugio to Antonio and Mellida to Antonio, represent two significant climaxes for the action, but both are, almost immediately, reversed. The romantic avowal of Antonio and Mellida is undermined by Balurdo's jests (IV.i.228ff.), and the tragic-philosophical resolve of Andrugio and Antonio is reversed, in Antonio's case, by his sudden collapse into the helpless despair of the foolish lover. Antonio never attains to Romeo's single-minded dedication to love and death; he remains always a youth caught up in a tragic web of circumstances over which he is never able to gain control. Marston's portrayal of Andrugio is sufficiently consistent for the impression of firm resolution to remain. In Antonio's case, however, his role as a parody of the lover causes the credibility of his passion for Mellida to fluctuate from incident to incident.

It is in the final stage of the action that there takes place the most drastic of all the play's alterations of direction and focus, involving the complete transformation of the character of Piero. The fourth act had ended on a note of foreboding: 'O, blood-true-honoured graves / Are far more blessèd than base life of slaves' (IV.ii.36–7), but in the fifth act these omens are simply ignored, or drastically altered in their significance, and the tragic potential of the action is reversed. The last act is wholly 'comical-pastoral', with romance overtones from Sidney's *Arcadia*. The first scene is preoccupied with the embryonic sub-plot of Rosaline and her suitors. One of them, Alberto, decides, like Orlando of *As You Like It*, to

> . . . go and breathe my woes unto the rocks
> And spend my grief upon the deafest seas.
> I'll weep my passion to the senseless trees
> And load most solitary air with plaints,
> For woods, trees, sea, or rocky Apennine
> Is not so ruthless as my Rosaline. (62–7)

This exaggerated lament is in keeping with the satire on lovers, on the whole romance convention, and also on the satire on courtly duplicity. Alberto, the exemplary honest lover of the play, abandons the world and his beloved because he is too poor to buy his way into her affections.

When Piero returns to the stage, his character has undergone a startling shift of emphasis. He is no longer the ruthless, tyrannical *condottiere* but has mellowed into a kindly uncle concerned with his niece's marriage prospects. Piero is now a Renaissance prince who is a patron of art and artists, perhaps modeled on Lodovico Sforza, the doyen of civilised Milanese society. There is some of the Old Capulet in him still, however, for he remains abrupt and imperious with Mellida, insisting that the marriage with Galeazzo go forward, but this element remains muted. More obvious is his compassion and regret for the death of Antonio, 'O, that my life, her love, my dearest blood / Would but redeem one minute of his breath!' (v.ii.221–2) which reminds us of the regret of Old Capulet for Romeo and 'his lady', both 'Poor sacrifices of our enmity!' (*R. & J.*, v.iii.303).

The concluding actions of the play are full of the implausibilies of literary romance, but the criticism of courtly excess now seems subdued. Andrugio presents himself to claim the reward for his own head; Antonio appears once again as a dead man, but soon 'arises'; Piero's extravagant hatred is turned to equally extreme affection, 'him whom I loathed before / . . . now I honour, love, nay more, adore' (185–6), by Andrugio's bravery; all other suitors drop their claims to Mellida and, through the lovers, the warring houses are united in affection. The conclusion of the action, where Piero and Andrugio 'drink a health while they two sip a kiss' (264), suggests that the scene has become one where Piero is now being presented as an exemplary Renaissance prince, presiding over a court that could suitably be called 'the flower of the world'.

The denouement artificially restores people, places, and events to 'nectar streams' of 'sweet airs' (278). This musical 'close' brings together, but does not obscure, the discrete events of the action. The plot shows romance obtruded upon by the alienation of 'tragical-historical' events, and the atmosphere produced is more often morally problematical than pastorally comic. The play has become the story of 'the comic crosses of true love' by a deliberate metamorphosis of character and incident. Piero Sforza's change of heart, however, may be motivated by his historical antecedents. As a representative Sforza, he can be seen to embody the elements of all three Dukes of Milan, but now, dominantly, he is Lodovico, the Moor. Antonio's pious hope that 'the passage' may 'most successful prove' (280) is not unreasonable in terms of the concluding notes of *Antonio and Mellida*, but will prove to be ominously detached from the realities of the situation in the sequel, *Antonio's Revenge*. Marston has created a drama in which is blended historical fact, theatrical realities, and romantic fancy: the historical Sforzas have become the unhistorical literary family of Piero; the characters of the Antonio/Mellida 'comedy' are the Children of Paul's, with all their own personal inexperience of life and action.

The world of the play is one where no value is constant, certainly not love, for while the love of Antonio and Mellida is the most sensitively and poignantly portrayed emotion in the play, the behaviour of lovers is the most consistently derided activity in the action. The plot suggests, however, that in both tragedy and history there is an element of literary fiction: the lives of the actors and the characters they personate have such similarity that each modifies the meaning of the other. Life may be as artificial as the arbitrary convention of the comic resolution to the play, for in both life and art when Piero promises 'My love be thine, the all I have be thine' (v.ii.262) there can be little certainty for how long it will remain true. In the denouement, the next phase in the development of the saga of the clash of the Sforza and the Genoese dynasty is prefigured. Piero Sforza may have made a wholly implausible conversion, but there is, as yet, no reason to anticipate that his hypocrisy may become evident, for the sound of 'Lydian wires' (277) dominates.

The many abrupt transitions between mood, theme, and purpose in *Antonio and Mellida* may have been deliberately intended to dazzle the original spectators with an amazing variety. The character of Antonio, voluble and inarticulate, passionate and foolish, tragic and inept, in particular, reflects the play's diverse moods and perceptions. The original spectators were offered an ending that was highly conventional and wholly unconvincing, but it was a closing of the action; they may, however, have remained more conscious of the fierceness of the satire and the utter helplessness of the lovers. The play, however, does not move towards a prearranged conclusion or end; its structure is less linear than circular. Since Marston is concerned with the demonstration of various kinds of dramatic form with which to display both his and his actors' expertise, the apparently bewildering changes of mood are one of the play's essential virtues. Without a constant shifting of perspective and idea, the exploratory quality of the play, revealing the range of talent from which it is drawn, could not be demonstrated effectively. The ending of *Antonio and Mellida* is a joyous conclusion to a potentially tragic love affair; the survival of the lovers, within the reconciliation of the Sforza dynasty with its enemies, is a romantic resolution denied to Romeo and Juliet. The denouement of *Antonio and Mellida* may, in fact, be less significant in its overall design than the design itself. As an advertisement to display a range of talent in author and actors, the play succeeded so well that Marston was able to return Antonio to the stage in a role which translated him from a burlesque Romeo to a childlike Hamlet. The public appears to have demanded that promised 'second part'.

6. THE PLAY AND ITS SEQUEL

In the Induction, Alberto dismisses Antonio's fears that he will not be able to 'play two parts in one' (70–1) on the grounds that it is usual to 'bear two subtle fronts under one hood' (78–9). The play's characters certainly bear witness to the truth of this remark, moving, between one scene and the next, from a 'tragical' identity to an ironic satiric 'vein', either as a criticism of the world or as a parody of the previous self. The Induction concludes with the promise that 'those persons ... that are but slightly drawn in this comedy, should receive more exact accomplishment in a second part which, if this obtain gracious acceptance, means to try his fortune' (143–7).

It is unlikely that Marston had *Antonio's Revenge* written or even plotted in detail when *Antonio and Mellida* was presented, since the creation of the sequel was contingent upon the 'gracious acceptance' (146) of the first part. It may well be that he waited to determine the reception *Antonio and Mellida* received before commencing work on a second part. Whatever the explanation about its composition, *The History of Antonio and Mellida* as we have received it is in two parts, and the second completes the action of the usurpation of Genoa by Piero with his assassination as a bloody tyrant.

G. K. Hunter has pointed out that *Antonio and Mellida* and *Antonio's Revenge* constitute a diptych, 'in which repetition of shape and design focuses attention on what is common to the two parts'.[57] The common elements in the design are, in both cases, the initial triumph of Piero (deposing Andrugio and killing him); the movement from abject romantic abandonment of life in Antonio to the assumption of the role of avenger; the decision by Andrugio to claim the reward for his own capture and the decision of the conspirators to assassinate Piero; and, finally, the reconciliation of the wedding masque and the vengeance masque of the second part.

While it is true that there was a significant time lapse between the performance of the first and second parts, and that it is unlikely that the sequel was written when the first part was performed, Marston did make considerable efforts to create a true two-part play pattern. There are significant additional ways in which the two plays constitute a developing and complementary sequence.

Antonio's Revenge is loosely co-ordinated in terms of the received Hamlet story, and the life of Piero Sforza is manipulated to conform to the general outlines of that legend. In a similar way *Antonio and Mellida* is 'historical' in the sense of using the story of the Sforza dynasty to provide a pseudo-factual, historical background to the romance plot. Marston was, also, obviously conscious that it is a simple matter to assume that Piero's reconciliation at the end of the first part is hypocritical, and thus it is easy to account for a change of heart in any sequel. The shift from comedy to tragedy is, also, in itself an obvious parallelism. Marston, in fact, created the first part with some skill, in the sense that it offers itself as an adaptable introduction to almost any kind of second part, for in that first part there are a multiplicity of themes and moods available to be exploited. *The History of Antonio and Mellida* is a sequential and interconnected two-part play, but the relationship was loose and capable, at least initially, of being adapted to whatever contingency determined the form of its second half.

There are additional, more specific ways in which the plays are a pair. In *Antonio and Mellida* aposiopesis is a symptom of the inertia which grips the protagonists. The only man capable of action is Andrugio, but his only act is to give up his body to his captor. In times of crisis Andrugio, Antonio, and Piero are all unable to act either through excessive emotionalism, too much *apathia*, or a failure to respond positively to a crisis. It is in *Antonio's Revenge* that this inertia is overcome by the intelligence from the ghost of Andrugio, the final rejection of the Stoic creed by Pandulpho, and the sheer bloodiness of Piero's deeds. Similarly the actors of the first part are singularly inexperienced and nervous in their roles, as the Induction bears witness, whereas in the second part they are more clearly matured, as actors and as human beings, by their sufferings under the tyranny of Piero.

In *Antonio and Mellida*, violence is rejected in favour of inaction and a dumb acceptance of fate; in *Antonio's Revenge*, violence is chosen as the only instrument to achieve a calmness of spirit and a meaningful retreat from the world to the 'holy verge of some religious order' (v.vi.35) where Antonio, Alberto, and Pandulpho will live 'Most constant votaries' (36). Inaction must be meaningful, and the right to it must be earned. The two parts of *Antonio and Mellida* are bound, then, by a common philosophy behind the diversities of plot and action. A commitment to meaningful action, at whatever personal cost, is the only way that man may translate an abstract philosophical system, whether it is Stoic or Christian, into a meaningful way of life.

Antonio and Mellida and *Antonio's Revenge*, then, do constitute a diptych in theme and mood. They do differ, however, in the form of their plots. *Antonio's Revenge* is essentially a revenge tragedy with the focus of the action in the culmination and fulfilment of that revenge; its climax is the bloody banquet where Piero consumes his son, Julio. In *Antonio and Mellida*, on the other hand, the demands of the plot are less rigid so as to allow for the requirements of display, both visual and literary.

7. THE PLAY IN ITS THEATRE

Antonio and Mellida is, as a whole, a demonstration of the various kinds of dramatic form that Marston is capable of creating, a display of the various talents that exist among the Children of Paul's, and an exhibition of the various facilities that are available in their playing place. It was performed in the Paul's Playhouse, which was, most probably, situated in the north-west quadrant of the Chapter House precinct of St Paul's Cathedral.[58] Richard Flecknoe, in his *Short Discourse on the English Stage*, 1664, tells how 'on weekdays after vespers ... the Children of ... St. Paul's acted plays ... behind the convocation-house [Chapter House] in Paul's'.[59] The building extended into and across both the garth and the cloisters, and the latter were probably used as the tiring-house; the cloisters were two-storeyed and the playhouse, therefore, had both upper and lower levels.

From the evidence supplied by *Antonio and Mellida*, Paul's playhouse had both upper and lower acting areas: '*Enter above,* MELLIDA, ROSALINE, *and* FLAVIA. *Enter below* GALEAZZO *with attendants* ...' (I.i.99.2–3). These areas were designated 'lower stage' (I.i.140.1) and, presumably, 'upper stage'. The distance from the upper to the lower level was short, requiring only ten lines for the exit and re-entry of three characters from one to the other (I.i.152–61). There were two

[handwritten marginal note: Paul's Playhouse are A Red Qair frontispiece or p471]

doors for entry to the stage (IV.i.225.1–3) and these may well have
been opposed: '*Enter* PIERO, CASTILIO, MAZZAGENTE, FOROBOSCO,
FELICE, GALEAZZO [*at one door*], BALURDO, *and his page* [DILDO, *and*
MELLIDA] *at another door.*' It is tempting to conjecture that procession-
al entry could have been made from a double opening at stage centre,
as for the inspection of the guard at II.i.160.1–7. The stage itself was
very small; as Piero explains to the masquers, 'The room's too scant.
Boys, stand in there, close' (v.ii.75). It could, however, hold some
twelve characters (I.i.34.1–5) on the 'lower stage', and another three
on the upper level (I.i.99.2–5). There was about 440 square feet of
usable space on the ground floor level to accommodate the stage and
the audience.

   From two other plays performed during the first months of the
revival at Paul's, *The Wisdom of Doctor Dodypoll* and *Jack Drum's
Entertainment*, it is apparent that the stage was organised in such a way
as to provide for an inner discovery space. This may perhaps have
been in the centre and was a wide double doorway, covered with a
curtain: '*A curtain drawn, Earl Lasingbergh is discovered (like a painter)
painting Lucilia, who sits working on a piece of cushion-work*' (*Dodypoll,
Q* 1600, A3). In addition, on the upper stage there was at least one
'casement' window, as in *Jack Drum*, C2v, '*The casement opens and
Katherine appears*', and later Camelia calls to Brabant Junior '*from her
window*' (D3). This upper acting area appears to have had a central
open balcony, flanked by at least one operating window, which could
be used to simulate the upper storeys of a house, as in *Jack Drum*, D3,
where first Winifred 'looks from above' and then, sixteen lines later,
Camelia shouts from her window; both ladies remain visible together
from two separate locations. There is no suggestion in any of these
three plays of the use of a trap.

   The theatre seems to have employed musicians to form an
orchestra, which was probably quite small and may have consisted of
a quintet of strings, and another quintet for cornet, sackbut, and
recorder.[60] In *Antonio and Mellida* the musicians provided a suitable
sound for signalling with cornets (I.i.34.1), for a measure (II.i.171.1),
and for a coranto pace (II.i.54.3); they also played a 'mournful sennet'
on the recorders (v.ii.186.1), and probably used the same instruments
for the concluding 'sweet airs' (v.ii.278). The actors themselves were
able to provide a harpist (v.ii.0.1), and a number of them could sing
well enough to compete with each other in solo performances (v.ii).
Antonio and Mellida has eight songs, II.i.54.1; III.i.105.1, III.ii.35.1,
270.1; IV.i.156.1; v.ii.9.1, 19.1, 25.1, and five catches or part songs,

II.i.54.2–3, 259; III.ii.36–8; IV.i.154.1; V.i.38–9. It is likely that the
singing was of a very high standard, and indeed was one of the most
distinguishing features of the performances. In 1614, Thomas
Ravenscroft, the lutenist and composer, testifies to Edward Pearce's
skills as a teacher and composer of music:

> Master Edward Pearce the first, sometimes master of the Children of Saint
> Paul's in London and there my master, a man of singular eminency in his
> profession, both in the educating of children for the ordering of the voice so
> as the quality might afterward credit him and prefer them, and also in those
> his compositions to the lute, whereof the world enjoys many, as from the
> master of that instrument; together with his skilfull instructions for other
> instruments too, as his fruits can bear him witness.[61]

The words of the songs from *Antonio and Mellida* have not, generally,
survived; they may have been composed by Pearce and kept in a
separate song book, now lost.

Balurdo describes Flavia as 'like a gentlewoman of fourteen years of
age' (V.ii.129–30), and this may well be a reasonably accurate estimate
of the upper age limit of the actor-choristers at the time of the
performance of this play. It is, however, possible that Antonio was
slightly older than this, for his voice had already broken; it was
'viragolike' (Ind. 76). On the other hand, Cazzo is 'diminutive' (II.i.2)
and Dildo is an 'urchin' (II.i.6), implying that both boys were younger
and shorter than the principals. As far as the audience for the play was
concerned, Marston and Stanley may well have initially simply invited
friends and acquaintances mainly from the Inns of Court, who
rewarded the actors by tossing coins on to the stage.[62] In this opening
period of the revival at Paul's, the spectators could be described as a
'good gentle audience' (*Jack Drum*, H3v), and the playhouse was a
place where 'A man shall not be choked / With the stench of garlic,
nor be pasted / To the barmy jacket of a beer-brewer' (H3v). The
emphasis, then, at the time of the first production of *Antonio and
Mellida* is on refinement and sophistication in literary taste and
setting, and on expertise and diversity of talent both in actor and
dramatist.

In 1598 one of the choristers was Thomas Ravenscroft, and he
became Pearce's star pupil. He seems to have been a child prodigy
who was described in these terms: 'A young man who is an old man in
his skill is a rare bird, but what is rarer still is if a man is young in
years, but old in moral character.' Ravenscroft, then, was a child with
the accomplishments of maturity and the wisdom to match.[63] He later

44 ANTONIO AND MELLIDA

preserved some of Pearce's songs and testifies that his master wrote
them not as mere embellishments to plays, but as integral parts of the
mood and themes. In them, he wrote, 'Music . . . gives both a relish,
and a beauty to . . . poetry . . . passionate tunes make amorous poems
both willinglier heard and better remembered.'[64] When Antonio is
convinced that Mellida is dead, he demands that his page sing:

> . . . but sirrah, mark you me,
> Let each note breathe the heart of passion,
> The sad extracture of extremest grief.
> Make me a strain. Speak groaning like a bell
> That tolls departing souls.
> Breathe me a point that may enforce me weep . . .
> Howl out such passion that even this brinish marsh
> Will squeeze out tears from out his spongy cheeks,
> The rocks even groan . . . (IV.i.138–43, 149–51)

If Ravenscroft's testimony is to be trusted and Antonio does not
exaggerate beyond all plausibility, then, Marston had a collaborator
for this play, Edward Pearce, the author of its songs. In 1599 Thomas
Ravenscroft was seven years old;[65] it is likely that he took part in
Antonio and Mellida, perhaps as Antonio's page. Two of his
companions in the choir at Paul's, Robert Coles and John Norwood,
also had parts, perhaps those of Andrugio/Alberto and Lucio
(IV.i.28.1n).

The Induction opens the play on a nervous and tentative note, with
the characters of the play hidden behind the anonymous cloaks of the
choristers, and Galeazzo is concerned lest his companions are not
ready to perform. The impression created is that this is a rehearsal for
the play proper, and the actors are tremulously analysing their ability
to play the parts allotted them. They go on to describe these parts so
as to outline for the audience the roles that they are supposed to
perform. By this detailed description of the characters, the audience is
offered a standard by which to judge the quality of the acting. It is
essential for the audience to appreciate both that the actors are
inexperienced and that they are highly talented.

Piero points out that the problem is not lack of preparation, for 'we
can say our parts' (3), but inexperience: 'we are ignorant in what
mould we must cast our actors' (3–4). Alberto advises on acting style,
and himself admits that he plays both Andrugio and Alberto, thus
revealing one of the necessary economies a company must make to
cast a play; Balurdo, Forobosco, and Felice express confidence in

their ability to personate their roles, but Antonio is convinced that he cannot play an Amazon. One of the reasons for his concern may be that his voice has broken. Alberto, behaving rather like the producer of the play, argues that the boy/man Antonio can perform his man/woman role because as a youth he is specially fitted for this part. Marston is pointing out one of the special properties of the chorister company, that their physical condition, on the verge of puberty, allows them to be both sexes at once. The audience is made intensely aware that this performance is a debut for the Children of Paul's. In the ensuing action Antonio's inarticulate emotional crises will be a manifestation of the inexperience the cast admits to in the Induction.

The Induction concludes with the promise of a sequel, if the response to *Antonio and Mellida* is sufficiently positive, and the Prologue continues this note of apology-in-advance:

> For wit's sake do not dream of miracles.
> Alas, we shall but falter if you lay
> The least sad weight of an unusèd hope
> Upon our weakness . . .
> . . . if our slightness your large hope beguiles,
> Check not with bended brow but dimpled smiles. (4–7, 22–3)

The nervous hesitation is intermingled with high praise for the perspicuity of the audience whose 'authentic censure' (9) is awaited with some apprehension.

After the entry of Antonio in his promised Amazonian guise, the first act parades the cast/company on the lower stage as Piero's guard (1.i.34.1–5), and places three ladies on the upper balcony (99.2–3). These three, Mellida, Rosaline, and Flavia, comment on the spectacle below which is conducted as a dumb show; this technique of commentary on a silent action is a new development for the old-fashioned dumb show. The same pattern of action recurs later in the scene at 1.i.116.1–3.

The effect of the Induction, the Prologue, and the first hundred lines of the first scene is to introduce a new company of actors to a new audience in a play by a novice dramatist. It has, moreover, already afforded an opportunity to show off the upper and lower playhouse acting areas, to display all the members of the acting company, and to allow Marston a chance to show his skill at innovating dramatic techniques. One of the essential purposes of the play, then, seems to be to provide a forum for the advertisement of the Paul's playhouse, the Children of Paul's, and John Marston.

The action often creates a sense of personal intimacy with the actors, as when Cazzo and Dildo are both described as 'diminutive urchins' for the play as characters, and for the choir as singers (II.i). So too the suggestion at II.i.161–2 that some form of relationship is possible between the Amazon Florizel (Antonio) and Piero reflects a consciousness of the erotic, homosexual appeal of the boys. The very name, Cazzo or 'penis', is also a cruder reflection of the same awareness. Similarly at III.ii.118.1–5, where Balurdo enters backwards with Dildo who holds a looking-glass for him as he preens himself, and Balurdo stands with Rosaline 'setting of faces' (118.4–5), the audience is reminded both of the Children of Paul's as actors making themselves ready for their parts, and the Choir of Paul's as children amusing themselves by making faces before mirrors.

The eight songs and five catches of the play are, of course, standard embellishments for a chorister company, and although here they may have been moulded to the action, the singing is none the less a form of display. The same is true of the dancing, as with Mellida '*in page's attire, dancing*' at III.ii.253.1, and Rosaline who runs a '*coranto pace*' (II.i.54.3), while Castilio sings '*fantastically*' (54.3). This density of song and dance was an essential part of the special attraction of the boy actors, and, in the second scene of the last act the action is manipulated to enhance it. While it is true that Piero, who presides over the singing contest for the golden harp, is at this stage in the play a patron of the arts rather than a despot, the competition is a conscious embellishment to use the special talents of the actors. Much more essential to the structure of the play as a whole is the device of using the special skills of trained singers to enhance emotional effects, as when Antonio 'breaks' a held tone by his singing page, IV.i.154.1. This exploits an ability peculiar to this kind of company, and here their ability is well integrated to the needs of the plot, intensifying Antonio's anguish by the sudden interruption of the vibrating chord.

A similar musical effect is found at II.i.172–205, where Mellida is forced to dance a measure by Piero's command but against her will, for she is grieving for the (supposed) death of Antonio. She exclaims that the music (playing in the background) is operating as an ironic counterpoint to her grief:

... O music, thou distill'st
More sweetness in us than this jarring world!
Both time and measure from thy strains do breathe,
Whilst from the channel of this dirt doth flow
Nothing but timeless grief, unmeasured woe. (201–5)

Once again this is an example of the use of an effect which the indoor theatre of the singing boys could perform exceptionally well, and which here is fully integrated to the action of the play.

Marston's attempt to advertise the range of talent among his actors, the facilities available in the playhouse, and the abilities of its musicians are more successful than his attempts to make himself known. In the first scene of the fourth act (189–206), Antonio and Mellida converse in Italian, probably to indicate the depth of their emotional commitment by this shift into the traditional language of love. A possible justification for the Italian dialogue might perhaps be that Marston wanted to intensify the audience's awareness of the historical Italian setting of the action, but this is not the explanation proffered. The Page explains that it is a private matter between the lovers themselves and also, perhaps, between the author and those who know him personally (223–4); as a result, the incident becomes somewhat extra-dramatic and partially underminines the dramatic illusion.

Similar damage to the dramatic form occurs when the portraits are introduced in v.i.7–13. To bring on a portrait of oneself is precious enough, but to comment upon it as blatantly as Balurdo does is to suggest that the future of the Paul's company is more important than the present dramatic illusion. The whole of the last act perhaps suffers from an excessive need to display, as with the rising-from-the-dead of Antonio (v.ii.223) which is gratuitous, for it repeats the theme of the living-dead Andrugio, who appears here already condemned. The effect of Antonio's resurrection is to dissipate the remains of the historical action and to intensify the concluding note of the play, which is wholly romantic. The historical action is a fiction, consciously manipulated to result in the comic convention of the reconciliation of a marriage. The extraordinary events of the last scene of the play may be designed to effect the metamorphosis from the 'tragical-historical' themes towards the 'comic-pastoral' conclusions.

In the Epilogue the audience is again made intensely conscious of the experimental, tentative, nervous nature of the performance. Andrugio/Alberto, who instructed the actors in the Induction, now pleads with the spectators not for conventional applause but for a form of contract. The Epilogue offers to modify plays to meet any criticism that the audience may have of what they have just seen. *Antonio and Mellida*, then, has many purposes: to display the range of Marston's abilities as a dramatist and satirist; to show off the Children of Paul's; to ask for help in building up the new theatrical venture in which Paul's are involved; and to show off dramatic effects never previously attempted. All of these purposes become dominant at various times, and they are in addition to the 'tragical-comical-historical-pastoral' plot; truly a play of many meanings.

Whether or not *Antonio and Mellida* was the first play at the second Paul's playhouse, it was certainly among the very first performed there, in the earliest days of the revival. As an advertisement it certainly seems to have succeeded in making known both the author and the company to a wider public. The war of words in the Poetomachia, which was soon to erupt, was certainly stimulated by this play. Not merely was this chorister company to enjoy an initial success which made it, along with the Blackfriar's company, the most fashionable group of entertainers in London, but this play appears itself to have been so remarkable for the contemporary audience that, a decade later, Thomas Dekker seems to have been able to recall details of its dialogue and action. *Antonio and Mellida* may well be the primary source of the popularity of the revived Children's Theatres in the opening decade of the seventeenth century.

NOTES

1. The printer is identified by W. W. Greg, *A Bibliography of the English Printed Drama to the Restoration*, London: Illustrated Monographs issued by the Bibliographical Society, No. 24, 1939, 1.185.
2. Since this is a modern spelling edition, I have made no attempt to describe the many variations which occur with the badly cast punctuation marks. I wish, however, to record my gratitude to all owners of copies of the 1602 quarto for access to these originals.
3. *Paul's*, p. 184.
4. *Paul's*, pp. 61–6.
5. *Malone Reprint*, p. vi.
6. For a more conventional biography of John Marston see G. K. Hunter's Introduction to *The Malcontent*, and my Introduction to *Antonio's Revenge*, both in the Revels Plays.
7. Chapter VI, p. 31.
8. Jonson may be alluding specifically to the Epilogue to *Antonio and Mellida*, where Marston promises to write whatever pleases the audience.
9. For a detailed study of the Poetomachia and the quarrel between Marston and Jonson, see both the Introduction to *Antonio's Revenge*, and *Paul's*, pp. 124–38.
10. The segment within the square brackets is a clause that was subsequently deleted; cited by D. G. O'Neill, 'The Commencement of Marston's Career as a Dramatist', *R.E.S.*, NS 22, 1971, 444. The will is in the Public Record Office, 82 Kidd.

11. See P. J. Finkelpearl, *H.L.Q.*, 29, 1966, 223–34. The text of *Histriomastix* is taken from H. H. Wood's edn. of Marston's plays, vol. 3, p. 264, III.i.
12. See further *Antonio's Revenge*, Introduction, pp. 6–7.
13. Oxford: J. Barnesius, F5*v*–F6, *Ad Joannem Marstonium*.
14. *Epigrams in the Oldest Cut and Newest Fashion*, ed. R. B. McKerrow, London: Sidgwick and Jackson, 1911.
15. Ed. C. Crawford, Oxford: Clarendon Press, 1913.
16. Spenser Society, Manchester: C. Sims, 1875 (no index); p. 28, *Pygmalion*; p. 50, *Satires, Dedn.*; pp. 168, 175, 220, *S. of V.* This work is often cited as edited by A. M., i.e., Anthony Munday.
17. C. Brown (ed.), *Poems by Sir John Salusbury and Robert Chester*, E.E.T.S., Extra Series, 113, 1914, p. lxxii.
18. *The Whipper Pamphlets*, ed. A. Davenport, Liverpool: Liverpool U. P., 1951.
19. Probably William Butler, who was famous for unconventional treatments.
20. *Q* 1606, B2–B2*v*; I.ii.269–84.
21. See 'The Play in its Theatre'.
22. Ed. R. D. Dunn, Toronto: Toronto U. P., 1984, p. 294.
23. The translation is by W. K. Marriott, Everyman's Library, London: Dent, 1931, p. 54; the later remark occurs at p. 115.
24. Cecilia M. Ady, *A History of Milan under the Sforza*, Methuen: London, 1907, p. 45.
25. Ady, p. 47.
26. Ady, p. 27.
27. L. Collison–Morley, *The Story of the Sforzas*, London: Routledge, 1933, pp. 114–19.
28. Morley, p. 119.
29. Morley, p. 119.
30. Ady, p. 125; Morley, p. 172.
31. Ady, pp. 280–1.
32. Morley, pp. 158–9.
33. *The Poems of John Marston*, ed. A. Davenport, Liverpool: Liverpool U.P., 1961, p. 30.
34. *Lettere del Conte Baldessar Castiglione*, ed. P. Serassi, Padova: G. Comino, 1769, I:5.
35. See the introduction to his Regents edition, p. xi.
36. The simile borrowed from Erasmus (IV.i.13–17) was first noticed by an anonymous correspondent to *N. & Q.*, 1st series, vol. 9, and the additional citation (II.i.234–41), from the same colloquy, was noted by Hunter. The indebtedness to Montaigne is catalogued by Charles Crawford in *Collectanea*, 2nd series, 1907; the ballad heroine, Mary Ambree, was, of course, familiar to nineteenth-century editors, as was Aesop's fable of the Ass and the Lion and Margaret Tyler's *Mirror of Princely Deeds*. It was Hunter who noted one of the similarities to Sylvester's *Du Bartas*, and Schoonover remarked on the intriguing similarity to Florio's *Second Fruits*, whereas Bullen found the tavern jest repeated in Peele, and noted the borrowing from Nashe's *Summer's Last Will and Testament*. The references to *The Spanish Tragedy*, Virgil and the Bible are, of course, generally known to most editors. The quotation from

C

the Harvey/Nashe controversy has not, however, been observed prior to this edition.

37. M. Shapiro, *The Children of The Revels*, New York: Columbia U. P, 1977, pp. 18–19, and also *N. & Q.*, NS 18, 1971, 14, has argued that the Children of Paul's were revived in 1597. He cites the phrase, 'if any man do appeal to any play at Paul's' in *Le Prince d'Amour*, a refurbished old play for the Christmas Revels at the Middle Temple 1597/8. While it is possible that some of the Paul's choristers could have acted on a casual basis in a play about this time, it is unlikely in the extreme that the company was reformed before late 1599, because their master, Gyles, was very ill (1598); no mention of their dramatic activities occurs in the extremely detailed *Visitation Report of Bishop Bancroft* of 1598/9, which exhaustively describes all of the activities at St Paul's; the cloisters where they customarily performed were let to trunkmakers (1597/8); see *Paul's*, pp. 46–7. The remark is likely to be either an uncorrected survival from the 'old' play or a reference to a play by the boys of Paul's grammar school (who had no connection with the choristers), located on the east side of Paul's churchyard. See further *Paul's*, p. 52n.
38. See further *Paul's*, p. 113.
39. For the details relating to Gyles, Pearce, and the choristers see my 'The Conditions of Appointment for Masters of Choristers at Paul's (1553–1613)', *N. & Q.*, 27, 2, 1980, 119–22.
40. *Paul's*, pp. 40–1.
41. *Henslowe's Diary*, ed. W. W. Greg, 1904, I: 112.
42. *Paul's*, p. 125.
43. *John Marston, Satirist*, Ithaca, New York: Cornell U. P., 1961, p. 260.
44. R. E. Brettle, 'Marston Born in Oxfordshire', *M.L.R.*, 22, 1922, 318–19.
45. Brettle, 'John Marston Dramatist at Oxford (1591(?)–1594, 1609)' *R.E.S.*, 3, 1927, 399.
46. 'A New Date for *Antonio's Revenge*', *P.M.L.A.*, 53, 1938, 135. Other scholars have argued that the play should be dated late in 1601 because of similarities between the Painter scene of *Antonio and Mellida*, v.ii, and the Painter scene in the Fourth Addition to *The Spanish Tragedy*. The Second Quarto of *The Spanish Tragedy*, in which the fourth addition first appears, was published in 1602, and it has been suggested that this was one of the additions to the play for which Jonson was paid by Henslowe on 25 September 1601 and 22 June 1602. There is, however, no certainty that the Fourth Addition is by Jonson: Philip Edwards, editor of the Revels edition of *The Spanish Tragedy*, doubts Jonson's authorship, pp. lxi–lxiv. It seems most unlikely that Marston would have had an opportunity to revise *Antonio and Mellida*, between the appearance of the new edition of *The Spanish Tragedy* and 24 October 1601, when *Antonio and Mellida* was entered in the Stationers' Register. The explanation is most probably either that the Fourth Addition precedes Jonson's work on Kyd's play or that the writer of that contribution was imitating Marston. There is, to my mind, no overwhelming evidence to suggest that Marston's painter scene is a parody of any other writer's work.
47. 'The Date of Marston's *Antonio and Mellida*', *M.L.N.*, 72, 1957, 331.
48. *John Marston of the Middle Temple: An Elizabethan Dramatist in his Social Setting*, Cambridge, Mass.: Harvard U. P., 1969, pp. 270–1.

49. See 'The Play in its Theatre'.
50. See my Revels edition, p. 15.
51. The most striking of these is perhaps the manipulation of the plot to allow a display of all the actors in the company and of all the features of the theatre, early in the first act; see further 'The Play in its Theatre'.
52. *Historical Manuscripts Commission, Lord de L'Isle and Dudley* (Penshurst Place), II:415.
53. Jonathan Dollimore, *Radical Tragedy*, Brighton: The Harvester Press, 1984, pp. 30–1, has studied this alienation effect both in *Antonio and Mellida* and in *Antonio's Revenge*.
54. Ellen Berland, 'The Function of Irony in Marston's *Antonio and Mellida*', *St. Phil.*, 66, 1969, 739–55, provides a detailed analysis of irony and satire in the play which she sees as a 'fabric of deceits'.
55. T. F. Wharton, 'Old Marston or New Marston: The *Antonio* Plays', *Essays in Crit.*, 25, 1975, 357–8, cites Marston's overuse of 'peise' in *A.R.*, and comments on the frequence of aposiopesis in *Antonio and Mellida*.
56. Roger Stilling, '*Antonio and Mellida I & II*', in *Love and Death in Renaissance Tragedy*, Baton Rouge, Louisiana: Louisiana U. P., 1976, pp. 83–9, points out some of the relationships between the two plays.
57. '*Henry IV* and the Elizabethan Two-Part Play', *R.E.S.*, 5, 1954, 237.
58. For further details concerning the history and design of Paul's playhouse, see *Paul's*, chapter 2 *passim*.
59. Chambers, *Elizabethan Stage*, IV:369.
60. *Paul's*, p. 65.
61. *Brief Discourse*, 1614, A2–A2v.
62. *Paul's*, p. 29.
63. *Brief Discourse*, *Theo-musophilus*.
64. *Brief Discourse*, A3v; for further details about Ravenscroft and Pearce, see *Paul's*, p. 168.
65. *Paul's*, p. 168.

ANTONIO AND MELLIDA

The History of Antonio and Mellida. The First Part.

[DEDICATION]

Satirical

To the only rewarder and most just poiser of virtuous merits,
the most honourably renowned Nobody, bounteous Maecenas
of poetry and Lord Protector of oppressed innocence, *do
dedicoque.*
Since it hath flowed with the current of my humorous blood   5
to affect a little too much to be seriously fantastical, here take,   × ×
most respected patron, the worthless present of my slighter
idleness. If you vouchsafe not his protection, then, O thou

---

1. *poiser*] weigher.

cf Twelfth Night -
"picture of nobody"

2. *Nobody*] John Day dedicates *Humour out of Breath* (1608) 'To Signor
Nobody. Worthless sir, I present you with these my unperfect labours,
knowing that what defect in me, or neglect in the printer hath left unperfect,
judgement in you will wink at, if not think absolute.' Marston's devotion to

IRONY

Nobody is both cynical and flippant; the flattery of a dedication is meaningless
in a self-centred and unheeding society. Cf. also the dedications to *Pygmalion's
Image*, 'To the world's mighty monarch, Good Opinion'; and to *Scourge of
Villainy*, 'To his most esteemed and best beloved Self'.
    Maecenas] patron of the arts: Maecenas, a Roman knight, was a friend of
Augustus and patron to both Virgil and Horace.
    3–4. do dedicoque] I give and dedicate [this play].
    5–6. *Since ... fantastical*] Probably an ironic comment by Marston on his
earlier career as a satirist, which had culminated in the doubtful achievement
of having his *Pygmalion* and *The Scourge of Villainy* condemned to be burnt by
the common hangman in June 1599. See Introduction, p. 14.
    5. *humorous*] whimsical, fanciful. Human nature was conceived as a blend of
four elements, or humours (blood, choler, phlegm, and melancholy) which
conditioned temperament, and this mixture produced effects both physical
and psychological.
    6. *affect*] ostentatiously assume; probably a combination of $O.E.D.$, $v.^{1}4$
and 5.
    fantastical] irrationally impassioned, $O.E.D.$, $a.1.b.$
    7. *slighter*] more trifling, even less significant. Marston's self-deprecation is,
of course, belied by the numerous italicised sententiae in the text of the play,
designed to give to it the serious weight here denied. See Introduction, p. 3.
    8–10. *If ... bottles*] This is an awkward and possibly deliberately obscure
sentence of which the meaning seems to be: 'If Nobody does not grant his
protection [i.e., unless someone protects me], I must appeal to the most
delightful perfection of all, women's beauty, to shield me from the effects of

?

the ban on hostile critics.' That 'women's beauty' is as unable as Nobody to do
this, is merely a continuation of Marston's ironic tone. The reference to the
'vinegar bottles' (10) is probably another allusion to Marston's condemnation
as a satirist.

sweetest perfection, female beauty, shield me from the stopping
of vinegar bottles. Which most wished favour if it fail me, then   10
si nequeo flectere superos, Acheronta movebo. But yet, honour's
redeemer, virtue's advancer, religion's shelter, and piety's
fosterer, yet, yet, I faint not in despair of thy gracious affection
and protection, to which I only shall ever rest most servingmanlike, obsequiously making legs and standing, after our   15
freeborn English garb, bareheaded.

Thy only affied slave and admirer,

John Marston.

18. John Marston] *This ed.; I. M. Q.*

---

8. *vouchsafe not*] not vouchsafe, not grant.

9. *stopping*] i.e., corking, inhibiting.

10. *vinegar bottles*] sourness of temper, hence 'attacks by critics'. Cf. *A.R.*,
IV.ii.44, 'These vinegar-tart spirits are too piercing.'

11. si ... movebo] 'if I cannot flex the will of the gods, I will move the
powers of hell.' From Virgil, *Aeneid* VII.312, but slightly modified; in Virgil
the line begins 'flectere si nequeo'.

11–16. *But yet ... bareheaded*] Marston's ironic tone continues as he credits
Nobody with the advancement of honour, virtue, religion, and piety, i.e.,
implying that these virtues do not exist in the world. He then resolves to attack
the vices of the world without the protection of a patron. The obscurity of this
avowal is probably deliberate, so as to avoid a new clash with the authorities.

14–15. *servingmanlike*] This compound, here used ironically to stress the
futility of fulsome dedications, predates any other similar usage, *O.E.D.*,
1.*comb.*

15. *obsequiously making legs*] bowing deferentially.

17. *affied*] betrothed. Cf. *A.R.*, II.iii.50, 'Thy dear affied love lately
defamed.' John Day signs his dedication to Nobody, 'One of your first
followers'; perhaps he has this dedication of Marston's in mind.

Antonio and Mellida

*ANDRUGIO, *lately Duke of Genoa.*
*ANTONIO, *his son.*
*PIERO SFORZA, *Duke of Venice.*
*FELICE.
*BALURDO.
*ALBERTO.   *Gentlemen of the*   5
*FOROBOSCO.   *Venetian Court.*
*CASTILIO BALTHAZAR.
CAZZO, *page to* CASTILIO.
DILDO, *page to* BALURDO.   10

D.P.] *Dilke, Bullen subst.*

---

3. *PIERO SFORZA*] Cf. Italian *sforzare*, 'to force, to enforce, to constrain, to compel, to ravish.' (The definition of the name(s) is taken from from G. Florio, *A World of Words, or A Dictionary in Italian and English*, 1598.) 'Sforza' was also a common term for a tyrant; a family with this name ruled the Duchy of Milan from 1450 to 1535. Marston partially derived his plot from an assemblage of incidents relating to at least three members of the Sforza house, see 'Sources', pp. 15–19.

4. *FELICE*] *felice*, 'happy, fortunate, blessed, lucky, prosperous, blissful'. Where sixteenth-century and modern usage differs, the character's names (Felice, Cazzo, Galeazzo, Mazzagente, Rosaline) are spelt as in modern form. In *Q*, however, their form (Feliche, Catzo, Galeatzo, Matzagente, Rossaline) may indicate how they are to be pronounced.

5. *BALURDO*] *balordo*, 'a fool, a noddy, a dizzard, an idiot, a giddyhead.'

7. *FOROBOSCO*] *forabosco*, 'a bird called a woodpecker. Also a sneaking, prying, busy fellow.'

8. *CASTILIO BALTHAZAR*] His name is designed to recall, satirically, Baldassare Castiglione, the author of the most famous of Elizabethan courtesy books, *Il Cortegiano* (1528). He appears again in *A.R.*, but it is very doubtful whether he is intended to retain this identity in that second play.

9. *CAZZO*] 'a man's privy member.'

10. *DILDO*] also 'a man's privy member', and used in a generic, contemptuous sense for a youth or servant. Middleton uses this device of naming characters after functions in *Blurt, Master Constable. C2v*, 'Enter *Imperia the courtesan, two maids, Trivia and Simperina, with perfumes.*'

57

*GALEAZZO, *son to the Duke of Florence.*
*MAZZAGENTE, *son to the Duke of Milan.*
*LUCIO, *friend and follower of* ANDRUGIO.
Page to ANDRUGIO.
A Painter.　　　　　　　　　　　　　　　　　　15
Three Pages.
*MELLIDA, *daughter to* PIERO.
ROSALINE, *niece to* PIERO.
FLAVIA, *gentlewoman to* MELLIDA.]

Those marked * *also appear in* ANTONIO'S REVENGE, The Second Part
of the History of ANTONIO and MELLIDA.

　　11. *GALEAZZO*] *galeazza*, 'a galliass'; ie., a heavy ship of war, larger than
a galleon.
　　12. *MAZZAGENTE*] 'a killer or queller of people, a man-queller.' Cf.
2H4, II.i.53, where Falstaff is described as 'a man-queller, and a woman-
queller', by Mistress Quickly. Marston uses the same device of naming his
characters from common Italian words in other plays, e.g., *The Malcontent*
(1603?), *The Fawn* (1604), *The Dutch Courtesan* (1604?), as does Jonson in
Volpone, or The Fox (1606).
　　17. *MELLIDA*] Probably intended to suggest 'honey' or 'sweet', from the
Latin *mel*, perhaps by association with the form *mellitus-a*, used by Plautus and
others, to mean 'honey-sweet' or 'darling'.

Induction

Enter GALEAZZO, PIERO, ALBERTO, ANTONIO,
FOROBOSCO, BALURDO, MAZZAGENTE, *and* FELICE, *with parts
in their hands, having cloaks cast over their apparel.*

Galeazzo. Come sirs, come! The music will sound straight for
   •entrance. Are ye ready, are ye •perfect?
Piero. Faith, we can say our parts, but we are ignorant in what
   mould we must cast our actors.
Alberto. Whom do you personate?
Piero. Piero, Duke of Venice.   5
Alberto. O, ho! Then thus frame your exterior shape
   To haughty form of •elate majesty,
   As if you held the•palsy-shaking head

0.1. GALEAZZO] *This ed.; Galeatzo Q.*   0.2. MAZZAGENTE] *This ed.;
Matzagente Q.*   FELICE] *This ed.; Feliche Q.*   1. S.P. *Galeazzo] 1633;
not in Q.*

0.1 INDUCTION] There is an Introduction to *Jack Drum* (1601); it is
spoken by the Tireman. *What You Will* (1601) has an Induction that merges
into the first act of the play, and the same device is used in *The Malcontent*
(1604), but, by 1606, Beaumont and Fletcher could declare in the The
Prologue to *The Woman Hater*—also a play 'lately acted by the Children of
Paul's'—'Gentlemen, inductions are out of date, and a prologue in verse is as
stale as a black velvet cloak, and a bay garland.'
0.2–3. with parts . . . apparel] i.e., they enter with their scripts in hand and
concealing their costumes. This entry takes place prior to the introductory
music, which was usually performed before the play's action commenced. At
Paul's, this music was probably played on recorders and viols; see *Paul's*, p.
65. This Induction is hesitant and full of nervous concern, perhaps suggesting
that it was designed as the first offering at the newly reopened Paul's
playhouse; see *Paul's*, pp. 118–19. The parts would consist only of each
individual's lines and his cue lines, pasted into long rolls.
2. entrance] the appearance of the actors upon the stage, as *O.E.D.,
sb.*1b.*spec.*
perfect] word perfect.
8. *elate*] exalted, lofty. Cf. *A.R.*, IV.i.2, 'Away with this disguise in any
hand! / Fie, 'tis unsuiting to your elate spirit.'
9. *palsy-shaking*] trembling with partial paralysis, *O.E.D., sb.C.attrib.* and
Comb. This was seen as a characteristic of old age, as with Ulysses's description
of Nestor (*T&C.*, I.iii.174), 'with a palsy fumbling on his gorget'.

Of reeling Chance under your fortune's belt,   10
In strictest vassalage. Grow big in thought
°As swoll'n with glory of successful arms.
Piero. If that be all, fear not, I'll suit it right.
Who cannot be proud,°stroke up the hair and°strut?
Alberto. °Truth! Such°rank custom is grown popular.   15
And now the vulgar fashion strides as wide
And stalks as proud upon the weakest stilts
Of the slight'st fortunes as if°Hercules
Or burly Atlas shouldered up their state.
Piero. Good. But whom act you?   20
Alberto. The necessity of the play forceth me to act two parts:
Andrugio, the distressed Duke of Genoa, and Alberto, a
Venetian gentleman enamoured on the Lady Rosaline,

---

23. Rosaline] *This ed.; Rossaline Q.*

---

10. *reeling Chance*] Like 'Nobody' (Dedication), this is an emblem; it is a
trembling, partially paralysed, staggering figure. Emblematic ideas abound in
this play; it is full of allegorical pictures designed to suggest moral adages. Cf.
Ind.48–9, Justice squints; Ind. 113, Madam Felicity is gracious; 1.i.23–4, the
fretting sea has a wrinkled brow; III.i.53–5, Fortune has a wrinkled forehead
and spits poison; III.i.97–8, Perfidiousness attends princes' courts; III.ii.204,
Death keeps an open, welcoming house; III.ii.220, Misery lives in a dark cave;
IV.i.120–2, Ruin, avenger of sin, pours scaldling liquid on the heads of the
guilty. These emblems compare with the figure of 'Vengeance' in *A.R.*,
III.i.45–6, 'Seize on revenge, grasp the stern-bended front / Of frowning
vengeance with unpeisèd clutch'; this figure has a bent-down forehead, with
'curled snaky locks' (II.i.7–8) and, perhaps, carries a knotted steel whip
(II.iii.127–8).
    12. *As*] as if
    14. *stroke . . . strut*] While 'stroke' has its modern meaning, it also means 'to
irritate, ruffle or cross' (*O.E.D.*, *v.*[1]I.d), and 'strut' means 'to behave
vaingloriously, to flaunt or triumph', and 'to walk with an affected air of
dignity or importance' (*O.E.D.*, *v.*[1]5 and 7); cf. 'to strut before a wanton
ambling nymph', *R3*, 1.i.17. This whole phrase seems to be a reference to
acting style, perhaps that used to portray Tamburlaine. To affect the character
of a proud, dictatorial ruler the player adopted a swollen-chested, stiff-legged
walk and, apparently, combed his hair into an upswept style, cf. p. 88n below.
    15–19] Alberto's rejection of the affectation of the histrionics of the stage is
similar to the refusal of Antonio in *A.R.*, II.iii.104–5, to 'swell like a
tragedian / In forcèd passion of affected strains'.
    15. *rank*] showy, coarse.
    18–19. *Hercules . . . Atlas*] Atlas, who bore heaven upon his head and
hands, and Hercules, the famous strong man of the twelve labours, are used as
symbols of the might which the pretentious in contemporary society lack.

whose fortunes being too weak to sustain the port of her,
he proved always disastrous in love, his worth being   25
much underpoised by the uneven scale that currents all
things by the outward stamp of opinion.
Galeazzo. [*To Balurdo*] Well, and what dost thou play?
Balurdo. The part of all the world.
Alberto. 'The part of all the world.' What's that?   30
Balurdo. The fool. Aye, in good deed, la, now, I play Balurdo, a wealthy, mountebanking, burgomasco's heir of
Venice.
Alberto. Ha, ha! One whose foppish nature might seem great
only for wise men's recreation, and like a juiceless bark,   35
to preserve the sap of more strenuous spirits. A servile
hound that loves the scent of forerunning fashion, like an
empty hollow vault still giving an echo to wit, greedily
champing what any other well-valued judgement had

---

34. great] *Q*; create *Hunter*.

24. *being . . . port of her*] i.e., being unable to afford to maintain her lifestyle
(with the implication of excessive expense).
26. *underpoised*] undervalued, with the additional sense of 'weight' (i.e.,
weighted down).
uneven scale] scale unevenly weighed, false measure.
currents] gives value to; i.e., creates coinage, or stamps everything merely on
the basis of outward show.
29. *part*] role.
32. *mountebanking*] smacking of chicanery, quackery.
burgomasco's] A corruption of burgomaster's, i.e., the heir of a city official of
Venice. Hunter adds that the word implies that he is from Bergamo, with the
implication of country stupidity. Middleton equates a burgomaster with
extravagant dress in *Blurt, Master Constable*, D2, 'A little simp'ring ruff, a
dapper cloak, / With Spanish buttoned cape, my rapier here, / Gloves like a
burgomaster here.'
34. *foppish*] dandyfied, a fool.
great] Hunter's emendation to 'create' is tempting, but the sense seems to be
that Alberto is referring to Balurdo's reference to a 'mountebank' of Venice,
i.e., he is one whose outer show of greatness does not deceive the wise.
35. *juiceless*] dried up. Cf. *A.R.*, *Prol.*, 4, 'snarling gusts nibble the juiceless
leaves' and *What You Will*, A3, 'squinting critics, drunken censure, splayfooted
opinion, juiceless husks.'
36. *strenuous*] energetic, valiant. Cf. *A.R.*, v.i.3, 'The fist of strenuous
Vengeance is clutched.' This was one of the words singled out by Jonson for
special condemnation in *Poetaster*, v.iii.291–2, 'we list / Of strenuous
vengeance to clutch the fist', but he has the *A.R.* context in mind.
39. *champing*] chewing noisily.

                beforehand chewed.   40
Forobosco. Ha, ha, ha! Tolerably good, good faith, sweet wag.
Alberto. Umph. Why 'Tolerably good, good faith, sweet wag'?
                Go, go! You flatter me.
Forobosco. Right. I but dispose my speech to the habit of my
                part.   45
Alberto. (*To Felice*) Why, what plays he?
Felice. The wolf that eats into the breast of princes, that breeds
                the lethargy and falling sickness in honour, makes justice
                look asquint, and blinks the eye of merited reward from
                viewing desertial virtue.   50
Alberto. What's all this periphrasis, ha?
Felice. The substance of a supple-chapped flatterer.
Alberto. O, doth he play Forobosco, the parasite? Good, i'faith!
                Sirrah, you must seem now as glib and straight in out-
                ward semblance as a lady's busk, though inwardly as   55
                cross as a pair of tailor's legs, having a tongue as nimble

---

40. chewed] *Dilke*; shew'd *Q*.

---

   40. *chewed*] Dilke's alteration to 'chew'd' seems most reasonable as it
continues the metaphor in 'greedily champing'. The *Q* text (shew'd) could
mean 'greedily chewing over what better judgements had already established
(shown)'—but this is very tortuous.
   44–5. *I . . . part*] i.e., I am merely seeking to speak in a manner which suits
the deportment necessary for my role.
   47. *The wolf*] i.e., the malignancy, the cancer. Schoonover cites Philip
Barrough, *The Method of Physic*, 1610, 'Lupus is a malignant ulcer quickly
consuming the nether parts, but specially annoying the thighs and legs, and it
is very hungry like unto a wolf . . . eating up the flesh that lieth next unto it',
v.xxiiii, p. 329.
   48. *falling sickness*] epilepsy (the disease), and the idea of 'falling away' from
greatness.
   49. *blinks*] shuts.
      merited] earned (apparently the first use in this sense), *O.E.D.*, *ppl.a.*
   51. *What's . . . periphrasis*] i.e., why are you speaking in such a circum-
locutious manner?
   52. *supple-chapped*] with jaws always ready to lie.
   55. *busk*] corset. Carroll Camden describes how 'the body beautiful was
achieved by the use of a garment, worn under the upper part of the kirtle,
which was stiffened with stays of whalebone or wood . . . The stays were called
busks' (*Elizabethan Women*, London: Elsevier Press, 1952, p.194).
   56. *cross . . . legs*] Tailors sat cross-legged to sew. There is also a play on the
idea of 'cross', vexed, or irritated.
   56–7. *as nimble . . . needle*] The phrase 'nimble as a needle' is proverbial,
Dent N94.11.

as his needle, with servile patches of glavering flattery to
stitch up the bracks of unworthily honoured.
Forobosco. I warrant you, I warrant you, you shall see me prove
the very periwig to cover the bald pate of brainless genti-   60
lity. Ho, I will so tickle the sense of *bella graziosa
madonna*, with the titillation of hyperbolical praise, that
I'll strike it in the nick, in the very nick, chuck.
Felice. Thou promisest more than I hope any spectator gives
faith of performance. (*To Antonio*) But why look you so   65
dusky, ha?
Antonio. I was never worse fitted since the nativity of my actor-
ship. I shall be hissed at, on my life now.
Felice. Why, what must you play?

68. shall] *1633*; shalt *Q.*

---

57. *glavering*] deceitful. Cf. *S. of V.*, VI.9, 'he glavers with his fawning
snout.'
58. *bracks*] cracks, breaks both in cloth, and honour. Cf. *A.R.*, II.v.41, 'To
plaster up the bracks of my defects.'
honoured] shown respect, *O.E.D., ppl.a.*
60–1. *very ... gentility*] This is probably a recollection of two passages from
Joshua Sylvester's translation of Du Bartas' *Divine Weeks* (1592–9). 'Instead of
flowers, chill shivering winter dresses / With icicles her self-bald borrowed
tresses: / About her brows a periwig of snow' (ed. A. B. Grosart, Edinburgh:
Constable 1880, I.58: 702–4) and I.124: 184–9, 'But, when the winter's
keener breath began / To crystallise the Baltic ocean, / To glaze the lakes, and
bridle up the floods, / And periwig with wool the bald-pate woods; / Our
grandsire, shrinking, 'gan to shake and shiver, / His teeth to chatter, and his
beard to quiver.'
61–2. *bella ... madonna*] my beautiful and gracious lady.
63. *the nick*] the exact point aimed at, the mark. There is also a sexual
connotation, for 'titillation' means 'tickling' or 'itching', and 'chuck' means
'love', or 'dear'; it is a familiar term of endearment. Dent N160 cites the phrase
'in the nick (nick of time)' as proverbial.
64–5. *Thou ... performance*] i.e., you are promising more than any
spectator expects you to be able to perform.
66. *dusky*] gloomy, melancholy.
67–8.] This comment may suggest that Antonio has acting experience prior
to this performance. If this play is indeed the first for the newly revived Paul's
company (see Introduction, pp. 47–8) then he had gained his acting
experience elsewhere. Paul's new master Edward Pearce did buy and sell
actors (although strictly prohibited from doing so), so the remark may well be
literally true; see *Paul's*, pp. 42, 64, 97. If Antonio was an experienced actor,
he seems to have been an exception among this particular group of players.
Hissing was a common way of showing disapproval of an actor's performance.

Antonio. Faith, I know not what, an hermaphrodite—two parts 70
in one, my true person being Antonio, son to the Duke
of Genoa, though for the love of Mellida, Piero's daughter, I take this feigned presence of an Amazon, calling
myself Florizel and I know not what. I a voice to play a
lady! I shall ne'er do it. 75

Alberto. O, an Amazon should have such a voice, viragolike.
Not play two parts in one? Away, away, 'tis common
fashion. Nay, if you cannot bear two subtle fronts under
one hood, idiot, go by, go by, off this world's stage! O
time's impurity! 80

Antonio. Aye, but when use hath taught me action to hit the
right point of a lady's part, I shall grow ignorant, when I
must turn young prince again, how but to truss my hose.

Felice. Tush, never put them off, for women wear the breeches
still. 85

70. *hermaphrodite*] Both playing two parts in one and behaving as if
effeminate. Cf. Nashe, *Strange News* (McKerrow, I:286), 'shrouded a picked,
effeminate, carpet knight under the fictionate person of Hermaphroditus.'

73. *an Amazon*] One of a mythical race of female warriors who had their
right breasts removed that they might more easily draw a bow. In Sidney's
Arcadia Pyrocles disguises himself as an Amazon as a wooing device, until
Musidorus shames him out of 'woman's apparel' (Feuillerat, I.81).

74–5.] Antonio's concern that he cannot play a lady because of his voice
may reflect the fact that he was no longer a boy soprano: his voice had broken.
Alberto reassures him that an Amazon should have a 'manlike' (virago-like)
voice; see *Paul's*, p. 119. It is also probably intentionally comic that Antonio,
the boy, should be so concerned at the offence to his 'manhood' implicit in
playing a lady.

78–9. *bear . . . hood*] be hypocritical. The idea is proverbial: 'he bears two
faces under one hood', Dent F20.

79. *idiot*] i.e., 'fool, noddy, dizzard, giddyhead'; see *Dramatis Personae*,
Balurdo. Alberto calls Antonio a fool if he cannot be a hypocrite, and so
dismisses him from the great stage of the world.

go by] keep out of the way! The whole phrase is derived from Kyd's *Spanish
Tragedy*, III.xii.31, 'Hieronimo, beware: go by, go by.'

82. *point*] Probably a recollection of the earlier reference to a 'lady's busk'
(55), for 'after the busks were inserted in sheaths in the bodice, they were held
there by ribbons or laces, which were called busk-points' (Camden, p. 194).
See also next note and 55n.

83. *truss my hose*] tie the laces with which the stockings were fastened to the
doublet, ('truss' *O.E.D.*, *v.5 trans.*b.*spec.*). 'Hose' can mean 'breeches'
(*O.E.D.*, *sb.*2), and so the remark also implies 'to turn into a man again'.

84. *women . . . breeches*] Proverbial, Dent B645. Cf. 'her husband's a fool . . .
she wears the breeches', *What You Will*, G4.

Mazzagente. By the bright honour of a Milanese,
    And the resplendent fulgor of this steel,
    I will defend the feminine to death,
    And ding his spirit to the verge of hell
    That dares divulge a lady's prejudice.   90
        Exeunt [MAZZAGENTE, FOROBOSCO, *and* BALURDO].
Felice. Rampum, scrampum, mount tufty Tamburlaine! What *Comment on 86–90*
    rattling thunderclap breaks from his lips?
Alberto. O, 'tis native to his part. For, acting a modern brag-
    gadoch under the person of Mazzagente, the Duke of
    Milan's son, it may seem to suit with good fashion of   95
    coherence.

---

86. Milanese] *This ed.; Millanoise Q.*   86–90. By ... prejudice] *Bullen;*
prose in Q.   90.1 S.D.] *Bullen; Exit Ant. & Al. Q.*

86. *Milanese*] a (female) citizen of Milan; see 'burgomasco', l. 32 above.
87. *resplendent fulgor*] dazzling brightness, splendour.
89. *ding*] dash violently. Cf. *A.R.*, IV.iii.83., 'as he headlong topsy-turvy
dinged down'; cf. also *The Spanish Tragedy*, I.iv.22, 'paunched his horse, and
dinged him to the ground'.
    verge] precinct, pale or limit of a community, *O.E.D., sb.*[1] III.12b. Cf.
A.R., V.vi.34–5, 'we will live enclosed / In holy verge of some religious
order.'
    90. *prejudice*] bias, favour, *O.E.D., sb.*II.3; Mazzagente is asserting the
absolute confidentiality of love's favours.
    90.1.] *Q* has here an exit for '*Ant. & Al.*', but Antonio remains on stage until
the end of the Induction and Alberto does not exit until l. 121.1. It is possible
that the compositor misread *Mat. & Al.* i.e., 'Mazzagente and others'.
    91. *Rampum ... Tamburlaine*] An ironic allusion to a now unfashionable
acting style of excessive and highflown rhetoric; Marston probably has Edward
Alleyn specifically in mind, for Alleyn dominated the roles of Barabas,
Faustus, and Tamburlaine.
    tufty] covered in tufts of hair. This was perhaps the way in which the actor
playing the role of Tamburlaine was dressed, i.e., very hirsute. Cf. l. 14 above,
'stroke up the hair and strut', which may also be a comment on the same
acting style. Hunter suggests also an allusion to wearing tuftaffeta and
thus 'proud'. Both ideas are present, as well as the idea of 'robustious' from
'rufty-tufty'.
    91–2. *What ... lips*] An allusion to Marlowe's resonant style. Cf.
Tamburlaine, Prol.5, 'Threatening the world with high astounding terms.'
    93. *modern*] common, worthless. Cf. *Poetaster*, V.iii.280–1, 'Alas! That were
no modern consequence, / To have cothurnal buskins frighted hence.'
    93–4. *braggadoch*] idle boaster. Marston may be glancing at Spenser's
boastful coward Braggadochio of Book II of *The Faerie Queene.*

Piero. But methinks he speaks with a spruce Attic accent of
adulterate Spanish.
Alberto. So 'tis resolved. For Milan being half Spanish, half
high Dutch, and half Italian, the blood of chiefest houses   100
is corrupt and mongreled; so that you shall see a fellow
vainglorious for a Spaniard, gluttonous for a Dutchman,
proud for an Italian, and a fantastic idiot for all. Such a
one conceit this Mazzagente.
Felice. But I have a part allotted me which I have neither able   105
apprehension to conceit nor what I conceit gracious
ability to utter.
Galeazzo. Whoop, in the old cut? Good, show us a draught of
thy spirit.
Felice. 'Tis steady, and must seem so impregnably fortressed   110
with his own content that no envious thought could
ever invade his spirit, never surveying any man so un-
measuredly happy whom I thought not justly hateful for
some true impoverishment, never beholding any favour
of Madam Felicity gracing another which his well-   115
bounded content persuaded not to hang in the front of
his own fortune, and therefore as far from envying any
man as he valued all men infinitely distant from accomplished beatitude. These native adjuncts appropriate to
me the name of Felice. [*To Galeazzo*] But last, good, thy   120
humour?

                        Exit ALBERTO.

---

103. Italian] *Dilke*; Italians *Q.*

97. *Attic*] pure, refined, classical (of style), *O.E.D.*, *a.*2.
98. *adulterate Spanish*] Spanish mixed with German and Italian.
99–101.] As Hunter points out, Milan was under the German (High
Dutch), Spanish rule bequeathed by Charles V.
104. *conceit*] understand.
108. *in the old cut*] in the old style or fashion, 'cut' *O.E.D.*, *sb.*[1] III.16.b.*fig.*
Cf. the Epistle Dedicatory to Thomas Nashe's *Strange News* . . . 1592, 'such a
man as I have described this Epistler to be, one that . . . hath made many
proper rhymes of the old cut in his days' (I:257).
Good] i.e., good fellow, friend.
110. *impregnably*] invincibly, unconquerably.
118. *as*] as if.
118–19. *accomplished*] attained.
adjuncts] traits, qualities of character, *O.E.D.*, *B.sb.*3.

Antonio. 'Tis to be described by signs and tokens, for, unless I
were possessed with a legion of spirits, 'tis impossible to
be made perspicuous by any utterance. For sometimes
he must take austere state as for the person of Galeazzo,   125
the son of the Duke of Florence, and possess his exterior
presence with a formal majesty, keep popularity in distance and, on the sudden, fling his honour so prodigally
into a common arm that he may seem to give up his in-
discretion to the mercy of vulgar censure; now as solemn   130
as a traveller and as grave as a puritan's ruff, with the
same breath as slight and scattered in his fashion as—
as—as—a—a—anything. Now as sweet and neat as a
barber's casting bottle, straight as slovenly as the yeasty
breast of an ale knight; now lamenting, then chafing,   135
straight laughing, then—
Felice. What then?
Antonio. Faith, I know not what. 'T had been a right part for

---

130. censure] *B. L. copy C.131.c.16 only; all other Qs have slur over first 'e.'.*
131. traveller *Dilke;* trauailer *Q.*

123–4. *'tis . . . utterance*] it is impossible to clarify in speech.
127. *popularity*] the people.
128–30. *fling . . . censure*] i.e., rashly commit his reputation to a test of
popular support, at the risk of suffering public condemnation.
131. *traveller*] Both a 'traveller', and 'one who travails or labours'; see also
I.i.189 and III.ii.113. Cf. *As You Like It*, IV.i.15–22, where Jaques explains
that his melancholy proceeds mainly from 'the sundry contemplation of my
travels' (17–18), and Rosalind exclaims 'A traveller! By my faith you have
great reason to be sad' (21–2).
   grave . . . ruff] i.e., restrained, not ostentatious.
   puritan's ruff] 'The English ruff seems to have come from Italy . . . and is at
first simply a pleated ruffle . . . Elizabethan ruffs . . . become larger and larger,
and the pleating becomes more intricate, being supported either by starch or
by pasteboard in the folds. The starched folds are set with 'poking-sticks' of
wood or bone. The width of the pleat can be varied by the width of the
poking-stick, Puritans seemingly using the narrowest' (Camden, p. 225). Cf.
55n.
134. *casting bottle*] scent bottle. Cf. III.ii.24.1–2 and *Cynthia's Revels*,
I.i.72–4, 'pray Jove the perfumed courtiers keep their casting bottles,
picktooths, and shuttle-cocks from you.'
134–5. *yeasty breast*] breath smelling of beer. Cf. *Jack Drum*, A3, 'Each
cobbler's spawn and yeasty, bousing [tippling] bench / Reeks in the face of
sacred majesty / His stinking breath of censure.'

Proteus or Gew. Ho! Blind Gew would ha' done't rarely,
rarely.   140
Felice. I fear it is not possible to limn so many persons in so
small a tablet as the compass of our play affords.
Antonio. Right. Therefore I have heard that those persons, as
he and you, Felice, that are but slightly drawn in this
comedy, should receive more exact accomplishment in a   145
second part which, if this obtain gracious acceptance,
means to try his fortune.
Felice. Peace, here comes the Prologue. Clear the stage.
                                                    Exeunt.

---

142. play affords] *This ed.*; playes afford   *Q.*

---

139. *Proteus*] The 'old man of the sea' of Greek myth, who tended the flocks
(seals) of Poseidon; he possessed the gift of prophecy, but sought to avoid
foretelling the future by adopting a bewildering variety of different shapes to
escape his interrogator. Proteus is, then, an image of versatility in acting styles.
   Gew] The word is an archaic form of 'jaw', but here is clearly a name; it is
that of a current celebrity. Edward Guilpin in *Skialetheia* (1598) addresses his
eleventh Epigram 'To Gue': 'Gue hang thyself for woe, since gentlemen / Are
now grown cunning in thy apishness. / Nay, for they labour with their
foolishness / Thee to undoe, procure to hang them then. / It is a strange
seld-seen uncharity, / To make fools of themselves to hinder thee.' Gew seems
to have been an actor specialising in apelike mannerisms, perhaps as a
caricature of contemporary manners. Gew may also, therefore, represent
acting versatility.
   141. *limn*] Both to portray or depict and to embody in human form (to
'limb'). Cf. v.i.1–6, 'And are you a painter, sir? Can you draw, can you draw?
. . . I did limn them.'
   142. *play affords*] Felice is talking about this present play, possibly the first
at the new Paul's. The Q compositor has placed the 's' at the end of the wrong
word.
   144. *he*] Galeazzo.
   Felice] Felice only appears in *A.R.* as a corpse: I.iii.129.1–2, '*The curtain's
drawn and the body of* FELICHE, *stabbed thick with wounds, appears hung up.*'
There is in that play, however, a comparable character, Pandulpho Feliche,
and the same actor probably performed both parts.
   146. *second part*] The sequel to this play is *Antonio's Revenge*, written well
over a year later and performed early in 1601. It replaces the 'comic crosses of
true love' (v.ii.279) by a 'sullen tragic scene', *A.R.*, Prol.7, where 'Never more
woe in lesser plot was found', *A.R.*, v.vi.59.
   gracious acceptance] This note of supplication is a conventional appeal for the
audience to tolerate the inadequacies of an inexperienced company of actors.

The Prologue

The wreath of pleasure and delicious sweets
Begirt the gentle front of this fair troop!
Select and most respected auditors,
For wit's sake do not dream of miracles.
Alas, we shall but falter if you lay   5
The least sad weight of an unusèd hope

0.1. Prologue] In *Jack Drum* there is a prologue, spoken by one of the children, very similar in tone to this. It is preceded by an Introduction spoken by the Tireman explaining that the author has snatched the book from the actors: 'So God help me, if we wrong your delights, 'tis infinitely against our endeavours, unless we should make a tumult in the tiring house.' The Child explains: 'You much mistake his [Marston's] action, tireman. / His violence proceeds not from a mind / That grudgeth pleasure to this generous presence, / But doth protest all due respect and love / Unto this choice, selected influence. / He vows, if he could draw the music fro[m] the spheres, / To entertain this presence with delight, / Or could distil the quintessence of heaven / In rare composed scenes, and sprinkle them / Among your ears, his industry should sweat / To sweeten your delights. But he was loth, / Wanting a prologue, and ourselves not perfect, / To rush upon your eyes without respect. / Yet if you'll pardon his defects and ours, / He'll give us passage and you pleasing scenes, / And vows not to torment your list'ning ears / With mouldy fopperies of stale poetry, / Unpossible dry musty fictions. / And for our parts, to gratify your favour, / We'll study till our cheeks look wan with care, / That you our pleasures, we your loves may share.' In direct contrast to the Prologues to *Antonio and Mellida* and *Jack Drum* is the Prologue to *Antonio's Revenge*, which expresses a much more assured tone of confidence in the ability of the actors to display the 'weighty passion' (14) of that tragedy.

1–2.] 'May both the laurel wreath of pleasure and sweet delight deck the noble brows of this distinguished company.'

1. *wreath*] garland (as of flowers).
delicious sweets] delightful perfumes (from the garland).

2. *gentle front*] noble brow.
fair troop] handsome assembled company, i.e., audience.

3. *Select ... auditors*] While this flattery is conventional, and the audience is 'chosen' or 'distinguished', it may also imply that they were 'invited' to attend, since this play was possibly written to launch the 'first night' of the newly revived Paul's company; cf. Introduction, pp. 47–8.

6. *least sad*] slightest, most trifling.
unusèd] unaccustomed.

Upon our weakness; only we give up
The worthless present of slight idleness
To your authentic censure. O that our muse
Had those abstruse and sinewy faculties   10
That, with a strain of fresh invention,
She might press out the rarity of art,
The pur'st elixèd juice of rich conceit,
In your attentive ears, that with the lip
Of gracious elocution we might drink   15
A sound carouse unto your health of wit!
But O, the heathy dryness of her brain,
Foil to your fertile spirits, is ashamed
To breathe her blushing numbers to such ears.

13. juice] *Dilke*; ioyce *Q*.

---

8. *The worthless* . . . *idleness*] i.e., this present poor play, which is the
unconsidered product of a moment of leisure; cf. Dedication.
9. *authentic censure*] respected judgement.
10. *abstruse*] recondite.
sinewy] tough (in an intellectual sense).
11. *a strain*] a stream or flow (with the suggestion of considerable effort
involved).
13. *elixèd*] distilled.
juice] *Q*'s 'ioyce' is merely a variant spelling.
conceit] conception.
14–16. *that* . . . *wit*] that with elegant rhetoric, we might be able to drink a
suitable toast to you (i.e., because the state of your wit will be such as to favour
what we offer).
17. *heathy*] i.e., as dry and as tough as a heath or heather. This seems to be a
unique figurative usage of this word. It is cited again in *Jack Drum* (F4) where
Brabant Junior, Brabant Senior, and Planet are discussing new plays,
including *Antonio and Mellida*: '*Bra. Jun.* Brother how like you of our modern
wits? How like you the new poet Mellidus? *Bra. Sig.* A slight bubbling spirit, a
cork, a husk. *Pla.* How like you Musus' fashion in his carriage? *Bra. Sig.* O
filthily, he is as blunt as Paul's [Paul's had no steeple; it burnt down in 1561]
. . . *Pla.* Brabant, thou art like a pair of balance, / Thou weighest all saving
thy self. *Bra. Sig.* Good faith, truth is they are all apes and gulls, / Vile
imitating spirits, dry heathy turves. *Bra. Jun.* Nay, brother, now I think your
judgement errs. *Pla.* Err? He cannot err, man, for children and fools speak
truth always.' The allusion to the 'new poet Mellidus' makes it clear that it is
this context, the Prologue to *Antonio and Mellida*, that is referred to.
18. *Foil*] i.e., The heathery dryness of my brain may be contrasted to the
lushness of your intelligence.
19. *numbers*] verses.

Yet, most ingenious, deign to veil our wants. 20
With sleek acceptance polish these rude scenes,
And if our slightness your large hope beguiles,
Check not with bended brow but dimpled smiles.

Exit Prologue.

20. *most ... wants*] most intellectually outstanding, witty [audience], condescend to conceal our deficiencies.

21. *sleek*] perfectly smooth, unruffled. Cf. *A.R.*, IV.i.42–3, 'the chub-faced fop / Shines sleek with full-crammed fat of happiness.'

22. *slightness*] Both 'small' in size, *O.E.D.*, 3, and 'small' in quantity or quality of performance, *O.E.D.*, 1.

23. *Check*] criticise, rebuke.

dimpled] Cf. *A.R.*, III.iii.11–12, 'I will laugh and dimple my thin cheek / With capr'ing joy.'

Act I

[Sc. i]

The cornets sound a battle within. Enter ANTONIO *disguised
like an Amazon.*

Antonio. Heart, wilt not break? And thou, abhorrèd life,
Wilt thou still breathe in my enragèd blood?
Veins, sinews, arteries, why crack ye not,
Burst and divulsed with anguish of my grief?
Can man by no means creep out of himself   5
And leave the slough of viperous grief behind?
Antonio, hast thou seen a fight at sea,
As horrid as the hideous day of doom,
Betwixt thy father, Duke of Genoa,
And proud Piero, the Venetian Prince,   10
In which the sea hath swoll'n with Genoa's blood
And made spring tides with the warm reeking gore
That gushed from out our galley's scupper holes,
In which thy father, poor Andrugio,
Lies sunk or, leapt into the arms of chance,   15
Choked with the labouring ocean's brackish foam;

Act I] *ACTVS PRIMUS Q.*   Sc. i] *Dilke, not in Q.*

0.1. cornets ... within] Instead of trumpets, cornets seem to have been
used at Paul's for all forms of signalling. This act is staged as a continuous
scene with one sequence merging into another; during it, all the principal
characters are introduced to the audience, and both the main areas for acting
(the upper and lower stages) are utilised.
    1. *abhorrèd*] hated, despised, *O.E.D.*, *ppl.a.*1.
    4. *divulsed*] burst, torn asunder.
    6. *slough*] Both the 'moral degeneration' caused by excessive grief and the
outer skin periodically shed by a snake; a combination of *O.E.D.*, *sb.*¹ b.*fig.*
and *sb.*².
    7–16.] This rhetorical question of Antonio's relating to the sea battle which
sealed Andrugio's fate, may be based on a recollection of the destruction of the
Venetian fleet at Casalmaggiore by Francesco Sforza in 1448. See 'Sources', p.
16 and cf. also II.i.17–38n.
    13. *scupper holes*] holes at deck level in a ship's side, to allow water to flow
away.

72

Who even, despite Piero's cankered hate,
Would with an armèd hand have seized thy love
And linked thee to the beauteous Mellida?
Have I outlived the death of all these hopes?   20
Have I felt anguish poured into my heart,
Burning like balsamum in tender wounds,
And yet dost live? Could not the fretting sea
Have rolled me up in wrinkles of his brow?
Is Death grown coy, or grim Confusion nice,   25
That it will not accompany a wretch,
But I must needs be cast on Venice' shore
And try new fortunes with this strange disguise
To purchase my adorèd Mellida?
                The cornets sound a flourish. Cease.
Hark how Piero's triumphs beat the air.   30
O rugged mischief, how thou grat'st my heart!
Take spirit, blood; disguise, be confident;
Make a firm stand. Here rests the hope of all:
Lower than hell there is no depth to fall.

The cornets sound a sennet. Enter FELICE *and* ALBERTO,
CASTILIO, *and* FOROBOSCO, *a* Page *carrying a shield,*
PIERO *in armour,* CAZZO *and* DILDO *and* BALURDO:
all these, saving PIERO, *armed with petronels. Being entered,*
they make a stand in divided files. [ANTONIO *stands aside.*]

34.3. CAZZO] *This ed.; Catzo Q.*   34.5. *files*] Dilke; *foyles Q.*

---

22. *balsamum*] aromatic, resinous, vegetable juice from which ointment was distilled.

23–4. *fretting sea . . . brow*] Possibly, as Hunter suggests, a recollection of Sidney's *Arcadia*. The description of the second shipwreck of Pyrocles and Musidorus contains the phrase 'their blood had, as it were, filled the wrinkles of the sea's visage' (Feuillerat, I.10). It is also another emblematic concept; the idea is probably based on the god Neptune.

25. *nice*] fastidious, dainty.

30. *triumphs*] celebrations of victory.

34. *Lower . . . fall*] Proverbial. Cf. Dent G464, 'He that lies upon the ground can fall no lower.'

34.1. *sennet*] A set of notes for the ceremonial entry of a king or governor; these notes would act as a recognisable signal for Piero's entry on stage.

34.4. *petronels*] large cavalry carbines.

34.5. *divided files*] i.e., in two ranks, drawn up for inspection, and also to act as a royal guard.

Piero. Victorious fortune with triumphant hand   35
Hurleth my glory 'bout this ball of earth,
Whilst the Venetian Duke is heavèd up
On wings of fair success to overlook
The low-cast ruins of his enemies,
To see myself adored and Genoa quake.   40
My fate is firmer than mischance can shake.
Felice. Stand! The ground trembleth.
Piero. Ha! An earthquake!
Balurdo. O, I smell a sound.
Felice. Piero, stay! For I descry a fume   45
Creeping from out the bosom of the deep,
The breath of darkness, fatal when 'tis whist
In greatness' stomach. This same smoke, called Pride,
Take heed, she'll lift thee to improvidence
And break thy neck from steep security;   50
She'll make thee grudge to let Jehovah share
In thy successful battles. O, she's ominous,
Enticeth princes to devour heaven,
Swallow omnipotence, outstare dread fate,
Subdue eternity in giant thought,   55
Heaves up their heart with swelling puffed conceit
Till their souls burst with venomed arrogance.
Beware, Piero, Rome itself hath tried;

56. heart] *Dilke*; hurt *Q*.

39. *low-cast*] cast down, overthrown.
43. *earthquake*] Earthquakes were usually interpreted as a sign of divine wrath, but here Felice uses the idea to mock Piero's pretensions.
44. *smell a sound*] Cf. Rosaline's remark, II.i.60–1. 'what a strong scent's here! Somebody useth to wear socks.'
47. *whist*] hushed, kept quiet, *O.E.D., v.*^{1}*2.trans.*
48. *stomach*] Both literal (stomach) and figurative (pride, valour).
smoke ... Pride] Schoonover compares Gascoigne's *Steel Glass*, (1585): 'And therefore pray, my priests, least pride prevail ... / That philosophy smell no secret smoke', *A Hundreth Sundry Flowers ...* Giiijv–Hj.
49. *improvidence*] Florio defines *improvidenza* as 'improvidence, rashness, oversight'. Marston seems to be the first to use this Italian borrowing; here the primary sense is 'rashness'.
50. *steep security*] i.e., the guilt or folly that arises from overconfidence.
58. *Rome ... tried*] i.e., Rome, in its pride, has already attempted to 'outstare fate' but has failed.

Confusion's train blows up this babel pride.
Piero. Pish! *Dimitto superos, summa votorum attigi.*   60
  Alberto, hast thou yielded up our fixed decree
  Unto the Genoan ambassador?
  Are they content, if that their duke return,
  To send his and his son Antonio's head,
  As pledges steeped in blood, to gain their peace?   65
Alberto. With most obsequious, sleek-browed entertain
  They all embrace it as most gracious.
Piero. Are proclamations sent through Italy
  That whosoever brings Andrugio's head,
  Or young Antonio's, shall be guerdoned   70
  With twenty thousand double pistolets
  And be endearèd to Piero's love?
Forobosco. They are sent every way. Sound policy,
  Sweet lord.
Felice. (*Aside*) Confusion to these limber sycophants!   75

---

72. endearèd] *1633*; indeened *Q.*   75. Aside] *Mod. edns.; tacitè. at end of l. 76 in Q.*

---

59. *train*] A combination of *O.E.D.*, *sb.*[1]*10.fig.*, 'set of consequences', and 13, 'line of gunpowder, a fuse'. Cf. *A.R.*, I.iii.55, 'A blazing comet shot his threat'ning train.'

babel] Used here as an adjective, 'towering', with the implication that this tower will be blown up by the gunpowder of confusion. Felice may also be suggesting that Piero is talking nonsense (babbling).

60. Dimitto . . . attigi] 'I release the gods, for the utmost of my prayers have I attained', Seneca, *Thyestes*, 888.

61. *yielded up*] delivered.

66. *sleek-browed*] in a deferential manner. Cf. *A.R.*, IV.i.42–3, 'the chub-faced fop / Shines sleek with full-crammed fat of happiness.'

entertain] acceptance.

71. *double pistolets*] A pistolet was a Spanish or Italian gold piece, a doubloon. According to Francis Thynne, *Chaucer: Animadversions*, 1598, E.E.T.S., OS, No. 9, 1875, p. 37, a florin was 'much about the value of 3/4d., being half a pistolet Italian or Spanish'. A double pistolet was, then, worth 13s 4d in 1599, and the whole reward of 'twenty thousand double pistolets' was worth in excess of £13,330, but the figure is simply used generically to indicate a very substantial sum.

72. *endearèd*] made precious to. Cf. *A.R.*, II.i.48, 'Endear thyself Piero's intimate.'

75. Aside] This aside is indicated in *Q* by the word *tacitè* at the end of the speech. This is the adverb, formed from 'taceo' meaning, in classical Latin, 'silently, in silence, secretly'.

limber] flaccid, easily led.

No sooner mischief's born in regenty
But flattery christens it with policy.
Piero. Why, then, *O me coelitum excelsissimum!*
The intestine malice and inveterate hate
I always bore to that Andrugio   80
Glories in triumph o'er his misery.
Nor shall that carpet-boy Antonio
Match with my daughter, sweet-cheeked Mellida.
No, the public power makes my faction strong.
Felice. Ill, when public power strength'neth private wrong.   85
Piero. 'Tis horselike not for man to know his force.
Felice. 'Tis godlike for a man to feel remorse.
Piero. Pish! I prosecute my family's revenge,
Which I'll pursue with such a burning chase
Till I have dried up all Andrugio's blood.   90
Weak rage, that with slight pity is withstood.
                        The cornets sound a flourish.

76. *regenty*] government, rule; not in *O.E.D.*
78. O ... excelsissimum] 'Oh, most exalted of the gods am I', Seneca, *Thyestes*, 911.
79. *intestine*] inner, internal, *O.E.D.*, *a.*1.*fig.*
82. *carpet-boy*] ladies' boy, weakling. A term of contempt coined by Marston from the common insult 'carpet-knight'; cf. Massinger, *The Unnatural Combat*, 1639, 'At court ... / ... your carpet knights, / That never charged beyond a mistress' lips, / Are still most keen, and valiant ...' (sig. G, III.iii).
83. *sweet-cheeked*] Probably a pun on the Latin derivation of Mellida's name, 'honied'.
86. *horselike*] beastlike; paraphrased from Seneca, *Octavia*, 453, 'Inertis est nescire quid liceat sibi': ''Tis a dullard's part not to know what he may do.'
87. *godlike*] Possibly based on *Octavia*, 454, 'Id facere laus est quod decet, non quod licet': ''Tis praiseworthy to do, not what one may, but what one ought.' Cf. *A.R.*, II.ii.69, ''Tis praise to do, not what we can, but should.'
remorse] compassion.
91.] i.e., It would be a weak rage indeed that would yield to such a slight pity.
91.1–116.3.] The sequence of action here is complex. It begins with a 'flourish' (91.1) to warn of the impending arrival of Mazzagente and Galeazzo. Piero leaves the stage momentarily, leaving behind his courtiers drawn up in two ranks (see 34.1–3). At this point another signal, a sennet (99.2), announces the entry above of the ladies and of Galeazzo with his attendants on the lower stage (99.3). Now Piero re-enters to greet and embrace Galeazzo, and he does this between the two ranks of courtiers (100). His earlier withdrawal from the stage was, presumably, to stress his superior rank to that of Galeazzo, son of the Duke of Florence. Piero's greeting of Galeazzo is signalled by a

What means that fresh triumphal flourish sound?
Alberto. The prince of Milan and young Florence' heir
Approach to gratulate your victory.
Piero. We'll girt them with an ample waist of love.   95
Conduct them to our presence royally.
Let volleys of the great artillery
From off our galleys' banks play prodigal
And sound loud welcome from their bellowing mouths.
                                        Exit PIERO *only.*

The cornets sound a sennet. Enter above, MELLIDA, ROSALINE,
    and FLAVIA. *Enter below* GALEAZZO *with attendants;*
PIERO [*enters,*] *meeteth him, embraceth; at which the cornets
    sound a flourish.* PIERO *and* GALEAZZO *exeunt.*
                The rest stand still.

---

98. off] of *Q.*   99.1. *Exit* PIERO *only*] *This ed.; Exeunt all but Piero Dilke;
Exit Piero tantum Q.*

'flourish' (99.5). Piero and Galeazzo then leave, but everyone else remains on
stage and, probably, the two ranks stay in position, for the action moves to the
ladies in the gallery. Next a 'sennet' (113.1) announces the arrival of
Mazzagente and the action, on the lower stage, repeats itself with Piero
entering to greet him once more, probably between the two ranks
of his 'guard'. The flourish from the cornets (116.2) is designed, as before, to
act as a fanfare for the embrace between Piero and his guest. The action once
again moves to the upper stage, but this time there is a dumb show below, for
Piero and Mazzagente '*stand, using seeming compliments*' (116.2–3). During the
whole of this sequence of action, Antonio, as Florizel, has remained on stage
but has taken no part in the proceedings (142–3).
    94. *gratulate . . . victory*] congratulate you on your victory.
    95. *We'll . . . love*] i.e., We will lavish (waste) so much love on them that no
matter how great their importance (literally, 'how ample their waist'), we will
embrace them.
    98. *banks*] i.e., the ranks or tiers of oars, but here used figuratively to mean
the sides of the galleys.
    play prodigal] fire without counting the cost.
    99.2. above] on the upper stage. The arrangement was probably a central
curtained space with a window (an operating casement) on at least one side.
Behind this window(s) were placed the musicians.
    99.3 below] on the lower stage. The commentary which ensues from the
ladies on the upper stage relating to the action on the lower is a new variation,
created by Marston, on the dramatic use of the dumb show.
    99.4. meeteth] There is some suggestion here that Galeazzo and Piero enter
from opposite sides of the lower stage and meet in the centre, between the
ranks of the royal guard.

eavesdropper
Comment
on inset
action:
(new development
in dramaturgy
(Disto Mechs))

Mellida. What prince was that passed through my father's
        guard?   100
Flavia. 'Twas Galeazzo, the young Florentine.
Rosaline. Troth, one that will besiege thy maidenhead,
    Enter the walls, i'faith, sweet Mellida,
    If that thy flankers be not cannonproof.
Mellida. O, Mary Ambree! Good thy judgement, wench.   105
    Thy bright election's clear. What will he prove?
Rosaline. H'ath a short finger and a naked chin,
    A skipping eye. Dare lay my judgement, faith,
    His love is glibbery; there's no hold on't, wench.
    Give me a husband whose aspect is firm,   110
    A full-cheeked gallant with a bouncing thigh—
    O he is the *paradiso delle madonne contente!*
Mellida. Even such a one was my Antonio.

---

106. election's] *Dilke;* electious *Q.*   112. *delle madonne contente*] *Hunter;*
dell madonne contento Q.

---

104. *flankers*] protective forts (thighs).
cannonproof] impregnable.
105. *Mary Ambree*] A famous military heroine of the ballads: 'Mary Ambree:
Captain courageous, whom death could [not] daunt, / Besieged the city
bravely, the city of Gaunt! / ... And the foremost in battle was Mary
Ambree!' When eventually forced to retire to a castle, as a result of betrayal,
she refused to surrender it without a fight despite the blandishments of the
English captain, Sir John Major, who was amazed at her prowess; *The Percy
Folio of Old English Ballads and Romances,* London: De La More Press, 1906,
2:84–7.
105–6. *Good ... prove*] i.e., It is obvious that you have made a good
judgement, your choice is clear and obvious, but what will he turn out to be?
Hunter omits the apostrophe in 'election's', and glosses 'Give reasons for your
choice'.
107–12.] This whole speech is full of suggestive sexual innuendoes, as with
'short finger', 'naked chin', 'no hold on't', 'bouncing thigh', and 'paradise of
contented women'.
108. *skipping*] inconstant.
109. *glibbery*] shifty, untrustworthy. Cf. II.i.6, IV.i.69, and *A.R.*, I.ii.17, 'is
glib rumour grown a parasite' and also *Poetaster,* v.iii.277–8, where Jonson
mocks Marston's use of this word, 'What, shall thy lubrical and glibbery
muse / Live, as she were defunct, like punk in stews?'
111. *full-cheeked*] i.e., well-fleshed and thus spirited.
112. paradiso ... contente] 'the paradise of contented women'. Cf. Florio's
Second Fruits, 1591, pp. 204–5, 'L'Inghilterra e il paradiso delle donne, il
purgatorio de gli huomini, e lo inferno de cavalli': 'England is the paradise of
women, the purgatory of men, and the hell of horses.'

The cornets sound a sennet.

Rosaline. By my nine-and-thirtieth servant, sweet,
    Thou art in love. But stand on tiptoe, fair,   115
    Here comes Saint Tristram Tirlery Whiff, i'faith.

Enter MAZZAGENTE; PIERO *[enters,] meets him, embraceth,*
at which the cornets sound a flourish. They two stand, using seeming
compliments, whilst the scene passeth above.

Mellida. Saint Mark, Saint Mark! What kind of thing appears?
Rosaline. For fancy's passion, spit upon him—fie!—
    His face is varnished. In the name of love,
    What country bred that creature?   120
Mellida. What is he, Flavia?
Flavia. The heir of Milan, Signor Mazzagent.
Rosaline. Mazzagent? Now by my pleasure's hope,
    He is made like a tilting-staff and looks
    For all the world like an o'er-roasted pig.   125
    A great tobacco taker too—that's flat,

---

115. tiptoe] *Dilke*; tiptoed *Q*; tiptoes *Hunter*.   116. Saint Tristram] *Q*; Sir
Tristram *J & N.*

114.] Cf. v.ii.56–8, where Rosaline declares, 'I have thirty-nine servants
and my monkey—that makes the fortieth.'

116.] *Tirlery Whiff*] a trifling puff, an insignificant breath. The phrase may
be a recollection of Nashe's attack on Gabriel Harvey in *Strange News*, where
he calls him a 'fanatical phobetor, garemumble, tirleriwhisco, or what you will,
called forth the biggest gunshot of my thundering terms, steeped in aqua fortis
and gunpowder, to come and try themselves on his paper target' (McKerrow
I:321); see also II.i.31n.

117. *Saint Mark*] Mellida probably cries to 'Mark' because of the reference
to Tristram. Mark was the name of the King of Cornwall in medieval romance,
and he was the uncle of the romance hero, Tristram. Saint Mark, the
evangelist, was also the patron saint of Venice.

119. *varnished*] painted, made-up (with cosmetics).

124. *tilting-staff*] a wooden staff, used in place of a lance, for jousting
tournaments. The remark is a continuation of Rosalind's sexual innuendoes as
in ll. 107–12 above.

126. *tobacco taker*] Rosaline clearly hates the tobacco habit and, in the last
act, responding to Piero's inquiry as to when she will marry, declares, 'when
men . . . forsake taking of tobacco . . . O, to have a husband with a mouth
continually smoking' (v.ii.46–9). Later, however, in *A.R.*, III.iv.44, Balurdo
refers favourably to tobacco's medicinal properties for curing colds. Rosaline's
dislike of the habit was of course shared by many contemporary authorities,

For his eyes look as if they had been hung
   In the smoke of his nose.
Mellida. What husband will he prove, sweet Rosaline?
Rosaline. Avoid him, for he hath a dwindled leg,   130
   A low forehead, and a thin coal-black beard,
   And will be jealous too—believe it, sweet—
   For his chin sweats and h'ath a gander neck,
   A thin lip, and a little monkish eye.
   Precious, what a slender waist he hath!   135
   He looks like a maypole or a notched stick.
   He'll snap in two at every little strain.
   Give me a husband that will fill mine arms,
   Of steady judgement, quick and nimble sense.
   Fools relish not a lady's excellence.   140

Exeunt all [except ANTONIO] *on the lower stage; at which the cornets*
     sound a flourish and a peal of shot is given.

Mellida. The triumph's ended. But look, Rosaline,
   What gloomy soul in strange accoutrements

---

134. monkish]   *Q*;   monkey'sh   *Hunter.*   142. accoutrements]   *Dilke*;
accustrements *Q*.

---

not least James I, who declared in *A Counterblast to Tobacco* (1604): 'Surely
smoke becomes a kitchen far better than a dining chamber, and yet it makes a
kitchen also oftentimes in the inward parts of men, soiling and infecting them
with an unctious and oily kind of soot, as hath been found in some great
tobacco takers, that after their death were opened' (edn. of 1672, pp. 10–11).

   130. *dwindled*] wasted away and, also, impotent.

   131. *A low forehead*] A sign of stupidity; so Caliban in *The Tempest* fears that
he and the drunken Stephano and Trinculo will 'be turn'd to barnacles, or to
apes / With foreheads villainous low' (IV.i.248–9).

   133. *a gander neck*] i.e., a neck like a gander, with the suggestion of aimless
stupidity.

   134. *monkish*] Probably a combination of two ideas: he has a beady eye that
makes him resemble both a monk and a monkey. It is tempting to emend, as
Hunter does, to 'monkey'sh' but this obscures the double meaning.

   136. *maypole*] It was a common insult to compare a person to a maypole; so
Hermia to Helena in *M.N.D.*, III.ii.296, 'thou painted maypole'. The phrase
'as slender as a maypole' is proverbial, Dent M778.

   140.2. *peal of shot*] discharge of guns to produce a loud sound, *O.E.D.*,
peal, *sb.*1.II.5.

   141. *triumph*] victorious parade.

Walks on the pavement?
Rosaline. Good sweet, let's to her, prithee, Mellida.
Mellida. How covetous thou art of novelties! 145
Rosaline. Pish! 'Tis our nature to desire things
    That are thought strangers to the common cut.
Mellida. I am exceeding willing, but—
Rosaline. But what? Prithee, go down, let's see her face.
    God send that neither wit nor beauty wants 150
    Those tempting sweets, affection's adamants.
        Exeunt. [MELLIDA, ROSALINE, *and* FLAVIA *descend.*] ——
Antonio. [*Alone*] Come down! She comes like—O, no simile
    Is precious, choice, or elegant enough
    To illustrate her descent. Leap heart! She comes,
    She comes. Smile, heaven, and softest southern wind 155
    Kiss her cheek gently with perfumèd breath!
    She comes. Creation's purity, admired,
    Adored, amazing rarity, she comes.
    O now, Antonio, press thy spirit forth
    In following passion, knit thy senses close, 160
    Heap up thy powers, double all thy man.

    Enter MELLIDA, ROSALINE, *and* FLAVIA.

143. *the pavement*] i.e., the paved portion of a square or walkway. The description of the lower stage as a paved walking area may, just possibly, be literally true. The Paul's boys were performing in a corner of the Chapter House garth using the cloisters as their tiring house; the floor of this garth was paved with squares and lozenges of Purbeck marble. There is some evidence to suggest that the facilities in their playhouse were primitive at first, but gradually improved later, e.g., there is no evidence to assume that they had a trap until *A.R.* over a year after this play. At the time this play was first performed, late autumn 1599, they may not have had a stage as such, but were acting on the floor of the garth. See *Paul's*, chapter 2.

147. *common cut*] everyday costume.

151. *affection's adamants*] i.e., wit and beauty, which are the magnets to attract affection. Cf. Lyly, *Euphues: The Anatomy of Wit*: 'It hath been a question often disputed, but never determined, whether the qualities of the mind, or the composition of the man, cause women most to like, or whether beauty or wit move men most to love' (Bond, I:201).

151.1 *descend*] i.e., they come down from the upper stage, by a stair not visible to the audience. Since Antonio's speech before their re-entry is only ten lines long (152–61), the height could not have been great.

158. *amazing*] astounding, astonishing.

160. *following*] conformable, commensurate (with its object).

161. *double ... man*] i.e., be twice the man you are.

She comes. O, how her eyes dart wonder on my heart!
Mount blood, soul, to my lips, taste Hebe's cup,
Stand firm on deck when beauty's close fight's up.
Mellida. Lady, your strange habit doth beget 165
Our pregnant thoughts, even great of much desire
To be acquaint with your condition.
Rosaline. Good, sweet lady, without more ceremonies,
What country claims your birth, and, sweet, your
name?
Antonio. In hope your bounty will extend itself 170
In selfsame nature of fair courtesy,
I'll shun all niceness. My name's Florizel,
My country Scythia. I am Amazon,
Cast on this shore by fury of the sea.
Rosaline. Nay, faith, sweet creature, we'll not veil our names. 175
It pleased the font to dip me Rosaline.
That lady bears the name of Mellida,
The Duke of Venice' daughter.
Antonio. (*To Mellida, kissing her hand*)

163. *Hebe's cup*] Hebe was cupbearer to the gods and filled their cups with nectar. She also had the power to make the old young again.
164. *close fight*] i.e., a fight at close quarters. Technically, the area between a ship's mainmast and foremast, which could be defended as a strong point in case of attack by a boarding party. As defined by Captain John Smith, Governor of Virginia, in 1627, 'close fights' are also specifically 'small ledges of wood laid cross one another like the grates of iron in a prison's window, betwixt the mainmast and the foremast' (*A Sea Grammar*, p. 58).
165. *habit*] dress, costume. Antonio is disguised as an Amazon.
166. *great*] pregnant. The phrase 'to be with child to hear' is proverbial, Dent C317. Mellida is consumed with desire to learn of the Amazon's adventures.
167. *To be acquaint . . . condition*] i.e., to know who and what you are. *acquaint*] acquainted.
170–1. *In . . . courtesy*] i.e., hoping that you will be equally civil and candid with me.
172. *niceness*] coyness, reserve.
173. *Scythia*] A name applied to different countries at different times. The Scythians were essentially nomads and, for the Romans, Scythia was a generic term for northern Asia. It is appropriate that Antonio should obscure his origin, since he is in disguise. The Amazons were associated with the general area of Asia Minor.
176. *It . . . Rosaline*] i.e., I was christened Rosaline.

Madam, I am obliged to kiss your hand
By imposition of a now-dead man.   180
Rosaline. Now, by my troth, I long beyond all thought
    To know the man. Sweet beauty, deign his name.
Antonio. Lady, the circumstance is tedious.
Rosaline. Troth, not a whit. Good fair, let's have it all.
    I love not, I, to have a jot left out   185
    If the tale come from a loved orator.
Antonio. Vouchsafe me then your hushed observances.
    Vehement in pursuit of strange novelties,
    After long travel through the Asian main,
    I shipped my hopeful thoughts for Britainy,   190
    Longing to view great nature's miracle,
    The glory of our sex, whose fame doth strike
    Remotest ears with adoration.
    Sailing some two months with inconstant winds,
    We viewed the glistering Venetian forts   195
    To which we made, when, lo, some three leagues off,
    We might descry a horrid spectacle:
    The issue of black fury strewed the sea
    With tattered carcasses of splitted ships,
    Half-sinking, burning, floating, topsy-turvy.   200
    Not far from these sad ruins of fell rage,
    We might behold a creature press the waves;
    Senseless he sprawled, all notched with gaping wounds.

---

189. travel] *Bullen*; trauaile *Q*.

179–80.] i.e., Florizel must kiss Mellida's hand, because she has promised
the (dead) Antonio that she will do so.
183. *circumstance*] details.
187. *Vouchsafe . . . observances*] i.e., keep silence and pay careful attention
while I speak.
189. *travel*] Both 'travel', and 'labour' or 'effort'. Cf. Ind. 131 and III.ii.114.
main] mainland.
190. *Britainy*] This trisyllabic spelling of 'Britain' is required for the
scansion.
192. *The . . . sex*] Probably a flattering reference to the Queen of Britain,
Elizabeth, despite the fact that there is no clear statement of the historical time
of the play's action.
195. *glistering*] shining (i.e., the sun glinting off the fortifications of Venice).
201. *fell*] savage, ruthless.

To him we made and, short, we took him up.
The first word that he spake was 'Mellida',   205
And then he swooned.
Mellida.   Ay me!
Antonio.   Why sigh you, fair?
Rosaline. Nothing but little humours. Good sweet, on.
Antonio. His wounds being dressed and life recoverèd,
We 'gan discourse, when, lo, the sea grew mad,
His bowels rumbling with windy passion.   210
Straight swarthy darkness popped out Phoebus' eye
And blurred the jocund face of bright-cheeked day,
Whilst curdled fogs masked even darkness' brow;
Heaven bade's good night, and the rocks groaned
At the intestine uproar of the main.   215

---

210. windy] *Schoonover*; winde *Q*.

204. *short*] in short.
207. *little humours*] trifling moodiness.
209–15. *grew mad* ... *main*] Perhaps a recollection of Seneca, *Agamemnon*,
470–4, 'cum subito luna conditur, stellae latent, / in astra pontus tollitur,
caelum perit. / nec una nox est, densa tenebras obruit / caligo et omni luce
subducta fretum / caelumque miscet.' 'Suddenly the moon is hid, the stars
sink out of sight, skyward the sea is lifted, the heavens are gone. 'Tis doubly
night; dense fog overwhelms the dark and, all light withdrawn, confuses sea
and sky.' This description of the sea battle compares with the lament of
Antonio (1.i.7–16) over Andrugio's defeat at sea by Piero. The description in
both contexts may be derived from the historical destruction of the Venetian
fleet at Casalmaggiore by Francesco Sforza; see 'Sources, p. 16. It is possible
also that this commentary on the sea battle may be in Pandulpho's mind in
A.R., II.ii.85–8, where he declares, 'The portholes / Of sheathèd spirit are
ne'er corbed up, / But still stand open, ready to discharge / Their precious
shot into the shrouds of heaven.'
211. *Straight*] immediately.
Phoebus' eye] the bright light of the sun. Phoebus was an epithet applied
to Apollo, a god of light. Apollo was also identified with Helios, the sun
god.
212. *blurred*] obscured. Cf. *A.R.*, I.v.41–2, 'Hast thou a love as spotless as
the brow / Of clearest heaven, blurred with false defames?'
213. *curdled*] *Q* reads 'crudl'd', a variant spelling of 'curdled', *O.E.D.*,
v.b.*fig.*, thickened, congealed. Cf. II.i.206–7., 'O how impatience ... / ...
curdles thick my blood with boiling rage.'
214. *Heaven* ... *night*] i.e., the sky was completely obscured.
bade's] bade us.
215. *main*] open sea.

Now gusty flaws struck up the very heels
Of our mainmast, whilst the keen lightning shot
Through the black bowels of the quaking air.
Straight chops a wave, and in his sliftered paunch
Down falls our ship, and there he breaks his neck,   220
Which in an instant up was belched again;
When thus this martyred soul began to sigh:
'Give me your hand', quoth he, 'now do you grasp
Th'unequal mirror of ragg'd misery.
Is't not a horrid storm? O well-shaped sweet,   225
Could your quick eye strike through these gashèd
    wounds
You should behold a heart—a heart, fair creature,
Raging more wild than is this frantic sea.
Wolt do me a favour if thou chance survive?
But visit Venice, kiss the precious white   230
Of my most—nay, all, all epithets are base,
To attribute to gracious Mellida;
Tell her the spirit of Antonio
Wisheth his last gasp breathed upon her breast.'
Rosaline. Why weeps softhearted Florizel?   235
Antonio. Alas, the flinty rocks groaned at his plaints.
'Tell her', quoth he, 'that her obdurate sire
Hath cracked his bosom.' Therewithal he wept
And thus sighed on, 'The sea is merciful.
Look how it gapes to bury all my grief.   240
Well, thou shalt have it. Thou shalt be his tomb.
My faith in my love live; in thee die woe,
Die unmatched anguish, die Antonio.'
With that he tottered from the reeling deck

216. *gusty flaws*] sudden bursts or squalls of wind.
216–7. *struck ... mainmast*] i.e., bowled it over.
219. *sliftered*] riven asunder, cleft.
221. *belched*] vomited. *Q* reads 'belked', which is a variant spelling of 'belched', *O.E.D.*, belch *v.*4.b.*fig.* Cf. *A.R.*, I.iii.63–4, 'methought the ground yawned and belched up the abominable ghost', and also I.iv.6. Elyot's *Dictionary* (1599) defines, 'Eructo ... to belk or break wind out of the stomach.'
224. *unequal ... misery*] unique exemplar of threadbare wretchedness.
237–8. *Tell ... bosom*] i.e., Piero's unyielding opposition to Antonio's marriage to Mellida has resulted in Antonio's death.

And down he sunk.   245
Rosaline. Pleasure's body! What makes my lady weep?
Mellida. Nothing, sweet Rosaline, but the air's sharp.
    [*To Antonio*] My father's palace, madam, will be proud
    To entertain your presence if you'll deign
    To make repose within. Ay me!   250
Antonio. Lady, our fashion is not curious.
Rosaline. Faith, all the nobler, 'tis more generous.
Mellida. Shall I then know how fortune fell at last,
    What succour came, or what strange fate ensued?
Antonio. Most willingly. But this same court is vast,   255
    And public to the staring multitude.
Rosaline. Sweet lady—nay, good sweet—now by my troth
    We'll be bedfellows. Dirt on compliment froth!
                        Exeunt, ROSALINE *giving* ANTONIO *the way.*

246. *Pleasure's body*] This seems to be an oath of Rosaline's, probably
meaning 'by my body, which is the source of pleasure'. It is in keeping
with her frequent sensual puns and sexual innuendoes, when she describes
Mellida's potential suitors. See above l. 102ff.
    251. *our . . . curious*] i.e., we Amazons are not difficult to satisfy.
    252. *'tis more generous*] i.e., that you do not stand on ceremony argues a
more open handed nature.
    255–6. *this . . . multitude*] i.e., We need privacy for me to recount the rest
of my adventures.
    258. *Dirt . . . froth*] i.e., We'll have no over-fastidious manners here.
Rosaline is making a distinction between the mere show of courtesy (the 'froth
of compliment') and sincere respect.
    258.1 *giving . . . way*] i.e., Rosaline allows the Amazon to precede her, in
deference to Florizel's higher rank.

Act II

Enter CAZZO, *with a capon, eating;* DILDO *following him.*

Dildo. Ha, Cazzo! Your master wants a clean trencher. Do you
hear? Balurdo calls for your diminutive attendance.
Cazzo. The belly hath no ears, Dildo.
Dildo. Good pug, give me some capon.
Cazzo. No capon. No, not a bit, ye smooth bully. Capon's no   5
    meat for Dildo. Milk, milk, ye glibbery urchin, is food
    for infants.
Dildo. Upon mine honour—
Cazzo. Your 'honour'—with a pah! 'Slid, now every jackanapes
    loads his back with the golden coat of honour, every ass   10
    puts on the lion's skin and roars his honour—'upon your

Act II] *ACTVS SECVNDVS Q.*   Sc. i] *Dilke, not in Q.*

    0.1. *capon*] A bawdy pun. Cazzo, meaning 'a man's privy member', is eating
a castrated cock (a capon), which is also slang for a eunuch.
    1. *trencher*] wooden plate.
    2. *diminutive*] tiny, i.e., the boy playing Cazzo is the smallest of the actors.
He was probably one of the youngest members of the choir, aged between
seven and ten, whereas the actor playing Flavia was about fourteen; cf.
v.ii.129–30. See also *Paul's*, p. 83 and Introduction, p. 43.
    3. *The belly . . . ears*] Proverbial: 'The belly has no ears', Dent B286.
    4. *pug*] A term of endearment (*O.E.D.*, *sb.*² I.i), and also meaning 'an imp,
a dwarf' i.e., a puck (II).
    5. *smooth*] hairless (i.e., Dildo did not need to shave).
    bully] fine fellow, good friend. Cf. v.i.73. Shakespeare's 'bully Bottom' is
Quince's friend (*M.N.D.*, III.i.8).
    6. *glibbery*] slippery. Cf. I.i.109.
    9. *'Slid*] Shortened form of 'by God's eyelid', a casual oath.
    jackanapes] i.e., ridiculous upstart.
    10. *golden coat*] Marston associates the royal coat of arms with a gold-braided
coat in *S. of V.*, I.66–9, 'Fabius' perpetual golden coat, / Which might have
Semper Idem for a mot, / Hath been at feasts and led the measuring / At court,
and in each marriage revelling.'
    10–11. *ass . . . skin*] One of the fables related by Aesop concerns: '. . . he
who puts on a show of learning, of religion, of a superior capacity in any

87

honour!' By my lady's pantable, I fear I shall live to hear
a vintner's boy cry, "'Tis rich neat canary, upon mine
honour!'
Dildo. My stomach's up.   15
Cazzo. I think thou art hungry.
Dildo. The match of fury is lighted, fastened to the linstock of
    rage, and will presently set fire to the touchhole of in-
    temperance, discharging the double culverin of my in-
    censement in the face of thy opprobrious speech.   20
Cazzo. I'll stop the barrel thus. [*He puts part of the capon in
    Dildo's mouth.*] Good Dildo, set not fire to the touch-
    hole.
Dildo. My rage is stopped, and I will eat to the health of the fool
    thy master, Castilio.   25
Cazzo. And I will suck the juice of the capon to the health of
    the idiot thy master, Balurdo.
Dildo. Faith, our masters are like a case of rapiers sheathed in
    one scabbard of folly.
Cazzo. Right Dutch blades. But was't not rare sport at the sea   30
    battle, whilst rounce-robble-hobble roared from the

21–2. *He . . . mouth*] *Dilke subst.*   22. Good] *1633*; god *Q.*

---

respect or, in short, of any virtue or knowledge to which he has no proper
claim, is, and will always be found to be, an ass in a lion's skin' (*The Fables of
Aesop and Others*, tr. J. Croxall, Edinburgh: Nimmo, 1722, fable 42). The
story of the ass and the lion is, of course, proverbial in its own right, as in
Doctor Dodypoll, 'an ass may wear a lion's skin', C4 (Dent A351).
    12. *pantable*] J & N point out that the word is a corruption of
'pantofle', a high-heeled, cork-soled Italian 'chopine'.
    13. *canary*] a light sweet wine, from the Canary Islands.
    15. *My stomach's up*] i.e., I am both hungry and angry.
    17. *match*] slow match or fuse to light gunpowder.
    linstock] a staff about three feet long, with a notch to hold a lighted match.
    18. *touchhole*] the vent in the cannon through which the charge was ignited.
    19. *culverin*] cannon.
    20. *opprobrious*] insulting, offensive.
    28. *case*] pair.
    30. *Right Dutch blades*] i.e., They are thin and ridiculous like sword blades,
and also incompetent swordsmen. It was a common slur for the Dutch to be
credited only with excessive drinking; cf. *Jack Drum*, 1601, D4v, 'Pour wine,
sound music, let our bloods not freeze, / Drink Dutch like gallants . . .'
    rare] excellent.
    31. *rounce-robble-hobble*] This is, ultimately, a recollection of Richard
Stanihurst's translation of Virgil's *Aeneid*, 8:426–8, 431–2: 'These three were

ship's sides, to view our masters pluck their plumes and
drop their feathers for fear of being men of mark?
Dildo. "Slud', cried Signior Balurdo, 'O for Don Besicleer's
armour in *The Mirror of Knighthood*! What coil's here?   35

32. ship's sides] *This ed.*; ship sides *Q.*   33. men] *all Qs except Ashley,*
which reads then.

---

upblotching, not shaped, but partly well onward, / A clapping firebolt, such as
oft, with ronce robel hobble / Jove to the ground clatt'reth . . . Now do they
raise ghastly lightnings, now grisly reboundings / Of ruff raff roaring, mens'
hearts with terror agrising' (*The first Four Books of the Aeneis of P. Virgilius
Maro*, 1582). The reference is, however, actually more specifically to Thomas
Nashe's ridicule of Stanihurst's translation in his Preface to Greene's
Menaphon, August 1589. Nashe declares: 'I will propound to your judgements,
as near as I can . . . part of one of his descriptions of a tempest, which is
thus / *Then did he make heaven's vault to rebound, with rounce, robble
hobble, / Of ruff, raffe, roaring, with twick, thwack, thurlery bouncing.* / Which
strange language of the firmament, never subject before to our common
phrase, makes us that are not used to terminate heaven's moving in the accents
of any voice, esteem of their triobolar [i.e., three obol, or worthless]
interpreter, as of some thrasonical huff snuff' (McKerrow, III: 319–20). And
later, in *Strange News* (1592), Nashe again remarks, 'Master Stanihurst . . .
trod a foul, lumbering, boistrous, wallowing measure in his translation of
Virgil' (McKerrow, I:299). The extreme dissonance of Stanihurst's style is due
to his attempt to render the Latin in English hexameters. Cf. I.i.116, where
there is another recollection of the word 'thurlery'. See also E. Arber's edn. of
Stanihurst in the *English Scholar's Library*, London, 1880, pp. 137–8.
        32. *ship's sides*] Here the compositor has omitted the 's' at the end of ship: a
normal Elizabethan usage.
        32–3. *pluck . . . feathers*] i.e., take off their plumed helmets of rank and thus
show their lack of courage. Cf. *R2*, IV.i.108, 'plume-pluck'd Richard'.
        33. *men*] Ashley's 'then' does not make sense. It is likely, therefore, to be a
compositor's mistake that was rectified in the printing house.
        men of mark] targets for the snipers in the rigging (marked out to aim at), and
persons of importance (marked with distinction).
        34. *'Slud*] An abbreviation for '[by] God's blood'; a mild oath.
        35. Mirror of Knighthood] *The Mirror of Princely Deeds and Knighthood* was
translated from the Spanish by Margaret Tyler (1578); its hero Rosicleer (but
Balurdo's Besicleer may be an intentional error, to reflect his stupidity) is the
brother of the Knight of the Sun and both are sons of the Emperor Trebetio.
The book, the subject of much mockery (satirised by Marston again in
Malcontent, v.ii.23), is a tale of amazing deeds by one who impressed others 'as
if they had seen in him some undoubted image of immortality'. He wore
impregnable armour and was always victorious. Typical is his battle with a
giant: 'The giant rashly ran upon the sword that it entered a little, and
therefore, made angry at his wound he gave back, lifting up his great bat with
both his hands to drive at Rosicleer. But Rosicleer, as destined to greater
exploits, watching the blow, start aside and closing with the giant thrust his

O, for an armour, cannonproof! O, more cable, more
featherbeds, more featherbeds, more cable!'—till he had
as much as my cable hatband to fence him.

Enter FLAVIA *in haste, with a rebato.*

Cazzo. Buxom Flavia, can you sing? Song, song!
Flavia. My sweet Dildo, I am not for you at this time. Madam   40
Rosaline stays for a fresh ruff to appear in the presence.
Sweet, away!
Dildo. 'Twill not be so put off, delicate, delicious, spark-
eyed, sleek-skinned, slender-waisted, clean-legged,
rarely shaped—   45
Flavia. Who? I'll be at all your service another season. Nay,
faith, there's reason in all things.
Dildo. Would I were 'Reason', then, that I might be in all
things.

sword into his guts. Rosicleer pulled out the sword hastily to have given him
another blow, but the giant fell upon the planks gasping for breath. Then
Rosicleer stepped unto him and, with main force, tumbled him over shipboard
where he lay drenched in the sea' (p. 78).
    coil] commotion, noisy disturbance. Cf. *A.R.*, I.v.89, 'To stab in fume of
blood, to keep loud coil.'
    36. *cannonproof*] impenetrable to cannon shot.
    36–7. *more* ... *cable*] Balurdo is shouting for more supplies of soft,
shock-absorbing materials used to protect seamen from the flying splinters
torn from a ship's timbers by cannon shot; 'feather-beds' and hammocks were
often used for this purpose. In his *Naval Tracts*, Sir William Monson expresses
a preference for 'the coiling of cables on the deck, and keeping part of the men
within them ... for the soldiers are in and out speedily upon all sudden
occasions to succour any part of the ship, or to enter an enemy, without trouble
to the sailors in handling their sails or to the gunners in plying their ordnance'
(*Collection of Voyages and Travels*, 1704, iii.358).
    38. *cable hatband*] a twisted cord of gold, silver, or silk worn around the hat.
In *Every Man Out of his Humour* (1599), IV.vi.84–5, Fastidious Brisk remarks:
'I had on a gold cable hatband, then new come up, which I wore about a
murrey [purple] French hat I had.' The fashion, then, was a recent one.
    fence] enclose, protect.
    38.1. rebato] a stiff collar or wire frame used to support a ruff.
    39. *Buxom*] lively, gay, blithe, *O.E.D.*, *a.*II.3.
    41. *the presence*] i.e., the presence chamber, where Piero holds court.
    43–4. *spark-eyed* ... *clean-legged*] A group of compound adjectives of
Marston's invention.
    48–9. *Would* ... *things*] Dildo responds to Flavia's remark with a bawdy
pun for, as a 'dildo', he wants to be 'in' all things. The adage 'there's reason in
all things' is proverbial, Dent R46.11.

Cazzo. The breve and the semiquaver is we must have the   50
     descant you made upon our names ere you depart.
Flavia. Faith, the song will seem to come off hardly.
Cazzo. Troth, not a whit, if you seem to come off quickly.
Flavia. Pert Cazzo, knock it lustily, then!

They sing.

Enter FOROBOSCO *with two torches [and two* Pages], CASTILIO
singing fantastically, ROSALINE *running a coranto pace, and*
     BALURDO, FELICE *following, wondering at them all.*

Forobosco. Make place, gentlemen! Pages, hold torches. The   55
     prince approacheth the presence.
Dildo. What squeaking cartwheel have we here, ha? 'Make
     place, gentlemen. Pages, hold torches. The prince ap-
     proacheth the presence.'
Rosaline. Foh, what a strong scent's here! Somebody useth to   60
     wear socks.
Balurdo. By this fair candlelight, 'tis not my feet. I never wore
     socks since I sucked pap.
Rosaline. Savourly put off.

54.1. *They sing*] *Keltie; CANTANT Q.*

_____

50. *breve* . . . *semiquaver*] Musical term used figuratively to mean 'a very
short space of time' and, thus, equivalent to the modern phrase 'the long and
the short of it'. Literally *Q*'s 'breefe' and 'semiquauer' refer to the longest and
the shortest notes in the scale. The phrase 'the long and the short of it' was
proverbial, Dent L419.
   51. *descant*] song. Neither this, nor any of the other songs from this play, or
its sequel has survived (with the possible exception of 'Monsieur Mingo'; see
v.ii.29).
   52. *hardly*] with difficulty. Flavia seems doubtful whether the song on their
names will be well received.
   54. *knock it*] strike up (the music).
   54.3. running . . . pace] i.e., proceeding very swiftly, using the steps of the
coranto, which Florio defines as 'a kind of French dance'.
   57–9. Dildo's parody of Forobosco's announcement is not, presumably,
intended to be heard by him, but it is designed to be heard by Balurdo,
Rosaline, Castilio, and Felice.
   60–1. *Somebody* . . . *socks*] i.e., Somebody has been wearing socks without
changing them. Cf. Balurdo's remark, 'I smell a sound', 1.i.44.
   63. *since* . . . *pap*] i.e., since I was a baby.
   64. *Savourly*] wittily. It also means 'unsavourly', i.e., the socks were
stinking.
   put off] A pun on (1) taken off the feet and (2) a neatly avoided volley of wit.

Castilio. Ha, her wit stings, blisters, galls off the skin with the   65
    tart acrimony of her sharp quickness. By sweetness, she
    is the very Pallas that flew out of Jupiter's brainpan.—
    Delicious creature, vouchsafe me your service. By the
    purity of bounty, I shall be proud of such bondage.
Rosaline. I vouchsafe it. Be my slave.—Signor Balurdo, wilt   70
    thou be my servant too?
Balurdo. O God, forsooth, in very good earnest, la, you would
    make me as a man should say—as a man should say—
Felice. 'Slud, sweet beauty, will you deign him your service?
Rosaline. O, your fool is your only servant. But good Felice,   75
    why art thou so sad? A penny for thy thought, man.
Felice. I sell not my thought so cheap. I value my meditation at
    a higher rate.
Balurdo. In good sober sadness, sweet mistress, you should
    have had my thought for a penny. By this crimson satin   80
    that cost eleven shillings—thirteen pence—threepence
    halfpenny a yard, that you should, la.
Rosaline. What was thy thought, good servant?
Balurdo. Marry, forsooth, how many strike of peas would feed

---

81. shillings—thirteen pence—threepence] *This ed.*; shillings, thirteene pence,
three pence *Q*.

65. *galls*] rubs off, removes by chafing, *O.E.D.*, *v.*¹1 trans.b. Cf. *A.R.*,
I.v.44–5, 'does thy heart / With punching anguish spur thy galled ribs?'
    67. *Pallas*] Pallas Athena was the daughter of Zeus and Metis ('wise
counsel'). Before her birth, Zeus swallowed her mother and Athena
subsequently sprang forth from the head of Zeus in complete armour.
    68. *vouchsafe me your service*] allow me to serve you.
    71. *servant*] servant in love (in a courtly sense).
    72. *O God*] This exclamation of Balurdo's was ridiculed by contemporaries
as an absurd affectation, as in Jonson's *Every Man Out of His Humour*, where
Cordatus, the author's friend, says of Orange, a coxcomb, 'as dry an Orange as
ever grew. Nothing, but salutation and "O God, sir."' When asked if he
understands what is being said, Orange replies 'O God, sir' (III.i.23–5, 35).
    76. *penny . . . thought*] Proverbial, Dent P203.
    79. *sadness*] seriousness.
    80–2. *crimson . . . yard*] Balurdo seems to be gradually reducing the amount
he claims as the cost of the 'crimson satin', perhaps because of the sceptical
look he sees on Rosaline's face, i.e., he claims that it cost 11s, then 1s 1d, and at
last he admits it was only 3½d per yard.
    84. *strike*] bushels (one bushel is approximately equivalent to three and a
half cubic metres). Balurdo's 'thought' is, characteristically, both incon-
sequential and absurd, and Rosaline ignores it.

a hog fat against Christtide.   85
Rosaline. Poh! [*She spits.*] Servant, rub out my rheum. It soils
   the presence.
Castilio. By my wealthiest thought, you grace my shoe with an
   unmeasured honour. I will preserve the sole of it as a
   most sacred relic for this service.   90
Rosaline. I'll spit in thy mouth, an thou wilt, to grace thee.
Felice. [*Aside*] O that the stomach of this queasy age
   Digests or brooks such raw unseasoned gobs
   And vomits not them forth! O slavish sots!
   'Servant', quoth you? Foh! If a dog should crave   95
   And beg her service, he should have it straight.
   She'd give him favours, too, to lick her feet,
   Or fetch her fan, or some such drudgery—
   A good dog's office, which these amorists
   Triumph of. 'Tis rare! Well, give her more ass,   100
   More sot, as long as dropping of her nose
   Is sworn rich pearl by such low slaves as those.
Rosaline. Flavia, attend me to attire me.
                              Exeunt ROSALINE *and* FLAVIA.
Balurdo. In sad good earnest, sir, you have touched the very
   bare of naked truth. My silk stocking hath a good gloss,   105
   and I thank my planets my leg is not altogether unpro-
   pitiously shaped. There's a word—'unpropitiously'! I
   think I shall speak 'unpropitiously' as well as any courtier in Italy.
Forobosco. So help me your sweet bounty, you have the most   110

---

86. *She spits*] Dilke.   103.1 *Exeunt*] *Exit* Q.

---

85. *against*] in anticipation of.
Christtide] Christmas.
86. *rheum*] spittle.
91. *spit . . . mouth*] 'Let me spit in your mouth' is a proverbial expression,
Dent M1255. The phrase was used to indicate strong feelings or passions, but
Rosaline appears to be using it ironically.
100. *give . . . ass*] i.e., let her find more fools (asses) like these.
104. *sad*] serious.
106–7. *unpropitiously*] unfavourably, unpleasingly and, by extension, sar-
castically. It also has a literal astrological meaning, i.e., Balurdo claims that
a favourable conjunction of the planets at his birth gave him a well-shaped
leg.

graceful presence, applausive elocuty, amazing volubil-
ity, polished adornation, delicious affability—
Felice. [*Aside*] Whop! Fut, how he tickles yon trout under the
  gills! You shall see him take him by and by with groping
  flattery.   115
Forobosco. —that ever ravished the ear of wonder. By your
  sweet self, than whom I know not a more exquisite, illustrate, accomplished, pure, respected, adored, observed,
  precious, real, magnanimous, bounteous—if you have
  an idle rich cast jerkin or so, it shall not be cast away,   120
  away, if—ha! here's a forehead, an eye, a head, a hair
  that would make a—or if you have any spare pair of
  silver spurs, I'll do you as much right in all kind offices—
Felice. [*Aside*] of a kind parasite.
Forobosco. —as any of my mean fortunes shall be able to.   125
Balurdo. As I am a true Christian, now, thou hast won the
  spurs.
Felice. [*Aside*]—for flattery!
  O how I hate that same Egyptian louse,

---

111. elocuty] *Hunter; conj. Dilke*; elecuty *Q.*

---

111. *applausive*] worthy of applause. Cf. Epil.9, 'applausive encouragements.'
  elocuty] eloquence; unlisted in *O.E.D.*
  114. *groping*] seeking to please. This figurative sense seems originated by
Marston, but it also relates to 'tickle', i.e., the process is one of insinuation by
implication. Cf. *Jack Drum*, B4, '[he] will not stick to spend some twenty
pound / To grope a gull.' The adage, 'to catch one like a trout with tickling' is
proverbial, Dent T537.
  117–8. *illustrate*] illustrious. Cf. *A.R.*, IV.iii.7, 'this grave senate, and
illustrate bloods.'
  119. *real*] royal. This was one of the words condemned, in *S. of V.*, *To* . . .
perusers, as an invention of 'the late perfumed fist of judicial Torquatus [with]
some of his new-minted epithets, as real, intrinsicate, delphic.' Marston seems
to be still satirising its use.
  120. *an idle . . . jerkin*] a richly finished jerkin that you have discarded.
  123. *silver spurs*] Perhaps a reference to the choristers' right to collect 'spur
money', a fee of 6*d* from anyone who came into St Paul's Cathedral wearing
spurs; see *Paul's*, pp. 28–9.
  123–4. *kind offices . . . kind parasite*] A pun on two meanings of 'kind'.
Forobosco promises to use sympathetic or well-disposed attitudes towards
Balurdo (*O.E.D.*, a.II.5), but Felice comments that Forobosco is by nature a
parasite, and thus his promises are worthless (*sb.*3.c).

A rotten maggot that lives by stinking filth   130
Of tainted spirits. Vengeance to such dogs
That sprout by gnawing senseless carrion!

Enter ALBERTO.

Alberto. Gallants, saw you my mistress, the Lady Rosaline?
Forobosco. My mistress, the Lady Rosaline, left the presence
    even now.   135
Castilio. My mistress, the Lady Rosaline, withdrew her graci-
    ous aspect even now.
Balurdo. 'My mistress, the Lady Rosaline, withdrew her graci-
    ous aspect even now.'
Felice. [*Aside*] Well said, echo.   140
Alberto. My mistress, and his mistress, and your mistress, and
    the dog's mistress—precious dear heaven, that Alberto
    lives to have such rivals!
    'Slid, I have been searching every private room,
    Corner, and secret angle of the court,   145
    And yet, and yet, and yet she lives concealed.
    Good sweet Felice, tell me how to find
    My bright-faced mistress out.
Felice. Why man, cry out for lantern and candlelight. For 'tis
    your only way to find your bright flaming wench with   150
    your light burning torch, for most commonly these light
    creatures live in darkness.
Alberto. Away, you heretic! You'll be burnt for—

129. *Egyptian louse*] 'And the Lord said unto Moses, Say unto Aaron,
Stretch out thy rod, and smite the dust of the land, that it may become lice
throughout all the land of Egypt. / And they did so; for Aaron stretched out
his hand with his rod, and smote the dust of the earth, and it became lice in
man, and in beast ...' Exodus, VIII.16–17. Cf. *What You Will*, G3*v*, 'he's
more pestilent than the plague of lice that fell upon Egypt.'
    149. *cry ... candlelight*] i.e., summon an escort to see you safe home. After
dusk, the tardy were escorted by a bellman with a lantern; cf. *Jack Drum*, B2*v*,
'Rely on me Christopher, I will be thy staff, / And thy master's nose shall be
thy lantern and candlelight.'
    150. *bright flaming wench*] i.e., a whore; cf. *1H4*, I.ii.9–10, 'a fair hot wench
in flame-coloured taffeta.'
    151. *light*] with the additional sense of 'promiscuous'.
    burning torch] A reference to the disastrous effects of uncontrolled passions;
cf. *Tit.*, v.i.43, 'here's the base fruit of her burning lust.'

Felice. Go, you amorous hound, follow the scent of your mistress' shoe. Away!   155
                                    [*Exit* ALBERTO.]
Forobosco. Make a fair presence. [*To the Pages*] Boys, advance
your lights. The princess makes approach.
Balurdo. An please the gods, now in very good deed, la, you
shall see me tickle the measures, for the heavens. Do my
hangers show?   160

Enter PIERO, ANTONIO [*as* FLORIZEL], MELLIDA, ROSALINE,
GALEAZZO, MAZZAGENTE, ALBERTO, *and* FLAVIA. *As they enter,*
FELICE *and* CASTILIO *make a rank for the Duke to pass through.*
FOROBOSCO *ushers the Duke to his state. Then, whilst* PIERO
speaketh his first speech, MELLIDA *is taken by* GALEAZZO *and*
MAZZAGENTE *to dance, they supporting her,* ROSALINE *in like*
manner by ALBERTO *and* BALURDO, FLAVIA *by* FELICE *and* CASTILIO.

Piero. [*To Antonio*] Beauteous Amazon, sit, and seat your
thoughts

---

156. presence. Boys] *Dilke subst.*; presence, boyes *Q*.

158. *An*] if it.
159. *for the heavens*] i.e., 'by heaven'; a mild oath. Other editors (e.g.,
Hunter and J & N) gloss the whole phrase 'tickle the measures for the heavens'
to mean, 'leap as high as the sky in my dance'. This is possible, and both
meanings may be intended.
160. *hangers*] the loops (usually fringed and ornamental) by which a sword is
suspended, *O.E.D.*, 4.b. Balurdo may simply be concerned that his sword
loops do not show beneath his tunic, but since 'hangers' was also a term
referring to a short ornamental sword itself, *O.E.D.*, 3, he may also be anxious
that his elaborate sword should be visible. Cf. *What You Will*, G3*v*, 'a pair of
massy silver spurs, . . . a hatch short sword and then your embroidered
hanger.'
160.1–7] This elaborate pageant provides, in dumb show, the proper
ceremonial for a tyrant to preside over his army and his court. Piero Sforza is
shown both as general, like Francesco Sforza, and as courtier, like Lodovico
Sforza. With his throne centrally placed, Piero presides over the dancing of the
'measure' in a masque-like tableau.
160.3. make a rank] create a line or file.
160.4 state] throne.
160.5–7. *MELLIDA . . . CASTILIO*] The dance is arranged in three
couples, with Mellida 'supported' (i.e., partnered on either side) by Galeazzo
and Mazzagente, Rosaline by Alberto and Balurdo, and Flavia by Felice and
Castilio.

In the reposure of most soft content.—
Sound music, there!—Nay, daughter, clear your eyes
From these dull fogs of misty discontent.
Look sprightly, girl! What though Antonio's
    drowned,   165
That peevish dotard on thy excellence,
That hated issue of Andrugio,
Yet mayst thou triumph in my victories,
Since, lo, the highborn bloods of Italy
Sue for thy seat of love. Let music sound!   170
Beauty and youth run descant on love's ground.
           [*Music sounds for the measure.*]
Mazzagente. [*To Mellida*] Lady, erect your gracious symmetry.
Shine in the sphere of sweet affection,
Your eye as heavy as the heart of night.
Mellida. My thoughts are as black as your beard, my fortunes 175
as ill-proportioned as your legs, and all the powers of my
mind as leaden as your wit and as dusty as your face is
swarthy.
Galeazzo. Faith, sweet, I'll lay thee on the lips for that jest.
Mellida. I prithee, intrude not on a dead man's right.   180
Galeazzo. No, but the living's just possession,
    Thy lips and love, are mine.

---

170. Let music sound!] *Dilke; printed as S.D. in Q.*   172. symmetry] *1633*;
summetry *Q.*

---

162. *reposure*] rest, repose.
163. *clear your eyes*] i.e., Mellida is weeping.
166. *dotard on*] one who dotes on something or someone, a doter (*O.E.D.*, *sb.*I.b).-
167. *issue*] offspring.
170. *Sue . . . love*] petition to be seated in the throne of your love.
171. *run . . . ground*] 'make sprightly melodies above the plainsong base-line of love' (Hunter).
172. *erect . . . symmetry*] i.e., stand up. Mazzagente is asking her to dance. Mellida seems initially to refuse the invitation and both Galeazzo and Mazzagente have to persuade her to agree; she does not clearly do so until l. 201.
173-4. *Shine . . . night*] i.e., Let your eye, now as dark and gloomy as night, shine in the proper realm of love.
179. *I'll lay . . . lips*] i.e., I'll kiss you.
180. *dead man's*] i.e., Antonio's.

Mellida. You ne'er took seisin on them yet. Forbear!
There's not a vacant corner of my heart,
But all is filled with dead Antonio's loss.   185
Then urge no more. O, leave to love at all!
'Tis less disgraceful not to mount than fall.
Mazzagente. Bright and refulgent lady, deign your ear;
You see this blade. Had it a courtly lip
It would divulge my valour, plead my love,   190
Jostle that skipping feeble amorist
Out of your love's seat. I am Mazzagent.
Galeazzo. Hark thee! I pray thee, taint not thy sweet ear
With that sot's gabble—by thy beauteous cheek,
He is the flagging'st bulrush that e'er drooped   195
With each slight mist of rain—but with pleased eye
Smile on my courtship.
Mellida. What said you, sir? Alas, my thought was fixed
Upon another object. Good, forbear.
I shall but weep. Ay me, what boots a tear!   200
Come, come, let's dance. O music, thou distill'st
More sweetness in us than this jarring world!
Both time and measure from thy strains do breathe,
Whilst from the channel of this dirt doth flow
Nothing but timeless grief, unmeasured woe.   205
Antonio. [*Aside*] O, how impatience cramps my crackèd veins

---

198. was] *1633*; wax *Q*.

---

183. *seisin*] legal possession, *O.E.D.*, *sb*.1.b.*fig.* Cf. Blackstone, II:311,
'livery of seisin is no other than the pure feudal investiture, or delivery of
corporal possession of the land or tenament, which was held absolutely
necessary to complete the donation' (*Commentaries on the Laws of England*).
    188. *refulgent*] radiant, gleaming—a term of compliment for a lady; invented
by Marston, *O.E.D.*, *a.c.*
    188–92.] Mazzagente, the 'man-queller', is boasting, on the strength of the
Italian meaning of his name, about his prowess.
    194. *sot's*] dolt's, blockhead's.
    195. *flagging'st*] most drooping or languid.
    199. *Good*] i.e., kind sir; cf. l. 222 below.
    200. *what boots*] what good is.
    203. *Both time . . . do breathe*] i.e., From the beat of the music we derive
both the rhythm and the timing for our earthly dance.
    204. *channel*] gutter or open sewer. Mellida seems to see this world as an
open drain.
    this dirt] i.e., this life, this earth.

And curdles thick my blood with boiling rage!
O eyes, why leap you not like thunderbolts
Or cannon bullets in my rivals' face?
Ohimè infelice misero, O lamentevol fato!   210
              [*He throws himself to the ground.*]
Alberto. What means the lady fall upon the ground?
Rosaline. Belike the falling sickness.
Antonio. [*Aside*] I cannot brook this sight. My thoughts grow
      wild.
  Here lies a wretch on whom heaven never smiled.
Rosaline. [*To Alberto*] What, servant, ne'er a word, and I here,
      man?   215
  I would shoot some speech forth, to strike the time
  With pleasing touch of amorous compliment.
  Say, sweet, what keeps thy mind—what think'st thou on?
Alberto. Nothing.
Rosaline. What's that nothing?   220
Alberto. A woman's constancy.
Rosaline. Good, why, wouldst thou have us sluts and never shift
      the vesture of our thoughts? Away, for shame!
Alberto. O no, th'art too constant to afflict my heart,
  Too, too firm fixèd in unmovèd scorn.   225
Rosaline. Pish, pish. I, 'fixèd in unmovèd scorn'?
  Why, I'll love thee tonight.
Alberto. But whom tomorrow?
Rosaline. Faith, as the toy puts me in the head.
Balurdo. And pleased the marble heavens, now would I might   230
      be the toy, to put you in the head kindly to conceit my—

210.1. S.D.] *Dilke subst.*

---

210. Ohimè . . . fato] Alas, miserable wretch; O, deplorable fate!
    212. *falling sickness*] epilepsy, but with a sexual connotation (i.e.,
willingness to be seduced).
    213. *this sight*] i.e., the attempted seduction of Mellida by Mazzagente and
Galeazzo.
    222–3. *never shift . . . our thoughts*] never change our minds, like whores
who never change their clothes.
    224. *constant to afflict*] consistent in afflicting.
    230. *And . . . heavens*] if the heavens be pleased; 'And' seems to stand for
'an', 'if'.
    231. *toy . . . head*] The phrase 'to have toys in one's head' is proverbial,
Dent T456.1.

my—my—pray you, give m'an epithet for love.
Felice. 'Roaring', 'roaring'.
Balurdo. O love, thou hast murdered me, made me a shadow,
　　and you hear not Balurdo but Balurdo's ghost.   235
Rosaline. Can a ghost speak?
Balurdo. Scurvily, as I do.
Rosaline. And walk?
Balurdo. After their fashion.
Rosaline. And eat apples?   240
Balurdo. In a sort, in their garb.
Felice. Prithee, Flavia, be my mistress.
Flavia. Your reason, good Felice?
Felice. Faith, I have nineteen mistresses already, and I not
　　much disdain that thou shouldst make up the full score.   245
Flavia. O, I hear you make commonplaces of your mistresses,
　　to perform the office of memory by. Pray you, in ancient
　　times were not those satin hose? In good faith, now they
　　are new dyed, pinked, and scoured, they show as well as
　　if they were new.—What, mute, Balurdo?   250
Felice. Ay, in faith, and 'twere not for printing and painting,
　　my breech and your face would be out of reparation.
Balurdo. 'Ay, in faith, and 'twere not for printing and painting,

232. m'an] *Hunter*; in an *Q.*   234. s.p. *Balurdo*] *Dilke; continuous from
233–5 to Felice in Q.*   253. in] *Dilke*; an *Q.*; painting *1633; pointing Q.*

234–41.] Derived from Erasmus' *Colloquies*, 'Proci et Puellae' (The Lovers
and the Maids), *Omnia Opera*, Lyons: P. Vander, 1703, I:692–3. Translated
in 1671 by H.M., it reads: '[*Pamphilius*] . . . even as that God [Mars] makes
sport on't to kill men, so dost thou too, but that thou, being more cruel than
Mars, killest even him that loveth thee . . . Thou seest one lifeless carcase, if so
be thou seest me. [*Mary*] What's this I hear? Dost thou speak and walk about
when thou art dead? I wish that more dreadful ghosts may never meet me . . .
do ghosts also walk? have they clothes on? Do they sleep? [*Pamphilius*] They
perform the act of generation too, but after their manner.' Cf. also iv.i.13–17.
246. *make commonplaces*] make trite, trivialise, *O.E.D.*, B.*adj*.a. The
suggestion is, perhaps, that Felice uses the mnemonic device of associating the
names of his mistresses with particular places.
251–2. *'twere . . . reparation*] The same joke occurs in *The Merry Jests of
George Peele*: 'if it were not for printing [i.e., stamping with new designs, or
darning] and painting [i.e., using cosmetics], my arse and your face would
grow out of reparations [repair]' (edn. of 1627, p. 30).
253. *in faith*] While the 'an faith' of Q makes good sense, Balurdo is echoing
Felice and is complimented on his accuracy, thus 'in faith' is more likely.

SC I]   ANTONIO AND MELLIDA   IOI

my breech and your face would be out of reparation.'
Felice. Good again, echo.   255
Flavia. Thou art, by nature, too foul to be affected.
Felice. And thou, by art, too fair to be beloved.
     By wit's life, most spark spirits but hard chance.
     [*Sings*] La ty dine.
Piero. Gallants, the night grows old, and downy sleep   260
     Courts us to entertain his company.
     Our tirèd limbs, bruised in the morning fight,
     Entreat soft rest and gentle hushed repose.
     Fill out Greek wines; prepare fresh cresset-light;
     We'll have a banquet. Princes, then good night.   265

The cornets sound a sennet and the Duke *goes out in state. As they are*
     going out, ANTONIO *stays* MELLIDA; *the rest exeunt.*

Antonio. What means these scattered looks? Why tremble you?
     Why quake your thoughts in your distracted eyes?
     Collect your spirits, madam. What do you see?
     Dost not behold a ghost?
     Look, look where he stalks, wrapped up in clouds of
          grief,   270
     Darting his soul upon thy wond'ring eyes.
     Look, he comes towards thee. See, he stretcheth out
     His wretched arms to gird thy lovèd waist
     With a most wished embrace. See'st him not yet?
     Nor yet? Ha, Mellida, thou well may'st err,   275
     For look, he walks not like Antonio,
     Like that Antonio that this morning shone
     In glistering habiliments of arms

256. *too . . . affected*] too ugly to be accepted as a lover.
257. *art . . . beloved*] i.e., cosmetics have made you too beautiful to be
believed/loved.
258. *most . . . chance*] i.e., most sparkling wits give their lovers harsh
treatment.
264. *Fill out*] add water to.
     cresset-light] This is possibly derived from the French 'croiset', which is
defined by Cotgrave as 'a cruet, crucible, or little earthen pot, such as
goldsmiths melt their gold in' (Keltie). These lights were often hung on a pole
and used as torches at night.
269–79.] See ll. 234–41n above.
278. *glistering . . . arms*] shining armour.

To seize his love, spite of her father's spite,
But like himself, wretched and miserable,   280
Banished, forlorn, despairing, struck quite through
With sinking grief, rolled up in sevenfold doubles
Of plagues unvanquishable. Hark, he speaks to thee!
Mellida. Alas, I cannot hear nor see him.
Antonio. Why? All this night about the room he stalked   285
And groaned and howled, with raging passion
To view his love—lifeblood of all his hopes,
Crown of his fortunes—clipped by strangers' arms.
[*Removing his disguise*] Look but behind thee.
Mellida. O, Antonio! My lord, my love, my—   290
Antonio. Leave passion, sweet, for time, place, air, and earth
Are all our foes. Fear and be jealous. Fair,
Let's fly.
Mellida. Dear heart, ha, whither?
Antonio. O, 'tis no matter whither, but let's fly.   295
Ha! Now I think on't, I have ne'er a home,
No father, friend, no country to embrace
These wretched limbs. The world, the all that is,

---

283. unvanquishable] *Dilke*; vanquishable *Q*.

280–3] Antonio sees himself as wholly isolated ('banished, forlorn') and the plaything of heaven's wrath ('plagues'). He is totally without hope for, like the Egyptians visited by the wrath of Jehovah, his miseries are unconquerable. The *Q* reading 'vanquishable' (283) could be a reference to Antonio being 'vulnerable', but the Biblical context of these plagues makes Dilke's emendation more probable; it is the plagues which are unvanquishable.
    282. *sinking*] that leads to despair.
    sevenfold doubles] The image seems to be that of a carpet or roll of cloth folded or rolled over in seven folds, but it may also refer to the Feast of the Passover; see next note.
    283. *plagues*] Probably a recollection of the 'Egyptian louse' (129) which was, of course, one of the plagues sent by Jehovah to effect the deliverance of the Israelites from Pharaoh. The last of the plagues was the death of the firstborn, as a result of which there was instituted the Feast of the Passover: 'Seven days shall ye eat unleavened bread ... for whosoever eateth leavened bread from the first day until the seventh day ... shall be cut off ... in the seventh day there shall be an holy convocation ... In the first month, on the fourteenth day of the month at even, ye shall eat unleavened bread ... Seven days shall there be no leaven found in your houses' (Exodus, xii.15–19).
    286. *passion*] Trisyllabic.
    288. *clipped*] embraced. Cf. *A.R.*, 1.i.63, 'having clipped them with pretence of love'.
    292. *jealous*] vigilant, suspiciously watchful, *O.E.D.*, *a*.3.

Is all my foe. A prince not worth a doit!
Only my head is hoisèd to high rate,   300
Worth twenty thousand double pistolets
To him that can but strike it from these shoulders.
But come, sweet creature, thou shalt be my home,
My father, country, riches, and my friend,
My all, my soul, and thou and I will live—   305
Let's think like what—and thou and I will live
Like unmatched mirrors of calamity.
The jealous ear of night eavesdrops our talk.
Hold thee, there's a jewel, and look thee, there's a note
That will direct thee when, where, how to fly.   310
Bid me adieu.
Mellida.   Farewell, bleak misery!
Antonio. Stay, sweet, let's kiss before you go.   [*They kiss.*]
Mellida. Farewell, dear soul.
Antonio.   Farewell, my life, my heart.
                              [*Exeunt separately.*]

299. *a doit*] a small Dutch coin worth only half of an English farthing (one fourth of a penny), hence 'worthless'. The phrase 'not worth a dodkin [doit]' was proverbial, Dent D430.

300. *hoisèd*] raised.

307. *unmatched mirrors*] unequalled as images (of misfortune).

308. *eavesdrops*] stands within the 'eaves' of a house to listen to secrets. Cf. *A.R.*, v.iii.24–5, 'as I walked / Muffled, to eavesdrop speech' and *Fawn*, III.i.220, 'look that nobody eavesdrop us.'

Act III

[Sc. i]

Enter ANDRUGIO *in armour,* LUCIO *with a shepherd gown in his
hand, and a* Page.

Andrugio. Is not yon gleam the shuddering morn that flakes,
　　With silver tincture, the east verge of heaven?
Lucio. I think it is, so please your excellence.
Andrugio. Away! I have no excellence to please.
　　Prithee, observe the custom of the world　　　　　　　　　　5
　　That only flatters greatness, states exalts.
　　'An please my excellence'!—O Lucio,
　　Thou hast been ever held respected, dear,
　　Even precious to Andrugio's inmost love.
　　Good, flatter not. Nay, if thou giv'st not faith　　　　　　10
　　That I am wretched, O, read that, read that.
Lucio. [*Reads*] *'Piero Sforza, to the Italian princes, fortune! Ex-
　　cellent, the just overthrow Andrugio took in the Venetian
　　Gulf hath so assured the Genoese of the injustice of his cause
　　and the hatefulness of his person that they have banished him*　15
　　and all his family, and for confirmation of their peace with us

---

Act III] *ACTVS TERTIVS Q.*　　Sc. i] *Dilke, not in Q.*　　12. S.P. *Lucio*]
Bullen; not in Q.　　14. *injustice*] *Dilke; iustice Q.*

0.1. a shepherd gown] as a disguise for Andrugio. Perhaps, as J & N
suggest, an ironic comment is intended upon Tamburlaine's rejection of his
shepherd dress for 'complete armour' and a 'curtle-axe', *I Tamb.*, I.ii.42.
　1–2.] Cf. *A.R.*, I.i.106–8, 'the dapple-gray coursers of the morn / Beat up
the light with their bright silver hooves / And chase it through the sky.'
　1. *flakes*] flecks, *O.E.D.*, v.[1] 2.*trans.*a.
　2. *tincture*] tint.
　6. *states exalts*] [and] exalts [the power of] kings.
　7. *An . . . excellence*] Andrugio paraphrases Lucio's respectful 'so please
your excellence' (3).
　10. *if . . . faith*] i.e., if you do not give credence, belief.
　12–13. Excellent] i.e., Your Excellencies.

have vowed that, if he or his son can be attached, to send us
both their heads. We therefore by force of our united league
forbid you to harbour him or his blood; but if you apprehend
his person, we entreat you to send him or his head to us. For   20
we vow, by the honour of our blood, to recompense any man
that bringeth his head with twenty thousand double pistolets
and the endearing to our choicest love.
                              From Venice: Piero Sforza.'
Andrugio. My thoughts are fixed in contemplation   25
        Why this huge earth, this monstrous animal
        That eats her children, should not have eyes and ears.
        Philosophy maintains that nature's wise
        And forms no useless or unperfect thing.
        Did nature make the earth, or the earth nature?   30
        For earthly dirt makes all things, makes the man,
        Moulds me up honour and, like a cunning Dutchman,
        Paints me a puppet even with seeming breath
        And gives a sot appearance of a soul.
        Go to, go to. Thou liest, Philosophy.   35
        Nature forms things unperfect, useless, vain.
        Why made she not the earth with eyes and ears,
        That she might see desert and hear men's plaints?
        That when a soul is splitted, sunk with grief,

17. attached] arrested, *O.E.D.*, *ppl.a.*1.

23. endearing] making cherished, *O.E.D.*, *ppl.a.* Cf. *A.R.*, II.i.48, 'Endear thyself Piero's intimate.'

27. eats] i.e., at burials.

28–34.] Based upon *The Essays of Montaigne*, as translated by John Florio in 1603: 'Our composition, both public and private, is full of imperfection. Yet is there nothing in nature unserviceable, no, not inutility itself. Nothing thereof hath been insinuated in this huge universe but holdeth some fit place therein. Our essence is cemented with crazed qualities; ambition, jealousy, envy, revenge, superstition, despair, lodge in us with so natural a possession as their image is also discerned in beasts—yea, and cruelty, so unnatural a vice, for in the midst of compassion we inwardly feel a kind of bitter-sweet pricking of malicious delight to see others suffer' (ed. W. E. Henley, *The Tudor Translations*, London: Nutt, 1893, III, bk. III. chap. I, p. 6).

32. *Moulds me up honour*] i.e., It is from the dust of the earth that all honour and its possessors derive.

a cunning Dutchman] a German or Dutch painter.

38. *desert*] deserving.

39. *splitted*] split asunder. Cf. *A.R.*, IV.iv.14–15, 'I am a poor, poor orphan; a weak, weak child, / The wrack of splitted fortune.'

He might fall thus [*He casts himself down.*] upon the
   breast of earth   40
And in her ear halloo his misery,
Exclaiming thus: 'O thou all-bearing earth,
Which men do gape for till thou cramm'st their mouths
And chok'st their throats with dust, O, chawn thy breast
And let me sink into thee! [*He beats the ground.*] Look
   who knocks;   45
Andrugio calls!' But O, she's deaf and blind.
A wretch but lean relief on earth can find.
Lucio. Sweet lord, abandon passion, and disarm.
   Since by the fortune of the tumbling sea
   We are rolled up upon the Venice marsh,   50
   Let's clip all fortune, lest more louring fate—
Andrugio. 'More louring fate?' O Lucio, choke that breath.
   Now I defy chance. Fortune's brow hath frowned,
   Even to the utmost wrinkle it can bend,
   Her venom's spit. Alas, what country rests,   55
   What son, what comfort that she can deprive?
   Triumphs not Venice in my overthrow?
   Gapes not my native country for my blood?
   Lies not my son tombed in the swelling main?
   And yet 'more louring fate'? There's nothing left 60
   Unto Andrugio but Andrugio,
   And that nor mischief, force, distress, nor hell can take.
   Fortune my fortunes, not my mind, shall shake.

40. s.d.] *Dilke subst.*

41. *halloo*] shout aloud, O.E.D., *v*.3.*trans.*
44. *chawn*] gape open, split asunder, O.E.D., *v*.2.*trans.* Cotgrave, *A Dictionary of The French and English Tongues*, 1611, defines 'se fendre' as 'To cleave, rive, gape, chap, chink, or chawn, to open, break, or go asunder of itself', and defines 'gercer' as 'To cleave, rive, cut in many places, and by small clefts, to chink, chap, chawn (as the north wind does) the face, hands etc.'
51. *clip*] embrace.
53. *Fortune's brow*] Fortune appears to have an extremely wrinkled forehead and spits poison; cf. Ind.9–10. The phrase 'to spit one's venom' was proverbial, Dent v28. The idea that Fortune frowns is common; cf. *Lr.*, v.iii.6, 'Myself could else out-frown false Fortune's frown.'
55. *rests*] remains.
63. *Fortune . . . shake*] Cf. 'Fortuna opes auferre, non animum potest': 'Fortune can take away my wealth, but not my spirit', Seneca, *Medea*, 176. Dent cites the adage 'fortune can take from us nothing but what she gave us (our goods but not our virtue)' as proverbial, F599.

SC I] ANTONIO AND MELLIDA 107

Lucio. Spoke like yourself! But give me leave, my lord,
To wish your safety. If you are but seen, 65
Your arms display you. Therefore, put them off
And take—
Andrugio. Wouldst thou have me go unarmed among my foes,
Being besieged by passion, ent'ring lists
To combat with despair and mighty grief, 70
My soul beleaguered with the crushing strength
Of sharp impatience? Ha, Lucio, go unarmed?—
Come, soul, resume the valour of thy birth.
Myself, myself will dare all opposites.
I'll muster forces, an unvanquished power; 75
Cornets of horse shall press th'ungrateful earth;
This hollow-wombèd mass shall inly groan
And murmur to sustain the weight of arms.
Ghastly amazement, with upstarted hair,
Shall hurry on before and usher us, 80
Whilst trumpets clamour with a sound of death.
Lucio. Peace, good my lord. Your speech is all too light.
Alas, survey your fortunes, look what's left
Of all your forces and your utmost hopes:
A weak old man, a page, and your poor self. 85

---

64. Spoke] *Dilke*; Speake *Q.*

66. *Your arms . . . you*] The heraldic device on your armour reveals your identity.
69. *lists*] the palisades enclosing the ground for tilting, *O.E.D.*, *sb.*³ 9.*spec.* Here it is used metaphorically.
71. *beleaguered*] beset.
72. *sharp*] keen.
73. *of thy birth*] which you were born to. Andrugio is speaking to himself.
74. *Myself, myself*] now restored to my proper self (i.e, with my valour regained). Cf. l. 114 below, 'I'll show myself myself' and *R3*, 'Then fly. What, from myself? Great reason why— / Lest I revenge. What, myself upon myself!', v.iii.184–5.
dare all opposites] Cf. *R3*, v.iv.2–3, 'The King enacts more wonders than a man / Daring an opposite to every danger.'
76. *Cornets of horse*] companies of cavalry.
ungrateful] i.e., resenting the weight (of the cavalry).
82. *light*] insubstantial, dealing with trivia, *O.E.D.*, *a.*III.13.
85. *A weak old man*] i.e., Lucio himself. Cf. Seneca, *Troades*, 507–8, 'en intuere, turba quae simus super— / tumulus, puer, captiva': 'See how small a company of us remains—a tomb, a child, a captive woman.'
a page] This is a chorister who sings at l. 105.1.

Andrugio. Andrugio lives, and a fair cause of arms.
Why, that's an army all invincible.
He who hath that hath a battalion royal,
Armour of proof, huge troops of barbèd steeds,
Main squares of pikes, millions of harquebus.   90
O, a fair cause stands firm and will abide;
Legions of angels fight upon her side.
Lucio. Then, noble spirit, slide in strange disguise
Unto some gracious prince and sojourn there
Till time and fortune give revenge firm means.   95
Andrugio. No, I'll not trust the honour of a man.
Gold is grown great and makes Perfidiousness
A common water in most princes' courts.
He's in the checkle-roll. I'll not trust my blood.
I know none breathing but will cog a die   100

88–9. He . . . royal, / Armour . . . steeds] *Dilke*; He . . . battalion / Royal . . .
steeds *Q*.   98. water] *Q*; waiter *1633*.

86. *a fair . . . arms*] a cause well worth fighting for.
87. *that's . . . invincible*] i.e., a worthy cause is like having an army for your
support; cf. *R2*, III.ii.85, 'Is not the King's name twenty thousand names?'
88. *a battalion royal*] an army fit for a king.
89. *of proof*] invulnerable.
barbèd steeds] horses with armour covering the breast and flanks.
90. *Main . . . pikes*] i.e., the major part of the army, consisting of infantry
drawn up in squares and armed with pikes. The pike was a steel-headed
wooden spear that preceded the bayonet as a principal infantry weapon.
harquebus] portable firearms.
92. *Legions . . . side*] A recollection of the dream sequence in Shakespeare's
R3, V.iii.175, where the spirits of those murdered by Richard curse him and
bless Richmond, promising that, at the battle on the morrow, 'God and good
angels fight on Richmond's side.'
her] i.e., the fair cause.
93. *noble spirit*] i.e., Andrugio.
slide] slip away.
98. *common water*] i.e., base treachery (paid by gold) is a common currency
at the courts of princes. The 1633 reading 'waiter' (which has a variant form
'water') means a spy, a scout, *O.E.D.*, I.3.a, and thus Perfidiousness becomes
an emblematic figure lurking to eavesdrop at the court. Cf. Ind.9–10.
99. *checkle-roll*] This, as Hunter points out, is a Marstonian term of abuse,
from 'chequer-roll', which is a list of persons (usually servants) whose support
is chargeable to the royal exchequer, and 'shekel-roll' or list of those to be
bribed.
my blood] i.e., people like me who are born to high station, my relatives.
100. *cog a die*] cheat at dice.

For twenty thousand double pistolets.
How goes the time?
Lucio.   I saw no sun today.
Andrugio. No sun will shine where poor Andrugio breathes.
My soul grows heavy.—Boy, let's have a song.
We'll sing yet, faith, even despite of fate.   105

They sing.

Andrugio. 'Tis a good boy and, by my troth, well sung.
O, an thou felt'st my grief, I warrant thee,
Thou wouldst have struck division to the height
And made the life of music breathe. [*The Boy weeps.*]
Hold boy, why so?
For God's sake, call me not Andrugio,   110
That I may soon forget what I have been.
For heaven's sake, name not Antonio,
That I may not remember he was mine.
Well, ere yon sun set, I'll show myself myself,
Worthy my blood. I was a duke, that's all.   115
No matter whither but from whence we fall.

Exeunt.

105.1. *They sing*] *Keltie*; *CANTANT Q.*   109. *The Boy weeps*] *Hunter.*
112. sake] *This ed.*; name *Q.*   116. whither] whether *Q.*

102–3. *I saw ... shine*] These lines may be another reminiscence of *R3*,
v.iii.277–8, where Richard asks 'Who saw the sun today?', and Ratcliffe
replies, 'Not I, my lord.' The idea is, however, commonplace.
   105.1 They sing] This translates the Q reading (CANTANT) but it is clear
from the context that it is primarily the Page who sings. Andrugio calls upon
him for a song (104) and then compliments him on his performance (106–9).
Andrugio also says, however, 'We'll sing yet' (105); perhaps the Page was
accompanied by Lucio and even by other choristers off stage.
   107. *an*] if.
   108. *struck ... height*] i.e., produced the most moving kind of music. In
Poetaster, IV.v.188–91, Hermogenes sings, 'Then, in a free and lofty
strain, / Our broken tunes we thus repair' and Crispinus (Marston) responds,
'And we answer them again, / Running division on the panting air.'
   division] part of a melody, a musical phrase; cf. *R&J*, III.v.29, 'Some say the
lark makes sweet division.'
   112. *sake*] Q's 'name' is probably an anticipation of the next word.
   116. *No ... fall*] The fact of falling into misery is not, in itself, significant;
what does matter is the height from which we fall. Adapted from Seneca,
Thyestes, 925–6, 'magis unde cadas / quam quo refert': 'more matters it
whence thou fallest, than to what'. Cf. also *Malcontent*, II.i.25, '*Unde cadis non
quo refert.*'

[Sc. ii]

Enter FELICE *walking, unbraced.*

Felice. [*Calls*] Castilio, Alberto, Balurdo!—None up?—
Forobosco! Flattery, nor thou up yet?—
Then there's no courtier stirring, that's firm truth.
I cannot sleep. Felice seldom rests
In these court lodgings. I have walked all night   5
To see if the nocturnal court delights
Could force me envy their felicity,
And by plain truth—I will confess plain truth—
I envy nothing but the traverse light.
O, had it eyes and ears and tongues, it might   10
See sport, hear speech of most strange surquedries.
O, if that candlelight were made a poet,
He would prove a rare firking satirist
And draw the core forth of impostumed sin.
Well, I thank heaven yet that my content   15
Can envy nothing but poor candlelight.
As for the other glistering copper spangs

Sc. ii] *Bullen, not in Q.*   8. *truth ... truth] Hunter*; troth ... troth] *Q.*
9. traverse] *Hunter, conj. Dilke*; Trauense *Q.*

0.1. unbraced] with dress unfastened, *O.E.D., ppl.a.*1. Cf. *A.R.*, 1.i.0.1,
'*Enter* PIERO *unbraced*'. This entrance indicates a lapse of time since the end of
the previous scene. Scene I took place late in the evening; the new scene begins
just before the following dawn.
    8. *plain truth*] simple honesty. The phrases 'truth's tale is simple' and 'truth
is plain' were proverbial, Dent T593.
    9. *the traverse light*] the light admitted by the window in the screen or
partition (i.e., because from it one can observe the true character of others).
This may be an allusion to the upper stage where there was at least one window
(light), set in the right or left side of the façade which was, probably, at an
angle to the rear wall. It is from the upper stage that the ladies observe the true
nature of the men on the lower stage in 1.i.100ff.
    11. *surquedries*] arrogance. Cf. *A.R.*, III.ii.71–2, 'making him drunk / With
fuming surquedries', and *Satire I*, 102–4, 'Thou that did'st fear to eat poor
Johns a space. / Lie close ye slave at beastly luxury; / Melt and consume in
pleasure's surquedry.'
    12. *that candlelight*] i.e., the light shining through the 'traverse'.
    13. *firking*] whipping, lashing.
    14. *impostumed*] abscessed. The whole phrase seems to mean 'lance the boil
of sin'.
    17. *spangs*] small glittering ornaments. The adjective 'copper' implies that
the wearers are pretending that the copper is gold.

That glisten in the tire of the court,
Praise God, I either hate or pity them.
Well, here I'll sleep till that the scene of up   20
Is past at court. [*He lies down to sleep.*] O calm,
     hushed, rich content,
Is there a being blessedness without thee?
How soft thou down'st the couch where thou dost rest,
Nectar to life, thou sweet ambrosian feast.

Enter CASTILIO *and* [CAZZO], *his Page;* CASTILIO *with a casting
     bottle of sweet water in his hand, sprinkling himself.*

Castilio. Am not I a most sweet youth, now?   25
Cazzo. Yes, when your throat's perfumed; your very words
     Do smell of ambergris. O, stay sir, stay!
     Sprinkle some sweet water to your shoes' heels,
     That your mistress may swear you have a sweet foot.
Castilio. Good, very good, very passing, passing good.   30
Felice. Fut, what treble minikin squeaks there, ha? 'Good, very
     good, very very good'!
Castilio. I will warble to the delicious concave of my mistress'
     ear and strike her thoughts with the pleasing touch of
     my voice.   35

They sing.

Castilio. Felice! Health, fortune, mirth, and wine—
Felice. To thee, my love divine.

21. S.D.] *Hunter subst.*   24.1. CAZZO] *Hunter.*   35.1. *They sing*] *This ed.;*
He [*LUCIO*] sings Keltie; Cantant *Q.*

---

18. *tire*] attire, dress.
20. *the . . . up*] the levée.
22. *Is . . . blessedness*] Does a state of blessedness exist?
23. *down'st*] line with down.
24. *ambrosian*] like nectar, the food of the gods.
24. 1–2. casting bottle] scent bottle (for sprinkling perfumed waters). Cf.
Ind.134.
27. *ambergris*] a secretion of the sperm whale, used in perfumery and
cooking.
30. *passing*] surpassingly.
31. *minikin*] a high pitched, or shrill, voice, *O.E.D., sb.* A.2.c.*trans.* Cf.
v.ii.10–12, 'I had rather have a servant with a short nose and thin hair than
have such a high-stretched minikin voice.'
33. *concave*] hollow, cavity.

Castilio. I drink to thee, sweeting.
Felice. Plague on thee for an ass!
Castilio. Now thou hast seen the court, by the perfection of it   40
    dost not envy it?
Felice. I wonder it doth not envy me.
    Why, man, I have been borne upon the spirit's wings,
    The soul's swift Pegasus, the fantasy,
    And from the height of contemplation   45
    Have viewed the feeble joints men totter on.
    I envy none, but hate or pity all.
    For when I view, with an intentive thought,
    That creature fair, but proud; him rich, but sot;
    Th'other witty, but unmeasured arrogant;   50
    Him great, yet boundless in ambition;
    Him highborn, but of base life; t'other feared,
    Yet fearèd fears, and fears most to be most loved;
    Him wise, but made a fool for public use;
    Th'other learned, but self-opinionate—   55
    When I discourse all these and see myself

49. proud; him rich, but sot;] *All Qs except Ashley, Texas, Harvard*; prout; him rich, but sot: *Ashley*; prout; him rich, but so: Texas, Harvard.

36–9.] Castilio may be inviting Felice to sing another impromptu song with him, and he proffers the first line 'Health, fortune, mirth, and wine' (36), to which Felice adds 'To thee, my love divine'. Castilio then goes on, 'I drink to thee, sweeting' (38), but Felice refuses to continue and dismisses the game with 'Plague on thee for an ass!' (39). The sequence is, also, an ironic series of toasts between Castilio and Felice.

44. *Pegasus*] the winged horse whose heel called forth the fountain Hippocrene, which was sacred to the Muses. He flew to heaven and dwelt among the stars, hence the association with 'soul' and 'fantasy'.

48. *intentive*] earnestly applied.

49. *proud*] Ashley's 'prout' is clearly a simple letter error, as is Texas's 'so:'.

49–50. *That ... him ... Th'other*] Felice alludes to a succession of typical instances of courtly vanity and pride.

53. *fearèd fears*] Cf. 'Odia qui nimium timet regnare nescit; regna custodit metus': 'He who fears hatred overmuch, knows not to rule; fear is guard of kingdoms', Seneca, *Oedipus*, 705–6. The phrase 'feared men be fearful' was proverbial, Dent M515.

fears ... loved] Cf. Kyd, *Spanish Tragedy*, III.i.9–10, 'kings, / That would be feared, yet fear to be beloved.' The whole phrase here seems to mean that the tyrant is the one who fears most to be highest in popular esteem, for that popularity is insecure in the extreme.

55. *self-opinionate*] has too high an opinion of himself.

56. *discourse*] go over, list.

Nor fair, nor rich, nor witty, great, nor feared,
Yet amply suited, with all full content,
Lord, how I clap my hands and smooth my brow,
Rubbing my quiet bosom, tossing up   60
A grateful spirit to omnipotence!
Castilio. Ha, ha! But if thou knew'st my happiness,
Thou wouldst even grate away thy soul to dust
In envy of my sweet beatitude.
I cannot sleep for kisses. I cannot rest   65
For ladies' letters that importune me
With such unusèd vehemence of love
Straight to solicit them, that—
Felice. Confusion seize me, but I think thou liest.
Why should I not be sought to, then, as well?   70
Fut! Methinks I am as like a man.
Troth, I have a good head of hair, a cheek
Not as yet waned, a leg, faith, in the full.
I ha' not a red beard, take not tobacco much,
And 'slid, for other parts of manliness—   75
Castilio. Pew, waw! You ne'er accourted them in pomp,
Put your good parts in presence graciously.
Ha, an you had, why, they would ha' come off,
Sprung to your arms, and sued, and prayed, and vowed,

78–9. off, / Sprung to] *Bullen*; off, sprung / To *Dilke*; of, sprung / To *Q.*

60–1. *tossing . . . omnipotence*] i.e., giving grateful thanks to the almighty for
my status in life.
64. *beatitude*] state of being blessed, happy.
65. *I . . . kisses*] i.e., I have no time to sleep, for I am being kissed
continually.
67. *unusèd*] unusual.
73. *waned*] made wan, diminished (by age).
74. *red beard*] In *Poetaster*, III.i.27–8, Jonson calls Marston, Rufus Laberius
Crispinus, which probably describes his appearance: he had red (rufus), curly
hair (crispus), and was a maker of mimes (Laberius). The historical Decimus
Laberius (*c.* 105–43B.C.) was humiliated by Caesar by being required to act
out his own mimes, which were critical of Caesar, in Caesar's presence. Horace
(Jonson) also refers to Crispinus's 'beard' (29).
take . . . much] and would, thus, be acceptable to Rosaline, who disliked the
'great tobacco taker' Mazzagente (I.i.127).
76. *accourted them*] paid court to them and accompanied them at the court.
78. *an*] if.
come off] i.e., given in, ceased their resistance.

E

And opened all their sweetness to your love.   80
Felice. There are a number of such things as then
    Have often urged me to such loose belief.
    But, 'slid, you all do lie, you all do lie.
    I have put on good clothes and smudged my face,
    Struck a fair wench with a smart speaking eye,   85
    Courted in all sorts, blunt and passionate,
    Had opportunity, put them to the 'ah!',
    And, by this light, I find them wondrous chaste,
    Impregnable—perchance a kiss or so,
    But for the rest, O, most inexorable!   90
Castilio. Nay then, i'faith, prithee look here.
            Shows him the superscription of a seeming letter.
Felice. [*Reads*] '*To her most esteemed, loved, and generous servant,*
    Signor Castilio Balthazar.'
    Prithee, from whom comes this? Faith, I must see.
    [*Reads*] '*From her that is devoted to thee in most private*   95
        sweets of love, Rosaline.'
    Nay, God's my comfort, I must see the rest.
    I must, sans ceremony, faith I must.
            Felice takes away the letter by force.
Castilio. O, you spoil my ruff, unset my hair; good, away!
Felice. [*Reads*] '*Item, for strait canvas, thirteen pence halfpenny;*   100
    item, for an ell and a half of taffeta to cover your old canvas
    doublet, fourteen shillings and three pence.'
    'Slight, this' a tailor's bill!

81. then] *Q*; thou *Dilke.*

---

81. *then*] Bullen and Hunter argue for 'thou', but *Q*'s 'then' makes sense,
i.e., I have often been persuaded by my experiences of courting women that
your beliefs may be correct.
84. *smudged*] i.e., smartened up, by applying cosmetics.
86. *Courted in all sorts*] paid court to women in all fashions.
100. strait] narrow, *O.E.D.*, *a.*I.4.
    thirteen pence halfpenny] 1s 1½d or 5p. At the end of the sixteenth century
canvas cost between 1s and 3s per yard.
101. an ell] a measure of length of some 45 inches. The total length of the
taffeta is 5 ft 6½ in. or 1.69 metres.
    taffeta] light, thin silk of a bright, lustrous texture. It usually cost between
10s and 13s per yard. Castilio's canvas and taffeta were cheap.
103. *'Slight*] by God's light, a mild oath.
    this'] this is.

Castilio. In sooth, it is the outside of her letter, on which I took
the copy of a tailor's bill.   105
Cazzo. [*Aside*] But 'tis not crossed, I am sure of that. Lord have
mercy on him, his credit hath given up the last gasp.
Faith, I'll leave him, for he looks as melancholy as a
wench the first night she—
                                                        Exit.
Felice. Honest musk-cod, 'twill not be so stitched together.   110
Take that, and that, [*Strikes him*] and belie no lady's
love. Swear no more by Jesu, this madam, that lady.
Hence, go! Forswear the presence, travel three years to
bury this bastinado. Avoid, puff-paste, avoid!
Castilio. And tell not my lady mother? Well, as I am true gentle-   115
man, if she had not willed me on her blessing not to spoil
my face, if I could not find in my heart to fight, would I
might ne'er eat a potato pie more.
                                                        [*Exit.*]

Enter BALURDO *backward,* DILDO *following him with a looking glass
in one hand and a candle in the other hand;* FLAVIA *following him
backward with a looking glass in one hand and a candle in the other;*
ROSALINE *following her.* BALURDO *and* ROSALINE *stand setting
of faces; and so the scene begins.*

---

106. S.P. *Cazzo*] *Dilke; Dil. Q.*   111. S.D.] *Dilke subst.*

106. *crossed*] written with lines crossing at right angles, thus, 'crossed off',
'paid'.
110. *musk-cod*] a scented fop. Cf. *Every Man Out*, V.vi.11, 'I believe you,
musk-cod, I believe you.'
113. *travel*] journey, with the suggestion of labour or effort; cf. Ind.131, and
I.i.189.
114. *bastinado*] cudgelling.
Avoid] i.e., remove yourself. Said to devils, spirits etc. to expel them; cf.
2H6., I.iv.40, 'False fiend, avoid!'
puff-paste] a flimsy character: a minor insult, perhaps equivalent to 'flaky
pie'. Cf. *Jack Drum*, B4v, 'Sweet sir, repute me as a, puffe!, selected spirit born
to be the admirer of your never enough admired, puffe!'
118. *potato pie*] Hunter suggests an allusion to its (supposed) qualities as an
aphrodisiac.
118.1–5] This mime reflects the boyish qualities of the actors. As characters
they are checking their appearance in mirrors before facing the court and they
are also making faces before mirrors as children do. More simply, of course, it

Felice. More fools, more rare fools! O, for time and place long
    enough and large enough to act these fools! Here might   120
    be made a rare scene of folly, if the plot could bear it.
Balurdo. By the sugar-candy sky, hold up the glass higher that
    I may see to swear in fashion. O, one look more would
    ha' made them shine. God's nigs, they would have shone
    like my mistress' brow. Even so the Duke frowns for all   125
    this cursoned world. O that girn kills, it kills. By my
    golden—what's the richest thing about me?
Dildo. Your teeth.
Balurdo. By my golden teeth, [*To Dildo*] hold up, that I may put
    in. Hold up, I say, that I may see to put on my gloves.   130
Dildo. O delicious sweet-cheeked master, if you discharge but

---

119. More fools] *Hunter.*; More foole *Q.*   121. plot] *Hunter*; plat *Q.*
123. look] *This ed.*; loofe *Q.*   124. nigs] neakes *Q.*   126. cursoned] *Q*
(Cursond)*;* Curson *Hunter.*

shows Rosaline making herself up to mimic Mellida. See also Introduction,
'The Play in its Theatre'.
    121. *plot*] synopsis of the action used by the theatre, *O.E.D.*, *sb*.II.4. Cf.
v.ii.63–4, '[he] makes six plots of set faces before he speaks one wise word',
but here it is used figuratively to mean 'a device or design', *O.E.D.*, *sb*.II.4.b
and also cf. *What You Will*, B2*v*, 'let's think a plot.'
    123. *look*] Hunter (and all other editors) retain *Q*'s 'loofe'. Hunter suggests
it is perhaps a dialect word for 'hand' and J & N suggest a Northern form of
'loaf'. It seems to me to be a simple letter error, for Balurdo is saying 'please let
me have just one more look in the glass to admire my shining teeth.'
    124. *nigs*] *Q*'s 'neakes' is simply a variant of 'nigs', a meaningless oath,
O.E.D., 'God' Cf. IV.i.241 and *A.R.*, II.i.54, 'Go to, God's neaks, I
think I tickle it' (Balurdo).
    126. *cursoned*] *Q*'s 'Cursond' is an adjective formed from the dialect 'curson'
meaning 'Christian'. It was probably chosen for its similarity to 'cursed', i.e.,
'this accursed world', under the Christian curse of the fall from grace, which
Balurdo compares to the condition of the courtiers under the 'frown' of the
Duke.
    girn] snarl, *O.E.D.*, *sb*.2.1. Cf. *A.R.*, I.iii.12–13, 'When thou dost girn, thy
rusty face doth look / Like the head of a roasted rabbit.'
    129. *golden teeth*] Balurdo seems to have had some gold dental work,
probably a false set of caps for his front teeth, which he puts on at this point.
Gold leaf was used by Giovanni of Vigo as early as the end of the fifteenth
century for filling cavities, and single teeth were sometimes replaced by a gold
tooth banded to the adjacent teeth as a bridge. This whole sequence is part of
the play's satire on courtly excess.
    hold up] i.e., hold up the looking glass.

one glance from the level of that set face, O, you will
strike a wench, you'll make any wench love you.
Balurdo. By Jesu, I think I am as elegant a courtier as—
How likest thou my suit?   135
Dildo. All, beyond all, no paregal. [*Aside*] You are wondered at
for an ass!
Balurdo. Well, Dildo, no Christian creature shall know here-
after what I will do for thee heretofore.
Rosaline. Here wants a little white, Flavia.   140
Dildo. Ay, but master, you have one little fault—you sleep
open-mouthed.
Balurdo. Phew, thou jestest. In good sadness, I'll have a looking glass nailed to the tester of the bed, that I may see
when I sleep whether 'tis so or not. Take heed you lie   145
not! Go to, take heed you lie not!
Flavia. [*To Rosaline*] By my troth, you look as like the princess now—
Rosaline. Ay, but her lip is—lip is—a little redder, a very little
redder, but by the help of art or nature, ere I change my   150
periwig, mine shall be as red.
Flavia. O ay, that face, that eye, that smile, that writhing of
your body, that wanton dandling of your fan, becomes

---

136. S.P. *Dildo*] *Hunter; Catz. Q.*   143. Phew] Pewe *Q.*   144. the tester]
1633; the the testarn *Q.*   149. S.P. *Rosaline*] *Dilke; not in Q.*

---

132. *glance*] An allusion to the Elizabethan convention of love-at-first-sight,
as with Romeo's first glimpse of Juliet, I.v.49–50, 'Did my heart love till now?
Forswear it, sight; / For I ne'er saw true beauty till this night.'
  level] aim, *O.E.D.*, *sb.*II.9.a.
  set] fixed and thus 'made-up', *O.E.D.*, *ppl.a.*6.a.
  136. *paregal*] equal.
  139. *heretofore*] formerly, in time past; i.e., no one will ever know in the
future what I plan to do for you.
  140. *Here ... white*] Rosaline is referring to the make-up which Flavia is
assisting her to apply.
  144. *tester*] bed canopy.
  147. *By my troth*] This is an asseration, 'by my oath of fidelity as your
servant', equivalent to 'on my honour'.
  149–50. *lip ... redder*] *Q*'s odd repetition of 'lip is' may just be an
unintentional repetition of a word, but it seems more likely that the phrase is
repeated to indicate Rosaline's hesitation as she applies the rouge. Rosaline is
striving, by the use of bright red lipstick, to make herself look like Mellida.
The wig which she is to change suggests also that both had red hair.

prethily, so sweethly—[*Rosaline rewards her.*]—'tis
even the goodest lady that breathes, the most amiable—   155
faith, the fringe of your satin petticoat is ripped. Good
faith, madam, they say you are the most bounteous lady
to your women that ever—[*Rosaline gives her another
gift.*]—O most delicious beauty! Good madam, let me
kith it.   160
        [*She kisses the hem of Rosaline's petticoat.*]

                    Enter PIERO.

Felice. Rare sport, rare sport! A female fool and a female flat-
    terer.
Rosaline. Body o'me, the Duke! Away the glass!
Piero. [*Seeing a letter on the ground*] Take up your paper,
    Rosaline.   165
Rosaline. Not mine, my lord.
Piero. Not yours, my lady? I'll see what 'tis.
Balurdo. [*To Rosaline*] And how does my sweet mistress? O
    lady dear, even as 'tis an old say, ''tis an old horse can
    neither wehee nor wag his tail', even so do I hold my set 170
    face still; even so 'tis a bad courtier that can neither dis-
    course nor blow 'his nose.
Piero. [*Reads*] '*Meet me at Abraham's, the Jew's, where I bought
    my Amazon's disguise. A ship lies in the port, ready bound
    for England. Make haste. Come private. Antonio.*'   175
    [*Shouts*] Forobosco, Alberto, Felice, Castilio, Balurdo!

        Enter CASTILIO, FOROBOSCO, [*and* ALBERTO].

---

175. *Antonio*] Dilke; *printed as the first of the following list of names in* Q.
176.1. S.D.] *before 176 in* Q; *and* ALBERTO] *Hunter*.

154–60. *prethily . . . sweethly . . . kith*] Flavia is now affecting a lisp,
probably as a sign of licentiousness. Her speech is also perhaps intended to
suggest 'baby-talk'. Cf. *Hamlet*, III.i.144–6, 'You jig and amble, and you lisp,
and nickname God's creatures, and make your wantonness your ignorance.'
    164. *paper*] the letter given to Mellida by Antonio (II.i.309), which she
confesses (at l. 192) to having lost.
    169. *say*] proverb, saying.
    170. *wehee*] whinny. Proverbial, 'It is an ill Horse that can neither whinny
nor wag his tail' (Dent H671), and cf. *Every Man Out*, II.i.65–6, 'the legerity
for that, and the wehee, and the daggers in the nose'.

Run, keep the palace, post to the ports, go to my daughter's chamber! Whither now? Scud to the Jew's! Stay,
run to the gates, stop the gondolets, let none pass the
marsh. Do all at once. Antonio—his head, his head! [*To*   180
Felice] Keep you the court. The rest stand still, or run,
or go, or shout, or search, or scud, or call, or hang, or
do—do—do, su—su—su, something. I know not who—
who—who, what I do—do—do, nor who—who—who,
where I am.   185

[*Exeunt* FOROBOSCO, ALBERTO, CASTILIO, *and* BALURDO.]

   O trista traditrice, rea, ribalda fortuna,
   Negandomi vendetta mi causa fera morte!
                                                                              [*Exit.*]
Felice. Ha, ha, ha! I could break my spleen at his impatience.

   [*Enter* ANTONIO *below and* MELLIDA *above.*]

Antonio. Alma e graziosa fortuna siate favorevole,
   E fortunati siano vuoti della mia dolce Mellida.   190
   [*Looking up*] Mellida!
Mellida. Alas, Antonio, I have lost thy note.

185.1. S.D.]   *Hunter   subst.*   187. *Exit*]   *Hunter.*   188.1. S.D.]   *Hunter.*
190. *della*] *Dilke; del Q; dolce Dilke; dulce Q.*   190–1.] *Mellida. / Mellida!*]
This ed.; printed as one turned-over line in Q, 'Et fortunati siano vuoti del mia
dulce Mellida, Mel-/lida.'

---

   177. *post*] hurry.
   178. *Scud*] dart. Cf. *A.R.*, IV.iii.103–4, 'quick observation scud / To cote
the plot', and *Jack Drum*, D4, '*Sir Ed[ward]*. Body of me! My heart misgives
me now, / Look, call, search, run all about. / My daughter gone? Go all and
search her out.'
   179. *gondolets*] small gondolas. Cf. l. 244 below, 'there's my signet, take a
gondolet'.
   186–7. O trista ... morte!] 'O gloomy traitress, guilty scoundrel fortune,
by preventing my revenge you cause me savage death.'
   188. *break my spleen*] i.e., burst out laughing, *O.E.D.*, *sb.*1.c. Felice literally
means 'break or rupture his spleen', for the spleen was regarded as the seat of
laughter.
   impatience] annoyance, failure to bear suffering.
   189–90. Alma ... Mellida] 'May benevolent and gracious fortune smile
upon me and may the vows of my gentle Mellida be auspicious.'
   192. *note*] the 'paper' found by Piero at l. 164.

A number mount my stairs. I'll straight return.
                                              [*Exit.*]
              [*Antonio casts himself down.*]
Felice. Antonio,
    Be not affright, sweet prince. Appease thy fear!   195
    Buckle thy spirits up, put all thy wits
    In wimble action, or thou art surprised.
Antonio. I care not.
Felice. Art mad, or desperate? Or—
Antonio. Both, both, all, all. I prithee, let me lie.   200
    Spite of you all, I can and I will die.
Felice. You are distraught. O, this is madness' breath!
Antonio. Each man takes hence life, but no man death.
    He's a good fellow and keeps open house.
    A thousand, thousand ways lead to his gate,   205
    To his wide-mouthèd porch, when niggard life
    Hath but one little, little wicket through.
    We wring ourselves into this wretched world
    To pule and weep, exclaim, to curse and rail,
    To fret and ban the fates, to strike the earth   210

193.2. S.D.] *Hunter subst.*   203. takes] *Dilke;* take *Q.*   206. wide-
mouthèd] wide mouth'd *Q.*

---

193. *A number*] Mellida is concerned because her staircase, to her room on
the upper stage, is used by a number of people. The implication may also be
that people are, even now, seeking her (mounting her stairs).

197. *wimble*] active, nimble. A dialect usage probably derived from Spenser;
so *Shep. Cal.* March, 91–2, 'He was so wimble and so wight, / From bough to
bough he leapèd light.'

art surprised] will be caught unawares.

203.] Cf. 'eripere vitam nemo non homini potest, / at nemo mortem': 'of life
anyone can rob a man, but of death no one', Seneca, *Phoenissae,* 152–3.

204. *He's*] i.e., Death is.

keeps . . . house] The phrase 'to keep open house' was proverbial, Dent H754.

205. *thousand*] This is proverbial, 'death has a thousand doors to let out life',
Dent D140. Cf. Webster's *Duchess of Malfi,* IV.ii.234–5, 'I know death hath ten
thousand several doors / For men to take their exits.'

206. *when*] whenas, whereas.

208. *wring*] force, squeeze (as in a narrow gate).

209. *pule*] whine.

210. *ban*] curse.

fates] The allusion is to the three Fates (Moirae or Parcae) who controlled
man's destiny; Clotho spun the thread of life, Lachesis gave out the thread,
and Atropos cut the thread.

SC II]   ANTONIO AND MELLIDA   121

As I do now. Antonio, curse thy birth
And die!
Felice. Nay, heaven's my comfort, now you are perverse.
You know I always loved you. Prithee, live.
Wilt thou strike dead thy friends, draw mourning tears— 215
Antonio. Alas, Felice, I ha' ne'er a friend,
No country, father, brother, kinsman left
To weep my fate or sigh my funeral.
I roll but up and down, and fill a seat
In the dark cave of dusky Misery.   220
Felice. 'Fore heaven, the Duke comes. [*To Antonio*] Hold you,
    take my key.
Slink to my chamber. Look you, that is it.
There shall you find a suit I wore at sea.
Take it and slip away. Nay, precious,
If you'll be peevish, by this light I'll swear   225
Thou rail'dst upon thy love before thou died'st
And called her strumpet.
Antonio.   She'll not credit thee.
Felice. Tut, that's all one. I'll defame thy love,
And make thy dead trunk held in vile regard.
Antonio. Wilt needs have it so? Why then, Antonio,   230
Vive speranza in despetto del fato.
                              [*Exit.*]

    Enter PIERO, GALEAZZO, MAZZAGENTE, FOROBOSCO,
        BALURDO, *and* CASTILIO, *with weapons.*

Piero. O my sweet princes, was't not bravely found?
Even there I found the note, even there it lay.

---

231. *speranza*] Dilke; *esperanza* Q; *del* Dilke; *dell* Q.

213. *heaven's my comfort*] as heaven is my comfort.
219. *I roll . . . down*] i.e., I am driven from pillar to post without direction.
220. *dusky*] gloomy. Cf. Ind.65–6, 'why look you so dusky, ha?'. Marston conceives of Misery emblematically, living a melancholy life in a dark cave. See also Ind.10n.
221. *Hold you*] i.e., here, wait a minute.
224. *precious*] most esteemed, most loved (master).
225–7. *If . . . strumpet.*] Felice threatens to malign Antonio to Mellida to try to force him to take this opportunity to escape.
231. *Vive . . . fato*] 'Long lives hope, despite fate.'

I kiss the place for joy that there it lay.
This way he went. Here let us make a stand.   235
I'll keep this gate myself. O gallant youth!
I'll drink carouse unto your country's health

Enter ANTONIO [*disguised in a sea-gown*].

Even in Antonio's skull.
Balurdo. Lord bless us! His breath is more fearful than a ser-
geant's voice when he cries, 'I arrest!'   240
Antonio. Stop Antonio! Keep, keep Antonio!
Piero. Where? Where, man, where?
Antonio. Here, here! Let me, me, pursue him down the marsh.
Piero. Hold, there's my signet, take a gondolet.
Bring me his head, his head, and by mine honour,
I'll make thee the wealthiest mariner that breathes.
Antonio. I'll sweat my blood out till I have him safe.
                                                    [*Exit.*]
Piero. Spoke heartily i'faith, good mariner.
O, we will mount in triumph soon, at night.
I'll set his head up. Let's think where.   250
Balurdo. 'Up?'—on his shoulders, that's the fittest place for it.
If it be not as fit as if it were made for them, say, 'Balurdo,
thou art a sot, an ass.'

Enter MELLIDA *in page's attire, dancing.*

---

248. Spoke] *Dilke*; Speake *Q.*   251. 'Up?'—on] *This ed.*; Vp on *Q*; Upon
1633.

237.1 sea-gown] This is the gown, mentioned earlier at l. 223, in which
Antonio appears at the beginning of the next act.
239. *His breath*] i.e., his threats.
239–40. *sergeant's*] of the officer who arrested felons or debtors.
241. *Keep*] guard.
250. *I'll ... up*] i.e., Piero is threatening to display Antonio's skull as a
trophy; see ll. 237–8 above. Balurdo picks upon the word 'up' (l. 251) and
denies the suitability of seeing Antonio's head on display, except on his own
shoulders.
251. *it*] i.e., Antonio's head.
253.1.] Mellida returns to the stage to display her disguise and to show her
escape in progress. It is also possible that the re-entry is deliberately exploited,
so that the actor playing her part could show off his dancing abilities.

Piero. Sprightly, i'faith. In truth, he's somewhat like
      My daughter Mellida. But alas, poor soul,   255
      Her honour's heels, God knows, are half so light.
Mellida. [*Aside*] Escaped I am, spite of my father's spite.
                                                          [*Exit*.]
Piero. Ho, this will warm my bosom ere I sleep.

                     Enter FLAVIA, *running*.

Flavia. O, my lord, your daughter!
Piero. Ay, ay, my daughter's safe enough, I warrant thee.   260
      This vengeance on the boy will lengthen out
      My days unmeasuredly.
      It shall be chronicled, time to come,
      Piero Sforza slew Andrugio's son.
Flavia. Ay, but my lord, your daughter—   265
Piero. Ay, ay, my good wench, she is safe enough.
Flavia. O, then, my lord, you know she's run away?
Piero. Run away? Away? How, run away?
Flavia. She's vanished in an instant. None knows whither.
Piero. Pursue, pursue, fly, run, post, scud away!   270

         Felice sing[*s*], '*And was not good King Solomon.*'

      Fly, call, run, row, ride, cry, shout, hurry, haste,
      Haste, hurry, shout, cry, ride, row, run, call, fly
      Backward and forward, every way about!

---

254. truth] *Hunter*; troth *Q.*   256. honour's] *This ed.*; honour *Q.*   257.1.
Exit] *Bullen*.

256. *Her honour's . . . light*] i.e., Mellida is twice as light on her feet as this
page.
257. *spite*] i.e., in spite of.
258. *this . . . sleep*] i.e., being revenged on Antonio will comfort me when I
go to bed.
270. *Pursue . . . away!*] Cf. *Spanish Tragedy*, 'See, search, show, send some
man, some mean, that may— / What's here? A letter? . . . / A letter written to
Hieronimo!', III.ii.22–5.
270.1] The text of this song of Solomon is known only by this single line.
Felice may feel that this song is appropriate because Mellida has fled to seek
her beloved Antonio, as with the lover in the Song of Solomon, 'I will rise now,
and go about the city in the streets, and in the broad ways I will seek him
whom my soul loveth' (ii.2).

Maledetta fortuna che con dura sorta—
Che faro, che diro, per fugir tanto mal?   275
        [*Exeunt all except* CASTILIO *and* FELICE.]
Castilio. 'Twas you that struck me even now, was it not?
Felice. It was I that struck you even now.
Castilio. You bastinadoed me, I take it.
Felice. I bastinadoed you and you took it.
Castilio. Faith sir, I have the richest tobacco in the court for   280
    you. I would be glad to make you satisfaction, if I have
    wronged you. I would not the sun should set upon your
    anger. Give me your hand.
Felice. Content, faith, so thou'lt breed no more such lies.
    I hate not man but man's lewd qualities.   285
        [*Exeunt.*]

---

274. *Maledetta*] *Dilke; Maldetta Q.; che Dilke; chy Q.; con dura Hunter; con omit Dilke; condura Q.*   275. *per*] *Dilke; pur Q.*

274–5. Maledetta . . . mal] O cursed fortune which with bad luck—What shall I do, what shall I say, to escape so great an evil?
    278. *bastinadoed*] thrashed, beat; cf. l. 114.
    280. *tobacco*] The attitudes of the characters vary as to tobacco; Rosaline despises it, I.i.126–8, but Castilio assumes that Felice will want some.
    282–3. *I . . . anger*] Cf. Ephesians, iv.26, 'Be ye angry, and sin not: let not the sun go down upon your wrath.'

Act IV

[Sc. i]

Enter ANTONIO *in his sea-gown, running.*

Antonio. [*Shouting*] Stop, stop Antonio! Stay Antonio!
[*Lowering his voice*] Vain breath, vain breath, Antonio's
    lost.
He cannot find himself, not seize himself.
Alas, this that you see is not Antonio.
His spirit hovers in Piero's court,   5
Hurling about his agile faculties
To apprehend the sight of Mellida,
But, poor, poor soul, wanting apt instruments
To speak or see, stands dumb and blind, sad spirit,
Rolled up in gloomy clouds as black as air   10
Through which the rusty coach of night is drawn.
'Tis so. I'll give you instance that 'tis so.
Conceit you me as, having clasped a rose
Within my palm, the rose being ta'en away,
My hand retains a little breath of sweet;   15
So may man's trunk, his spirit slipped away,
Hold still a faint perfume of his sweet guest.

Act IV] *ACTVS QVARTVS Q.*   Sc. i] *Dilke; not in Q.*   17. Hold] *1633;*
Holds *Q*; guest] *Dilke;* ghest *Q*; ghost *Keltie.*

0.1. sea-gown] the mariner's disguise provided by Felice at III.ii.223.

2–4.] Cf. *R&J*, I.i.197–8, 'I have lost myself, I am not here: / This is not Romeo, he's some other where.'

6. *Hurling about*] flinging ideas vehemently about, *O.E.D.*, *v.5.fig.*

7. *apprehend*] take possession of.

11. *rusty coach*] Cf. Marlowe, *I Tamburlaine*, V.i.294–5, 'ugly darkness with her rusty coach / Engirt with tempests.'

13. *Conceit*] understand.

13–17.] This simile is derived from Erasmus' colloquy 'Proci et Puellae': 'Anima quae moderatur utcumque corpus animantis, improprie dicitur anima, cum revera sint tenues quaedam animae reliquiae, non aliter quam odor rosarum manet in manu, etiam rosa submota', *Opera Omnia*, I:693. In the translation by H.M. of 1671, it reads, 'The soul which governs the body of a

'Tis so, for when discursive powers fly out
And roam in progress through the bounds of heaven,
The soul itself gallops along with them   20
As chieftain of this wingèd troop of thought,
Whilst the dull lodge of spirit standeth waste
Until the soul return from—what was't I said?
O, this is nought but speckling melancholy
That morphews tender skin. I have been   25
Cousin german—bear with me, good Mellida—

24–7. O . . . melancholy / That . . . been / Cousin . . . Mellida— / Clod . . .
fall.] *This ed.*; O . . . melancholy / That morphews tender skins— / I have
been . . . Bear with me / Good—Mellida . . . clod thus fall *J & N*; O . . .
melancholie. / I haue beene / That Morpheus tender skinp Cousen germane /
Beare with me good / *Mellida*: clod . . . fall. *Q*.   25. morphews tender skin]
This ed.; morphews tender skins *J & N*; Morpheus tender skinp *Q*.

---

living creature after a sort, is unproperly called a soul, seeing that in very deed
they are some certain small relics of the soul; just as the sweet scent of roses is
left in one's hand although the rose be gone', *The Colloquies . . . of Desiderius
Erasmus*, p. 132. Cf. II.i.234–41.

18. *discursive*] digressive, i.e., the faculties which deal with a wide range of
subjects, *O.E.D.*, *a.2.fig.* Cf. *S. of V.*, III.xi.209–10, 'Boundless discursive
apprehension / Giving it wings.'

22. *lodge*] i.e., body.

24. *speckling*] which produces blemishes.

25. *morphews*] causes leprous or scurvy eruptions on the skin. This is the
emendation suggested by J & N for *Q*'s 'Morpheus'. They cite *O.E.D.*'s
'morphue' (a scurvy eruption) as the word intended by Marston, but which the
compositor corrupted to the more familiar 'Morpheus' (god of dreams and son
of sleep). Hunter argues that the *Q* version of these lines is another example of
Marston's use of aposeopesis, but elsewhere the breakdown of speech is not
represented by incoherent nonsense, but rather by the inability to find an
appropriate word (e.g., I.i.152–4, IV.i.270–3). If this explanation of *Q*'s
'Morpheus' is accepted (and I believe it is a plausible Marstonian usage, given
his fondness for unusual vocabulary), then the rest of the speech, while
reflecting some groping for words ('I have been / Cousin german—', 25–6)
makes sense, and becomes like the other instances of aposeopesis in the play.

skin] *Q*'s reading may be the result of the compositor mistaking 'skine' or
'skinn' for 'skinp', which was probably set because the preceding word was
completely misunderstood. It could, as J & N argue, be read as 'skins' but the
other comments are singular, and Antonio's remarks are about the effects of
melancholy upon himself. These fragmented statements, although they make
some sense in themselves, are designed to indicate Antonio's fractured
consciousness.

26. *Cousin german*] first cousin.

Clod upon clod thus fall.
[*He casts himself down.*]
Hell is beneath, yet heaven is over all.

Enter ANDRUGIO, LUCIO, [*and a* Page].

Andrugio. Come, Lucio, let's go eat. What hast thou got?
Roots, roots? Alas, they are seeded, new cut up.   30
O, thou hast wrongèd nature, Lucio.
But boots not much; thou but pursu'st the world,
That cuts off virtue 'fore it comes to growth
Lest it should seed and so o'errun her son,
Dull purblind error. Give me water, boy.   35
There's no poison in't, I hope, they say
That lurks in massy plate; and yet the earth
Is so infected with a general plague

27.1. S.D.] *Bullen subst.*   28.1.] *Dilke subst.; Enter Andrugio, Lucio, Cole,
and Norwod Q.*   37. lurks] *Dilke*; lukes *Q.*

---

27. *Clod ... fall*] One clod (I, myself) falls upon another (the ground).

28. *Hell ... all*] Gnomic remarks are often found italicised in sixteenth-century editions. Here, in *Q*, italics are used to indicate a proverb: 'Heaven (God) is above all' (Dent H348).

28.1.] The 'Cole and Norwod' of *Q* are the names of two of the choristers listed on the Paul's establishment in 1598. It seems likely that Robert Coles played the part of Andrugio and John Norwood that of Lucio, although it does remain possible that one of them took the part of the Page. In the same year the other members of the choir were John Taylor, William Thaire, Richard Brackenbury, John Thomkins, Samuel Marcupp, Thomas Rainescroft (Ravenscroft), Russel Gyrdler, Charles Pytcher, Charles Pendry, and Anthony Hitchman; see *Paul's*, Appendix 2, p. 184.

30. *seeded*] run to seed, matured.

new cut up] i.e., newly rooted up by cutting.

32. *boots not much*] it doesn't much matter.

but pursu'st the world] merely do like everyone else.

35. *purblind*] i.e., stupid, obtuse, *O.E.D., a.3.fig.*, also probably with the sense of a.1., totally blind, i.e., obtuse error, blind to all argument.

36–7. *There's ... plate*] Cf. 'Scelera non intrant casas, / tutusque mensa capitur angusta cibus; / venenum in auro bibitur': 'Crime enters not lowly homes, and in safety is food taken at a slender board; poison is drunk from cups of gold', Seneca, *Thyestes*, 451–3. Cf. Lyly, *Sapho and Phao*, 1584, 1.i.13–14, 'Thou needest not fear poison in thy glass, nor treason in thy guard.'

37. *massy*] solid. Cf. v.i.35.

That he's most wise that thinks there's no man fool,
Right prudent that esteems no creature just.   40
Great policy the least things to mistrust.
Give me assay. [*The Page tastes the food.*] How we mock
    greatness now!
Lucio. A strong conceit is rich, so most men deem.
    If not to be, 'tis comfort yet to seem.
Andrugio. Why, man, I never was a prince till now.   45
    'Tis not the barèd pate, the bended knees,
    Gilt tipstaves, Tyrian purple, chairs of state,
    Troops of pied butterflies that flutter still
    In greatness' summer, that confirm a prince.
    'Tis not the unsavoury breath of multitudes,   50
    Shouting and clapping with confusèd din,
    That makes a prince. No Lucio, he's a king,
    A true, right king, that dares do aught save wrong,
    Fears nothing mortal but to be unjust,
    Who is not blown up with the flattering puffs   55

---

39. *he's most wise . . . fool*] i.e., the man who thinks no man a fool is the
wisest man (because, then, he will suspect all men).

42. *Give me assay*] Taste the food before I eat. It was usual for rulers to have
their food tasted to avoid the danger of poison.

How . . . now] Andrugio bitterly reflects that courtly ceremony, like the
tasting of his food, merely mocks his lost greatness.

43–4.] Lucio responds to Andrugio's bitterness by observing that it is better
to appear to have, or to pretend to have, comfort than to confront one's
comfortlessness.

45–65.] Cf. 'regem non faciunt opes, / non vestis Tyriae color, / non frontis
nota regiae / non auro nitidae fores; / rex est qui posuit metus / et diri mala
pectoris, / quem non ambitio inpotens / et numquam stabilis favor / vulgi
praecipitis movet': 'A king neither riches make, nor robes of Tyrian hue, nor
crown upon the royal brow, nor doors with gold bright-gleaming; a king is he
who has laid fear aside and the base longings of an evil heart; whom ambition
unrestrained and the fickle favour of the reckless mob move not,' Seneca,
Thyestes, 344–52.

46. *the barèd pate*] the head bared in deference.

47. *tipstaves*] staves, tipped with metal, carried as a badge of office by
officials. Cf. the staff carried by a churchwarden.

Tyrian purple] imperial or royal purple. The name derives from the dye
traditionally made in ancient Tyre (a city on the coast of Phoenicia, besieged
by Nebuchadnezzar and later by Alexander).

48. *butterflies*] i.e., fashionable courtiers.

54.] Cf. Seneca, *Octavia*, 441, 'Iustum esse facile est cui vacat pectus metu',
''Tis easy to be just when the heart is free from fear.'

Of spongy sycophants, who stands unmoved
Despite the jostling of opinion,
Who can enjoy himself maugre the throng
That strive to press his quiet out of him,
Who sits upon Jove's footstool, as I do,   60
Adoring, not affecting, majesty,
Whose brow is wreathèd with the silver crown
Of clear content. This, Lucio, is a king,
And of this empire every man's possessed
That's worth his soul.   65
Lucio. My lord, the Genoese had wont to say—
Andrugio. Name not the Genoese! That very word
Unkings me quite, makes me vile passion's slave.
O you that made open the glibbery ice
Of vulgar favour, view Andrugio!   70
Was never prince with more applause confirmed,
With louder shouts of triumph launchèd out
Into the surgy main of government;
Was never prince with more despite cast out,

---

69. made open] *Q*; slide upon *Bullen*; wade upon *Schoonover*.

56. *spongy*] parasitic, sponging, *O.E.D.*, *a*.3.c.
58. *maugre*] in spite of.
58–9. *the throng . . . him*] i.e., the crowds who, by thronging around him,
seek to force him to renounce his calmness.
59. *quiet*] the Stoic's state of 'apathia' (passionlessness), in which the blows
of fate can be resisted.
60. *Jove's*] Jupiter's, the Lord of Heaven's.
61. *Adoring . . . affecting*] i.e., showing profound love for the majesty of
heaven without attempting to become like a god.
67. *Genoese*] Andrugio's anger with the inhabitants of Genoa (his own
subjects) springs from their compliance with Piero's demand that he and his
son be banished after their defeat at sea; see III.i.12ff.
68. *passion's slave*] This is proverbial, Dent P89.11.
69. *made open*] broke through, saw beyond; i.e., you who had the foresight
to realise that popularity was no form of security. Bullen suggests emending to
'slide upon', but the change is unnecessary; J & N emend to 'wade upon'
(Schoonover's conjecture), but it is very difficult to see how Andrugio could
'wade' upon ice.
glibbery] slippery; cf. 1.i.109.
73. *surgy*] moving in huge surges, like the sea.
main] sea.
74. *despite*] contempt, disdain.

Left shipwrecked, banished, on more guiltless ground.   75
O rotten props of the crazed multitude,
How you still falter under the lightest chance
That strains your veins! Alas, one battle lost,
Your whorish love, your drunken healths, your shouts,
Your smooth 'God save's', and all your devils last,   80
That tempts our quiet, to your hell of throngs.
Spit on me Lucio, for I am turned slave.
Observe how passion domineers o'er me.
Lucio. No wonder, noble lord, having lost a son,
A country, crown, and—   85
Andrugio. Ay, Lucio, having lost a son, a son,
A country, house, crown, son. *O lares, miseri lares!*

77–80. How you ... chance / That strains ... lost, / Your whorish ...
shouts, / Your smooth ... last,] *This ed.*; How you stil double, faulter, vnder
the lightest chance / That straines your vaines. Alas, one battle lost, / Your
whorish loue, your drunken healths, your houts / and shouts, / Your smooth
God saue's, and all your diuels last *Q.*   87. *miseri*] *Bullen; misereri Q.*

---

75. *on ... ground*] with less just cause, with a subsidiary meaning for
'ground' of shore, i.e., shipwrecked on a shore but without guilt.
76–8.] i.e., O you mindless multitude, weak props that you are, how fickle
you are at the slightest challenge of fortune!
77–9.] These lines in *Q* seem to betray an earlier and a later version of the
same idea i.e., 'How you still double, falter' (77) and 'your drunken healths,
your houts and shouts' (79). If either 'double' or 'falter', and either 'houts
and' or 'and shouts' is omitted, the lines become metrical, and there is no
significant change of sense created by the omissions. I suspect that these are
undeleted revisions in the literary manuscript which was used in the printing
house. There is no clear indication, however, which was Marston's final
intention. I have, therefore, assumed that the second version is, in each case,
the final one.
80. *devils*] i.e., the devils which possess you (and disturb our calm).
83. *domineers*] prevails, *O.E.D., v.3.* Cf. *A.R.*, v.ii.10, 'O hunger, how thou
domineerest in my guts!'
86–8.] Cf. Seneca, *Hercules Furens*, 1259–61, 'cuncta iam amisi bona: /
mentem arma famam coniungem natos manus, / etiam furorem!': 'All that was
dear to me I've lost: reason, arms, honour, wife, children, strength—and
madness too!'
87–90.] Cf. *Spanish Tragedy*, 'O poor Horatio, what hadst thou misdone, /
To lose thy life ere life was new begun / ... Ay me most wretched, that have
lost my joy, / In losing my Horatio, my sweet boy!', II.iv.90–1, 94–5.
87. *house*] dynasty.
O lares ... lares!] 'O household gods, O wretched household gods!',
Seneca, *Hercules Oetaeus*, 757. The 'household gods'—sometimes used as a
synonym for 'home'; Loeb translates the line, 'O home, O wretched

Which shall I first deplore? My son, my son,
My dear sweet boy, my dear Antonio.
Antonio. Antonio?   90
Andrugio. Ay, echo, ay. I mean Antonio.
Antonio. Antonio! Who means Antonio?
Andrugio. Where art? What art? Know'st thou Antonio?
Antonio. Yes.
Andrugio. Lives he?   95
Antonio. No.
Andrugio. Where lies he dead?
Antonio. Here.
Andrugio. Where?
Antonio. [*Stepping forward*] Here.   100
Andrugio. Art thou Antonio?
Antonio. I think I am.
Andrugio. Dost thou but think? What, dost not know thyself?
Antonio. He is a fool that thinks he knows himself.
Andrugio. Upon thy faith to heaven, give thy name.   105
Antonio. I were not worthy of Andrugio's blood
     If I denied my name's Antonio.
Andrugio. I were not worthy to be called thy father
     If I denied my name, Andrugio.
     And dost thou live? O, let me kiss thy cheek   110
     And dew thy brow with trickling drops of joy!
     Now heaven's will be done, for I have lived
     To see my joy, my son, Antonio.
     Give me thy hand. Now, Fortune, do thy worst!
     His blood, that lapped thy spirit in the womb,   115
     Thus, in his love, will make his arms thy tomb.
                              [*Embraces Antonio.*]

home!'—were the spirits of dead ancestors who watched over the household;
for Andrugio they have hopelessly failed.
   103. *know thyself*] The famous motto of the oracle at Delphi, the most
distinguished oracle of the ancient world, was 'know thyself'. This is,
of course, also a common philosophical theme both classical and biblical.
   114. *Fortune ... worst*] A proverbial phrase, Dent F614.11.
   115. *His*] i.e., Andrugio's.
   lapped] embraced and, figuratively, 'nurtured'.
   thy] i.e., Antonio's.
   116. *Thus ... tomb*] i.e., I, Andrugio, will bury (smother) you (Antonio) in
love.

Antonio. Bless not the body with your twining arms
　Which is accursed of heaven. O, what black sin
　Hath been committed by our ancient house,
　Whose scalding vengeance lights upon our heads,   120
　That thus the world and Fortune casts us out
　As loathèd objects, Ruin's branded slaves?
Andrugio. Do not expostulate the heavens' will.
　But, O, remember to forget thyself.
　Forget remembrance what thou once hast been.   125
　Come, creep with me from out this open air.
　Even trees have tongues and will betray our life.
　I am a-raising of our house, my boy,
　Which Fortune will not envy, 'tis so mean,
　And like the world, all dirt, there shalt thou rip   130
　The inwards of thy fortunes in mine ears
　Whilst I sit weeping, blind with passion's tears.
　Then I'll begin, and we'll such order keep
　That one shall still tell griefs, the other weep.
　　　　　　　　Exeunt ANDRUGIO [*and* LUCIO],
　　　　　　　　leaving ANTONIO *and his* Page.
Antonio. I'll follow you. Boy, prithee stay a little.   135

134.1 *Exeunt*] *Exit* Q.

117. *twining*] entwining.
118–19. *black sin ... house*] An allusion both to the idea of Original Sin
(i.e., the sin of Adam and Eve in Paradise, of which all mankind are the
inheritors), and to the classical tragic notion of inherited guilt (like that of
Oedipus in Sophocles' *Oedipus the King*). Both of these forms of guilt are
unavoidable and damning, but the victims, in later generations, seem
innocent.
120–2.] Marston seems here to conceive of Ruin as the avenger of inherited
sin, pouring scalding liquid upon the heads of the guilty, who are thus
branded, marked with infamy. Cf. Ind.9–11.
123. *expostulate*] complain about.
125. *remembrance what*] remembrance of what.
126.] Andrugio urges Antonio to quit the 'cold marsh' (136), where they
currently find themselves, and avoid the 'open air', by retiring into their house
which is metaphorically 'mean' (129) and of 'dirt' (130), but which he will raise
(128). This house is off-stage, but in it they will 'sit weeping, blind with
passion's tears' (132). Cf. *Lr.*, III.iv.
127. *trees have tongues*] The phrase is proverbial; cf. 'fields have eyes and
woods have ears', Dent F209.
134.2. *his Page*] i.e., the page who entered with Andrugio and Lucio at l.
28.1.

SC I]   ANTONIO AND MELLIDA   133

Thou hast had a good voice, if this cold marsh,
Wherein we lurk, have not corrupted it.

Enter MELLIDA, *standing out of sight, in her page's suit.*

I prithee sing, but sirrah, mark you me,
Let each note breathe the heart of passion,
The sad extracture of extremest grief.   140
Make me a strain. Speak groaning like a bell
That tolls departing souls.
Breathe me a point that may enforce me weep,
To wring my hands, to break my cursèd breast,
Rave and exclaim, lie groveling on the earth,   145
Straight start up frantic, crying, 'Mellida!'
Sing but 'Antonio hath lost Mellida',
And thou shalt see me, like a man possessed,
Howl out such passion that even this brinish marsh
Will squeeze out tears from out his spongy cheeks,   150
The rocks even groan, and—
Prithee, prithee, sing,
Or I shall ne'er ha' done. When I am in,
'Tis harder for me end than to begin.

The Boy runs a note; Antonio breaks it.

For look thee, boy, my grief that hath no end   155

---

139. breathe] breath *Q* (*also at 143*).   153. done. When] done when *Q*.

140. *extracture*] extract, essence.
141. *a strain*] a melody, a tune, *O.E.D., sb.*12.
141–2. *bell . . . souls*] the funeral bell, as in Donne's well-known *Devotions Upon Emergent Occasions*, 1623, XVII: 'any man's death diminishes me, because I am involved in mankind, and therefore never send to know for whom the bell tolls. It tolls for thee.'
143. *Breathe . . . point*] sing me a note.
145–6. *lie . . . Mellida*] Cf. *Spanish Tragedy*, fourth Addition (the Painter Scene), III.xiia.12–13, where Pedro describes Hieronimo as 'starting in a rage, falls on the earth, / Cries out, "Horatio! Where is my Horatio?"'
153. *in*] in [this vein or frame of mind].
154.1. *runs a note*] holds and elaborates a single note which is suddenly cut off by Antonio. This is the 'point' which Antonio asked him to 'breathe' at l. 143. This interruption was, apparently, a successful effect, for Marston uses it again in *What You Will*, Bv, '*He sings and is answered. From above a willow garland is flung down and the song ceaseth.*'

I may begin to plain, but—prithee, sing.

They sing.

Mellida. Heaven keep you, sir.
Antonio. Heaven keep you from me, sir.
Mellida. I must be acquainted with you, sir.
Antonio. Wherefore? Art thou infected with misery,   160
Seared with the anguish of calamity?
Art thou true sorrow, hearty grief? Canst weep?
I am not for thee if thou canst not rave,
                              Antonio falls on the ground.
Fall flat on the ground, and thus exclaim on heaven:
'O trifling Nature, why inspir'dst thou breath?'   165
Mellida. Stay sir. I think you naměd Mellida.
Antonio. Know'st thou Mellida?
Mellida. Yes.
Antonio. Hast thou seen Mellida?
Mellida. Yes.   170
Antonio. Then hast thou seen the glory of her sex,
The music of nature, the unequalled lustre
Of unmatched excellence, the united sweet
Of heaven's graces, the most adoreěd beauty
That ever struck amazement in the world.   175
Mellida. You seem to love her.
Antonio.   With my very soul.
Mellida. She'll not requite it. All her love is fixed
Upon a gallant, on Antonio,
The Duke of Genoa's son. I was her page,
And often as I waited she would sigh,   180

156.1. *They sing*] *This ed.; Boy sings Keltie; Cantant Q.*   178. on] *Q;* one
1633.

156.1. *They sing*] The Boy is clearly one of the singers and, perhaps,
Mellida joins in, but the other voices could well have been supplied by
additional choristers off-stage; cf. III.i.105.1.
158. *Heaven . . . me, sir*] i.e., Antonio does not want to be interrupted in his
grief.
.165. *why . . . breath?*] i.e., why did you breathe life into me?
178. *on*] The emendation of 1633 to 'one' makes good sense and 'on' was
sometimes written for 'one', but elsewhere (III.ii.251) Marston uses a similar
linkage between 'upon' and 'on', and thus the *Q* reading is likely to have been
what he wrote.

'O dear Antonio!' and to strengthen thought
Would clip my neck, and kiss, and kiss me thus.
                                        [*Embracing Antonio*]
Therefore leave loving her. Faugh, faith, methinks
Her beauty is not half so ravishing
As you discourse of. She hath a freckled face,   185
A low forehead, and a lumpish eye.
Antonio. O heaven, that I should hear such blasphemy!
Boy, rogue, thou liest and—[*Recognising Mellida*]
Spavento del mio core, dolce Mellida,
Di grave morte ristoro vero, dolce Mellida,   190
Celeste salvatrice, sovrana Mellida
Del mio sperar, trofeo vero Mellida.
Mellida. Diletta e soave anima mia Antonio,
Godevole bellezza, cortese Antonio.
Signior mio e virginal amore bell' Antonio,   195
Gusto dei miei sensi, car' Antonio.

183. Faugh] *This ed.*; fa *Q*.   190. *grave*] *Dilke; graua Q*.   196. *dei miei*]
Hunter; delli Q; miei Dilke; mei Q.

---

182. *clip*] embrace.
186. *lumpish*] sluggish, slow (with the implication of stupidity). Cf. v.ii.38
and *Blurt, Master Constable*, C3, 'I cannot abide these dull and lumpish tunes.'
188.S.D. Recognising] Antonio may gesture in such a way that he uncovers
Mellida's disguise.
189.] The ensuing dialogue in Italian reflects Marston's command of the
language, derived from his mother's teaching, for she was Mary Guarsi,
descendant of an Italian barber surgeon. This 'foreign' quality in Marston may
be hinted at by Jonson in *Poetaster*, III.i.185–6, where Horace remarks of
Crispinus, 'You have much of the mother in you, sir: your father is dead?'
Schoonover points out that this scenario merges two of the traditional themes
of the *commedia dell'arte*, 'the confrontation of the female page and disguised
lover, and the young swain courting a young lady'.
189–206. Spavento . . . morir.] Terror of my heart, sweet Mellida, / True
medicine of sad death, sweet Mellida, / Heavenly saviour, sovereign Mellida /
Of my hope, true trophy, Mellida. / *Mel.* Antonio, my beloved and gentle
soul, / Courtly Antonio, handsome delight, / Fair Antonio, my lord and first
love, / Dear Antonio, food for my senses. / *Ant.* O, the heart dissolves in a
gentle kiss. / *Mel.* The senses die in the object of desire. / *Ant.* Can there be a
more bright beauty in heaven? / *Mel.* Can there be a more bright beauty on
earth? / *Ant.* Bestow upon me a kiss from your blessed mouth. / Let me gather
up the sweet-smelling breath / Which [resides] in its royal seat in those sweet
lips. / *Mel.* Grant me rule over your most welcome love, / Which blesses me,
with an everlasting honour; / Thus, in this way, it is fitting that I die.'

Antonio. O svanisce il cor in un soave bacio.
Mellida. Muoiono i sensi nel desiato desio.
Antonio. Nel cielo può esser beltà più chiara?
Mellida. Nel mondo può esser beltà più chiara?   200
Antonio. Dammi un bacio da quella bocca beata.
 Lasciami coglier l'aura odorata
 Che in sua reggia, in quelle dolci labbra.
Mellida. Dammi l'impero del tuo gradit' amore,
 Che bea me, con sempiterno onore,   205
 Così così, mi converrà morir.
 Good sweet, scout o'er the marsh, for my heart trembles
 At every little breath that strikes my ear.
 When thou returnest, and I'll discourse
 How I deceived the court, then thou shall tell   210
 How thou escap'dst the watch. We'll point our speech
 With amorous kissing, kissing commas, and even suck
 The liquid breath from out each other's lips.
          [*Exit* MELLIDA.]

197. *svanisce*] *Bullen; suamisce Q.* 198. *Muoiono*] *Dilke; Murono Q.* 199.
può esser beltà più] *Dilke; puo lesser belta pia Q.* 200. *può esser beltà più*]
Dilke; pol esser belta pia Q. 202. *Lasciami*] *Dilke; Bassiammi Q.* 203. *in
sua reggia*] *This ed.; in sua neggia Q; in seco reggia Dilke; ha sua seggia Bullen;
in su anneggia Hunter; in su aleggia Schoonover; quelle dolci*] *Dilke; quello dolce
Q.* 204. *l'impero*] *Hunter; pimpero Q.* 205. *con sempiterno*] *Dilke; cosem-
piterno Q.* 208. *ear.*] *J & N; eare, Q.*

203. *in sua reggia*] *Q*'s reading is clearly corrupt, but opinions differ sharply
as to the correct reading. My suggestion is put forward for two reasons: firstly,
it requires the least emendation of *Q*, and the substitution of 'n' for 'r' is an
easy compositorial error; secondly, it allows both Antonio and Mellida to use
the same royal metaphor. The whole speech is, of course, couched in the
extravagant language of the *commedia dell'arte.*
 207. *scout*] reconnoitre, *O.E.D., v.*[1]4.
 208.] Hunter feels that some words have dropped out of *Q* at this point.
Punctuation with a period after 'ear' does, however, make sense, but Antonio
never explains why he is about to leave, nor why Mellida has to do the
scouting.
 211–12.] The verse in these two lines verges on prose. Bullen omitted the
repetition of 'kissing' to restore the metre, but the punctuation metaphor
('point', 'commas') requires it.
 211. *point*] punctuate.
 212. *kissing commas*] with a kiss at every punctuation mark.
 211–13.] Cf. *Jack Drum*, II.i, D2*v.*, 'when she clips and clings about my
neck, / And sucks my soul forth with a melting kiss.'

Antonio. [*To himself, as he leaves*]
Dull clod, no man but such sweet favour clips.
I go, and yet my panting blood persuades me stay. 215
Turn coward in her sight? Away, away!
[*Exit.*]
Page. I think confusion of Babel is fallen upon these lovers,
that they change their language; but I fear me my master,
having but feigned the person of a woman, hath got their
unfeigned imperfection and is grown double tongued. As 220
for Mellida, she were no woman if she could not yield
strange language. But howsoever, if I should sit in judgement, 'tis an error easier to be pardoned by the auditors
than excused by the authors, and yet some private respect may rebate the edge of the keener censure. 225

Enter PIERO, CASTILIO, MAZZAGENTE, FOROBOSCO, FELICE,
GALEAZZO [*at one door*], BALURDO, *and his page* [DILDO,
and MELLIDA] *at another door.*

Piero. This way she took. Search, my sweet gentlemen!
How now, Balurdo, canst thou meet with anybody?
Balurdo. As I am true gentleman, I made my horse sweat, that
he hath ne'er a dry thread on him, and I can meet with
no living creature but men and beasts. In good sadness, 230
I would have sworn I had seen Mellida even now, for I
saw a thing stir under a hedge, and I peeped and I spied

---

217. S.P. *Page.*] Bullen; *not in* Q.

214. *Dull ... clips*] He is a mere insensitive soul, not a man, who fails to
enjoy such a proferred delight (a kiss), i.e., man is made whole by love.
217. *Babel*] 'the Lord did there confound the language of all the earth',
Genesis, xi.9. Cf. I.i.59, 'Confusion's train blows up this babel pride', and
Spanish Tragedy, IV.i.173–5, 196–7, 'Each one of us must act his part / In
unknown languages, / That it may breed the more variety ... Now shall I see
the fall of Babylon, / Wrought by the heavens in this confusion.'
220. *double tongued*] deceitful. According to W. P. Tilley, *A Dictionary of
Proverbs in England in the Sixteenth and Seventeenth Centuries*, 1950, the adage,
'one tongue is enough for a woman', is proverbial, T398. Dent cites 'a woman's
heart and her tongue are not relatives', W672. Cf. *What You Will*, H2v, 'truth
seeks not to lurk under farthingales'.
223–5. *'tis ... censure*] this error (of writing in Italian) is more easily
forgiven by the audience than excused by the author, but servile criticism may
be toned down by the personal knowledge of individuals (probably that
Marston had an Italian mother).

a thing, and I peered and I twired underneath, and truly
a right wise man might have been deceived, for it was—
Piero. What, in the name of heaven?   235
Balurdo. A dun cow.
Felice. She'd ne'er a kettle on her head?
Piero. [*To Mellida*] Boy, didst thou see a young lady pass this
    way?
Galeazzo. [*To Mellida*] Why speak you not?   240
Balurdo. God's nigs, proud elf, give the Duke reverence. Stand
    bare with a—[*Peering closely at her*] Whoa! Heavens
    bless me—Mellida, Mellida!
Piero. Where, man, where?
Balurdo. Turned man, turned man. Women wear the
    breeches. Lo here!   [*Removing her hat*]
Piero. Light and unduteous! Kneel not, peevish elf,
    Speak not; entreat not. Shame unto my house,
    Curse to my honour! Where's Antonio,
    Thou traitress to my hate? What, is he shipped   250
    For England now? Well, whimpering harlot, hence!
Mellida. Good father—
Piero. Good me no goods! See'st thou that sprightly youth?
    Ere thou canst term tomorrow morning old,
    Thou shalt call him thy husband, lord, and love.   255
Mellida. Ay me!
Piero. Blurt on your 'Ay me's'!—Guard her safely hence.

253–5. Good ... youth? / Ere ... old, / Thou ... love] *1633 subst.; prose in
Q.*

233. *twired*] peered, peeped, *O.E.D., v.*¹1.
236. dun] dingy brown.
237. *a kettle*] As Hunter points out, Marston may be recalling an inn sign.
Guy of Warwick had a kettle and a dun cow. Felice is, of course, implying that
Balurdo was drunk when he saw the dun cow.
241. *give ... reverence*] take off your hat (as commoners did before royalty).
253. *Good me no goods*] Cf. *R&J*, III.v.152, where Old Capulet abruptly
dismisses Juliet's pleas to be heard, 'Thank me no thankings, nor proud me no
prouds'. See Introduction, pp. 19, 34.
youth] Galeazzo.
257. *Blurt*] Q's 'Blirt' is a northern dialect variant of 'blurt', a contemptuous
expletive, i.e., 'blow'. Cf. the title of the play 'sundry times privately acted by
the Children of Pauls', by Thomas Middleton, *Blurt, Master Constable, or The
Spaniard's Night Walk*, 1602.

SC I]   ANTONIO AND MELLIDA   139

Drag her away. I'll be your guard tonight.
[*To Galeazzo*] Young prince, mount up your spirits and
  prepare
To solemnise your nuptial's eve with pomp.   260
Galeazzo. The time is scant. Now, nimble wits, appear!
Phoebus begins to gleam; the welkin's clear.
              Exeunt all but BALURDO *and his Page* [DILDO].
Balurdo. 'Now, nimble wits, appear!' I'll myself appear;
Balurdo's self, that in quick wit doth surpass,
Will show the substance of a complete—
Dildo. [*Aside*]   Ass—ass.   265
Balurdo. I'll mount my courser and most gallantly prick—
Dildo. 'Gallantly prick' is too long, and stands hardly in the
  verse, sir.
Balurdo. I'll speak pure rhyme, and will so bravely prank it
That I'll toss love like a prank—   270
'Prank it?'—a rhyme for 'prank it'?
Dildo. Blanket.
Balurdo. 'That I'll toss love like a dog in a blanket!'
Ha, ha, indeed la,—I think—ha, ha—I think—ha, ha—
I think I shall tickle the muses. An I strike it not dead,   275
say, 'Balurdo, thou art an arrant sot.'
Dildo. [*Aside*] 'Balurdo, thou art an arrant sot.'
                                                    [*Exeunt.*]

---

260. pomp] popme *Q*.   262. to] *1633; not in Q*.   269-71. I'll ... it /
That ... prank— / 'Prank ... it'?] *This ed.; prose in Q*.   272. Blanket]
Blankit *Q*.

262. *Phoebus*] the bright sun god (Apollo); i.e., the dawn is breaking.
welkin] heaven, sky.
264. *Balurdo's self*] i.e., in my true character.
266. *courser ... prick*] spur (my) charger.
267. *prick ... long ... stands*] A sequence of bawdy expressions.
269. *prank it*] dance, caper, *O.E.D., v.*³.
270. *prank*] mad frolic, *O.E.D., sb.*²c.
272. *Blanket*] *Q*'s 'blankit' creates the pun on 'blanket' and 'blank it' i.e.,
Balurdo will toss love like a dog in a blanket, and thus throw it away (blank it
out). See also Introduction, p. 8. The phrase is proverbial, Dent D513.1.
275. *tickle the muses*] become a poet.
275-6.] i.e., If I do not hit the target in the centre, then say 'Balurdo, you
are an arrant drunkard.' Dildo responds by agreeing with him in an aside.

[Sc. ii]

Enter ANDRUGIO *and* ANTONIO *wreathed together*; LUCIO
[*and a* Page].

Andrugio. Now come, united force of chap-fall'n death!
    Come, power of fretting anguish, leave distress.
    O, thus enfolded, we have breasts of proof
    'Gainst all the venomed stings of misery.
Antonio. Father, now I have an antidote   5
    'Gainst all the poison that the world can breathe:
    My Mellida, my Mellida doth bless
    This bleak waste with her presence. [*To the Page*] How
      now, boy,
    Why dost thou weep? Alas, where's Mellida?
Page. Ay me, my lord!   10
Antonio. A sodden horror doth invade my blood,
    My sinews tremble, and my panting heart
    Scuds round about my bosom to go out,
    Dreading the assailant, horrid passion.
    O, be no tyrant, kill me with one blow!   15
    Speak quickly, briefly, boy.
Page. Her father found and seized her. She is gone.

Sc. ii] *Hunter; not in Q.*   10. S.P. *Page.*] *Bullen; Ant. Q.*   11. S.P. *Antonio.*]
Dilke; And. Q; sodden *Q*; sudden *1633*.

    Sc. ii] A new scene is demanded by the clearing of the stage and the
complete transition in the action from the jesting of Balurdo and Dildo to the
lamentation of Andrugio and Antonio.
    0.1. wreathed together] with arms linked.
    1. *chap-fall'n*] with lower jaw hanging down, gaping open-mouthed. Cf.
A.R., v.i.8–10, 'now is his fate grown mellow, / Instant to fall into the rotten
jaws / Of chap-fall'n death.' Jonson speaks of Marston (Crispinus) and Dekker
(Demetrius) in *Poetaster*, v.iii.341, as 'a couple of chap-fallen curs'.
    2. *leave distress*] abandon useless grief (i.e., replace lamentation with action).
    3. *of proof*] furnished with impregnable armour. Cf. *A.R.*, II.ii.18–21, 'A
wise man wrongfully but never wrong / Can take; his breast's of such
well-tempered proof / It may be rased, not pierced by savage tooth / Of
foaming malice.'
    11. *sodden*] made dull and pale (with shock), *O.E.D.*, *ppl.a.*2. The 1633
reading 'sudden' is probably a substitution of the common for the unusual
word.
    13. *Scuds*] drives, as before the wind.

Andrugio. Son, heat thy blood; be not froze up with grief.
Courage, sweet boy, sink not beneath the weight
Of crushing mischief. O, where's thy dauntless
    heart,   20
Thy father's spirit? I renounce thy blood
If thou forsake thy valour.
Lucio. See how his grief speaks in his slow-paced steps.
Alas, 'tis more than he can utter. Let him go.
Dumb solitary path best suiteth woe.   25
                                        [*Exit* ANTONIO.]
Andrugio. Give me my arms, my armour, Lucio.
Lucio. Dear lord, what means this rage? When lacking use
Scarce saves your life, will you in armour rise?
Andrugio. Fortune fears valour, presseth cowardice.
Lucio. Then valour gets applause when it hath place,   30
And means to blaze it.

25.1] *This ed.*; *not in Q.*   29. cowardice] cowardize *Q.*

18–20. *Son* ... *mischief*] Cf. 'pectus antiquum advoca / victasque magno robore aerumnas doma; / resiste; tantis in malis vinci mori est': 'Summon up thine old-time courage; conquer thy sorrows and with all thy might be master of them, resist them; amidst such woes, to be conquered is to die,' Seneca, *Phoenissae*, 77–9.

19.] Andrugio is urging Antonio to live despite the 'sodden horror' (shock) which has invaded him. According to contemporary belief, life itself depended upon the maintenance of the body's 'vital heat', and a failure to sustain it could only result in death; cf. J. B. Bamborough, *The Little World of Man*, London: Longmans, 1952, p. 55.

21. *thy blood*] my kinship in you.

25. *Dumb* ... *woe*] J & N compare Seneca, 'Curae leves loquuntur, ingentes stupent': 'light griefs talk, heavy ones strike dumb', *Hippolytus*, 607.

27–8. *When lacking* ... *rise*] i.e., When remaining out of battle can scarely save your life, will you now arm and deliberately seek a fight?

29–32. *Fortune* ... *esse*] Cf. 'Fortuna fortes metuit, ignavos premit. / Tunc est probanda, si locum virtus habet. / Nunquam potest non esse virtuti locus': 'Fortune fears the brave, the cowardly overwhelms. If there is place for courage, then should it be approved. It can never be that for courage there is no place,' Seneca, *Medea*, 159–61.

29. *Fortune* ... *cowardice*] i.e., Fortune or fate is made afraid by the brave, whereas it intimidates the cowardly. Antonio is essentially citing Seneca's 'Fortuna fortes metuit, ignavos premit'.

30–1. *Then* ... *it*] i.e., Valour is applauded only in those whose station in life gives them opportunity to display it; a paraphrase of *Medea*, 160–1.

Andrugio. Numquam potest non esse—
Lucio. Patience, my lord, may bring your ills some end.
Andrugio. What patience, friend, can ruined hopes attend?
    Come, let me die like old Andrugio,   35
    Worthy my birth. O, blood-true-honoured graves
    Are far more blessèd than base life of slaves.
                                              Exeunt.

36. blood-true-honoured] *Q* (blood-true-honour'd); blood! true-honour'd
Dilke.

---

32. Nunquam . . . esse] i.e., It can never be that [for courage there is no
place]. Andrugio cites the first half of *Medea*, 161.

34.] Andrugio's rejection of the Stoic advice to suffer fortune patiently finds
numerous parallels in *A.R.*, e.g., v.iii.59–63, 'Resolved hearts, time curtails
night, Opportunity shakes us his foretop. Steel your thoughts, sharp your
resolve, embolden your spirit, grasp your swords, alarum mischief, and with
an undaunted brow out-scout the grim opposition of most menacing peril.'

36. *blood-true-honoured*] (graves) made truly honourable by the shedding of
blood, i.e., by those who die an honourable death in being true to their
blood-line.

Act V

Enter BALURDO, *a* Painter *with two pictures, and* DILDO.

Balurdo. And are you a painter, sir? Can you draw, can you
draw?
Painter. Yes, sir.
Balurdo. Indeed, la! Now so can my father's fore-horse. And
are these the workmanship of your hands?   5
Painter. I did limn them.
Balurdo. 'Limn them'. A good word, 'limn them'. Whose picture is this? [*Examining the portrait*] '*Anno Domini 1599.*'
Believe me, Master Anno Domini was of a good settled
age when you limned him—1599 years old! Let's see   10
the other, '*Aetatis suae twenty-four*'—by'r Lady, he is
somewhat younger. Belike *Master Aetatis suae* was *Anno
Domini*'s son.

Act V] *ACTVS QUINTVS Q.*   Sc. i] *Dilke; not in Q.*   4. fore-horse]
Dilke; forehore horse *Q.*

0.1. Painter] Paintings figure largely in another play of the 1599 period at
Paul's. In *The Wisdom of Doctor Dodypoll*, 1.i.o.1–3, occurs the direction: '*A
curtain drawn, Earl Lassinbergh is discovered like a painter painting Lucilia, who
sits working on a piece of cushion work.*' Later, in the same act, 70–1, Haunce
says of the painter, 'We have the finest painter here at board wages that ever
made fleur-de-lis.'
    4. *fore-horse*] the foremost horse in a team, the leader. Balurdo's feeble joke
is that since a horse can 'draw' (pull) a load, an artist who 'draws' (paints) is no
better than a horse.
    6. *limn*] paint.
    7. *'Limn them'*] Balurdo is frequently in the habit of savouring words so as to
draw attention to them. Here he may be commenting on 'limn' because of its
association with 'limb'. Cf. 'proclivity', l. 15 below.
    8. Anno Domini] In the Year of the Lord. Balurdo is assuming that
'Domini' refers to the 'master' of a household, so that one of the portraits is of
the other's father.
    9. *settled*] established (in a way of life), *O.E.D.*, *ppl.a.*8.
    11. Aetatis suae] In the [twenty-fourth] year of his age. In 1599 Marston was
in his twenty-fourth year and this portrait is almost certainly of him.
    12–13. Anno Domini*'s son*] There is no indication in the text as to the

143

Painter. Is not your master a—

Dildo. He hath a little proclivity to him.   15

Painter. 'Proclivity', good youth? I thank you for your courtly
    'proclivity'.

Balurdo. Approach, good sir. I did send for you to draw me a
    device, an impresa, by synecdoche, a mot. By Phoebus'
    crimson taffeta mantle, I think I speak as melodiously—   20
    look you, sir, how think you on't? I would have you
    paint me for my device a good fat leg of ewe mutton
    swimming in stewed broth of plums. [*To Page*] Boy,
    keel your mouth; it runs over.—And the word shall be,
    'Hold my dish whilst I spill my pottage.' Sure, in my   25
    conscience, 'twould be the most sweet device, now.

Painter. 'Twould scent of kitchen-stuff too much.

Balurdo. God's nigs, now I remember me, I ha' the rarest
    device in my head that ever breathed. Can you paint me
    a drivelling, reeling song and let the word be, 'Uh'?   30

Painter. A belch?

Balurdo. O, no, no—'Uh'. Paint me 'Uh', or nothing.

Painter. It cannot be done, sir, but by a seeming kind of
    drunkenness.

---

identity of the *Anno Domini* portrait, but Marston at twenty-four could
possibly have been considered the 'son' of William Stanley, aged forty-two in
1599, who was the financier of the revival at Paul's. To introduce portraits of
both the financial backer and the dramatist would be useful publicity (see
Introduction pp. 43, 47).

18–19. *a device*] an emblematic figure or design, used as a heraldic bearing
and frequently accompanied by a motto, *O.E.D.*, 9. *spec.*

19. *impresa*] A synonym for 'device'.

mot] motto.

19–20. *Phoebus' . . . mantle*] An allusion to Apollo as sun god.

24. *keel*] cool (i.e, the page is open-mouthed, like a pot boiling over). Cf.
What You Will, A2, 'thy brain boils, keel it, keel it, or all the fat's in the fire.'
To 'keel' a pot was to stir it gently to prevent it boiling over.

word] motto. Cf. Jonson's *Every Man Out*, III.iv.86, 'Let the word be, "Not
without mustard".'

25. *Hold . . . pottage*] Proverbial, Dent D369.

pottage] a thick soup; Esau sold his birthright to Jacob for a 'pottage of
lentils', Genesis, XXV.34.

33–4. *a seeming . . . drunkenness*] i.e., by representing drunkenness visually.
Balurdo's request that the painter depict him 'a drivelling, reeling song', and
'uh or nothing', may be compared with the painter scene in the Fourth
Addition to *The Spanish Tragedy*, III.xiia, where Hieronimo asks 'Canst paint

Balurdo. No? Well, let me have a good massy ring, with your   35
   own posy graven in it, that must sing a small treble,
   word for word, thus:
            And if you will my true lover be
            Come follow me to the greenwood.
Painter. O Lord, sir, I cannot make a picture sing.   40
Balurdo. Why? 'Slid, I have seen painted things sing as sweet.
   But I have't will tickle it for a conceit, i'faith.

                Enter FELICE *and* ALBERTO.

Alberto. O dear Felice, give me thy device.
   How shall I purchase love of Rosaline?
Felice. 'Swill, flatter her soundly.   45
Alberto. Her love is such I cannot flatter her,
   But with my utmost vehemence of speech
   I have adored her beauties.
Felice. Hast writ good, moving, unaffected rhymes to her?
Alberto. O, yes, Felice, but she scorns my wit.   50
Felice. Hast thou presented her with sumptuous gifts?

---

me a tear, or a wound, a groan, or a sigh?' (109–11), '. . . Canst paint a doleful
cry?' (128), and the painter (Bazardo) responds, 'Seemingly, sir' (129).
   35. *massy*] solid (gold); cf. IV.i.37.
   36. *posy*] the motto inscribed inside the ring.
   37. *word for word*] Balurdo insists on accuracy and then, inaccurately, cites
lines from two popular songs.
   38–9. And . . . greenwood] The second of these lines is taken from the
refrain to 'In Sherwood lived stout Robin Hood', which runs 'Hey jolly robin,
Ho jolly robin / Hey jolly Robin Hood, / Love finds out me as well as
thee, / To follow me, follow me to the greenwood' (published by Robert
Jones, in *Fourth Book of Airs*, 1609); cf. Ophelia's song 'For bonny sweet robin
is all my joy', *Ham.*, IV.v.183–95. Balurdo's first line may be adapted from the
popular song, 'How should I your true love know / From another one?', which
is also sung by Ophelia, *Ham.*, IV.v.23–6. See F. W. Sternfeld, *Music in
Shakespearian Tragedy*, London: Routledge and Kegan Paul, 1963, pp. 71,
59.
   41. *'Slid*] God's eyelid.
   painted things] courtly ladies.
   42. *I have't . . . conceit*] I have that (i.e., an idea for the device) which will
ensure a satisfactory result.
   conceit] ingenious notion.
   43. *device*] opinion, advice, *O.E.D.*, 4.
   45. *'Swill*] His (God's) will.
   46. *Her love . . . her*] i.e., The way she loves (with her ironic wit), she cannot
be flattered (because she will see through it).

F

Alberto. Alas, my fortunes are too weak to offer them.
Felice. O then I have it—I'll tell thee what to do.
Alberto. What, good Felice?
Felice. Go and hang thyself! I say, go hang thyself.   55
     If that thou canst not give, go hang thyself.
     I'll rhyme thee dead, or verse thee to the rope.
     How think'st thou of a poet that sung thus:
     Munera sola pacant, sola addunt munera formam;
     Munere solicites Pallada, Cypris erit.   60
     Munera, munera?
Alberto. I'll go and breathe my woes unto the rocks
     And spend my grief upon the deafest seas.
     I'll weep my passion to the senseless trees
     And load most solitary air with plaints,   65
     For woods, trees, sea, or rocky Apennine
     Is not so ruthless as my Rosaline.
     Farewell, dear friend, expect no more of me;
     Here ends my part in this love's comedy.
                         Exeunt ALBERTO [*and the*] Painter.

69.1. s.d.] *Halliwell subst.; Exit Alb. / Exit Paynter. Q.*

---

57. *I'll . . . rope*] D. K. Hendrick (*The Explicator*, 35: 1976, 15–16) points out that this is an allusion to Archilochus of Paros (*c.* 714–676 B.C.). Archilochus had been a suitor to Neobule, one of the daughters of Lycambes, who first approved of the betrothal but afterwards denied his permission for the marriage. In revenge, Archilochus attacked the whole family in a satiric poem of such power that the daughters of Lycambes are said to have hanged themselves for shame.

59–61. Munera . . . munera] 'Gifts alone subdue, gifts alone bestow beauty; should you solicit Pallas [Athene] with a gift, she will become a Venus [a beauty]. Gifts, gifts.' The use of the word 'Cypris' for 'Venus' establishes that this is essentially a post-classical construct. It is an elegiac couplet, made up of a dactylic hexameter followed by an elegiac pentameter and is, of course, a cynical seduction poem (i.e., bribe a beauty and she will become a passionate lover). It is probably Marston's own composition, perhaps created from fragments of classical and post-classical sources, e.g., Ovid, *Ars Amatoria*, I.69, 'sua munera mater addidit' and Statius, *Silvae*, 5.i.51, 'laudantur pulchrae . . . munere formae'.

62–9.] Possibly a faint recollection of Orlando's verses in praise of Rosalind, *A.Y.L.*, III.ii.78–85. This speech by Alberto is the actor's farewell to the audience in that character; he now appears only as Andrugio, in which part he had previously doubled; see Ind.21–3.

66. *Apennine*] the mountain chain running throughout Italy from north to south.

Felice. Now, master Balurdo, whither are you going, ha?   70
Balurdo. Signor Felice, how do you, faith? And by my troth,
     how do you?
Felice. Whither art thou going, bully?
Balurdo. And, as heaven help me, how do you? How do you,
     i'faith, hee?   75
Felice. Whither art going, man?
Balurdo. O God, to the court. I'll be willing to give you grace
     and good countenance, if I may but see you in the
     presence.
Felice. O, to court? Farewell.   80
Balurdo. If you see one in a yellow taffeta doublet cut upon
     carnation velour, a green hat, a blue pair of velvet hose,
     a gilt rapier, and an orange-tawny pair of worsted silk
     stockings, that's I, that's I.
Felice. Very good, farewell.   85
Balurdo. Ho, you shall know me as easily—I ha' bought me a
     new green feather with a red sprig. You shall see my
     wrought shirt hang out at my breeches. You shall know
     me.
Felice. Very good, very good, farewell.   90
Balurdo. Marry, in the masque 'twill be somewhat hard, but if
     you hear anybody speak so wittily that he makes all the
     room laugh—that's I, that's I. Farewell, good signor.
                                                    [*Exeunt.*]

---

75. ifaith, hee?] ifaithhe? *Q.*   82. velour] valure *Q.*

73. *bully*] good friend; cf. II.i.5.
75. *hee*] *Q*'s 'ifaithhe' could simply be an error for 'ifaithe', but the 'ha' at
the end of l. 70 makes it likely that 'hee' is intended, to parallel the remarks.
77–8. *give you . . . countenance*] speak favourably of you and help you.
81–2. *yellow . . . velour*] i.e., tailored in such a way that the red velvet shows
through the yellow silk; 'cut', *O.E.D.*, *ppl.a.*3. Cf. *What You Will*, D2v, 'row
with the tide, / Pursue the cut, the fashion of the age.'
82. *hose*] literally 'stockings', but here equivalent to 'trousers'.
83. *orange-tawny*] dull yellowish-brown.
worsted] finely woven.
87. *sprig*] a spray-shaped decoration, probably a brooch, *O.E.D.*, *sb.*^{2}4.
88. *wrought*] embroidered, *O.E.D.*, *ppl.a.*3.b. Cf. *Every Man Out*, IV.vi.117–
18, where Fastidious Brisk boasts of 'having bound up my wound with a piece
of my wrought shirt'.
91. *hard*] i.e., difficult to recognise me.

[Sc. ii]

Enter FOROBOSCO, CASTILIO, *a* Boy *carrying a gilt harp,*
PIERO, MELLIDA *in night apparel,* ROSALINE, FLAVIA,
[*and*] *two* Pages.

Piero. Advance the music's prize! Now, cap'ring wits,
Rise to your highest mount. Let choice delight
Garland the brow of this triumphant night.
Forobosco. [*Aside*] 'Sfoot, 'a sits like Lucifer himself.
Rosaline. Good sweet Duke, first let their voices strain for   5
music's prize. Give me the golden harp. Faith, with
your favour, I'll be umpiress.
Piero. Sweet niece, content. [*To Pages*] Boys, clear your voice
and sing.

[*First Page*] *sings.*

Rosaline. By this gold, I had rather have a servant with a short   10
nose and thin hair than have such a high-stretched mini-
kin voice.
Piero. Fair niece, your reason?
Rosaline. By the sweets of love, I should fear extremely that he
were an eunuch.   15
Castilio. Spark spirit, how like you his voice?
Rosaline. 'Spark spirit, how like you his voice'?—So help me,
youth, thy voice squeaks like a dry cork shoe. Come,
come, let's hear the next.

[*Second Page*] *sings.*

Sc. ii] *Hunter; not in* Q.   4. S.P. *Forobosco*] *Hunter; speech continued to Piero
in* Q.   6. prize] *1633*; price Q.   9.1. *First Page sings*] *Dilke subst.*; 1.
CANTAT. Q.   11. thin] *J & N*; a thinne Q.   14. sweets] *Hunter*; sweete
Q.   19.1 *Second Page sings*] *Dilke subst.*; 2. CANTAT. Q.

1. *the music's prize*] i.e., the gilt harp.
4. 'Sfoot] God's foot.
7. *umpiress*] a female umpire. The first use, in print, of this feminine form.
11–12. *minikin*] shrill.
16. *Spark*] smart (with the implication of affectation), *O.E.D.*, sb.^{2}4, i.e.,
'brilliant wit'.
18. *squeaks*] Cf. *Jack Drum*, G4v, 'the howling dog / Shall be more gracious
than thy squeaking voice.'

Piero. Trust me, a good strong mean. Well sung, my boy.   20

                    Enter BALURDO.

Balurdo. Hold, hold, hold! Are ye blind? Could you not see my
    voice coming for the harp? An I knock not division on the
    head, take hence the harp, make me a slip, and let me go
    but for ninepence. [*To Piero*] Sir, mark! [*To Rosaline*]
    Strike up for Master Balurdo!   25

                    [*Balurdo*] *sings.*

Judgement, gentlemen, judgement! Was't not above
line?

24. Sir, mark!] *This ed.*; Sir Marke, *Q*; Sir Mark *Hunter*; Saint Mark! *J & N.*
25.1. BALURDO *sings*] *Keltie*; 3. CANTAT. *Q.*

20. *mean*] the intermediate part in a harmony, a tenor or alto, *O.E.D.*,
sb.^{2}2.a.
    22–3. *An . . . head*] If I do not render the music to perfection (and thus take
the prize).
    23–4. *make me . . . ninepence*] i.e., (If I do not sing perfectly,) pay me in
counterfeit money and throw me out with only a few coppers.
    23. *a slip*] a counterfeit coin. Robert Greene describes 'a slip' in *Thieves
Falling Out*, 1637, E4, 'he went and got him certain slips, which are counterfeit
pieces of money, being brass, and covered over with silver, which the common
people call slips'. When detected, slips were nailed to a shop counter. Cf.
A.R., I.iii.19–20, 'your nose is a copper nose and must be nailed up for a slip',
and Skialetheia, 1598, satire 2, 'Is he not fond then which a slip receives / For
current money? She which thee deceives / With copper guilt is but a slip, and
she / Will one day show thee a touch as slippery.'
    24. *Sir, mark!*] i.e., Sir, take note—pay special attention to me. When
Balurdo enters (20.1), Piero has just expressed considerable approval for the
second singer, 'a good strong mean. Well sung, my boy' (l. 20), and the
assumption is that Balurdo overhears this commendation as he enters. Balurdo
assumes that Piero will determine the winner of the contest despite Rosaline's
claim (l. 7) that she will be 'umpiress', for Piero is the senior person present.
Balurdo, then, calls upon Rosaline to play the harp to accompany him, as she
has apparently done for the two previous contestants.
    25. *Strike*] touch or play (the harp), *O.E.D.*, *v.*29.d.
    26. *Judgement, gentlemen*] Balurdo gives the impression that he is appealing
to the courtiers (and perhaps also to the audience at large) to show, by their
applause, that he is the winner. The 'Silver Fiddlestick' to which he refers
(30–1) immediately after his song may be purely imaginary (and is, of course,
introduced to make a bawdy jest), but it may have been real, and Balurdo may
have used it to conduct his own accompaniment.
    above line] above the (written) line of the stave; i.e., Balurdo claims that he
has sung the song in a manner beyond the strict requirements of the music,

I appeal to your mouths that heard my song:
[*Sings*] *Do me right and dub me knight, Balurdo.*
Rosaline. Kneel down, and I'll dub thee Knight of the Golden
  Harp.   30
Balurdo. Indeed, la, do, and I'll make you Lady of the Silver
  Fiddlestick.
Rosaline. Come, kneel, kneel.

Enter a Page *to* BALURDO [*to carry the harp*].

Balurdo. [*Accepting the harp from Rosaline*]
  My troth, I thank you. It hath never a whistle in't?
Rosaline. [*To Mellida*] Nay, good sweet coz, raise up your   35
  drooping eyes. An I were at the point of 'To have and to
  hold from this day forward', I would be ashamed to look
  thus lumpish. What, my pretty coz, 'tis but the loss of an
  odd maidenhead. Shall's dance? Thou art so sad. Hark

O.E.D., *sb.*² II.7.b. There is probably also the idea of winning a game or
contest intended, i.e., Balurdo has got the ball over the net or has passed the
test.
  28. Do ... knight] This is a version of the concluding phrase of the catch
'Monsieur Mingo', based on Orlando di Lasso's 'Un jour vis un foulon'
(published in *Mellange*, 1570). The same song may be alluded to in *A.R.*,
I.iii.66 and it also occurs in *2H4*, v.iii.73–5, with 'Samingo' in place of
'Balurdo'. See F. W. Sternfeld, 'Lasso's music for Shakespeare's "samingo"',
Sh. Q., 9 (1958) 105–16. Cf. Thomas Nashe's *Summer's Last Will and
Testament*, 1592, where Bacchus and his companions enter singing, 'Monsieur
Mingo, for quaffing doth surpass, / In cup, in can, or glass. / God Bacchus do
me right, / And dub me knight Domingo', *Q* 1600, D–F. Shortly afterwards
Bacchus expresses irritation by the use of the expletive 'A fiddlestick', and the
company then sing once again, 'Monsieur Mingo for quaffing did surpass, / In
cup, in can, or glass', concluding with the cry, 'God Bacchus do him right and
dub him knight.' Bacchus duly knights Will Summer 'with the black Jack', as
Sir Robert Tosspot. The scene concludes with the entire company exiting
while singing 'Monsieur Mingo'.
  31–2. make ... Silver Fiddlestick] a bawdy pun; i.e., make you the lady
(lover) of my silver baton.
  34. It ... in't?] i.e., Is this an instrument that I can blow?
  36–7. 'To ... forward'] The moment of public commitment of taking to
wife or husband in the marriage service.
  38. lumpish] dejected. Cf. IV.i.185–6, 'She hath a freckled face, / A low
forehead, and a lumpish eye.'
  39. odd] single, unique, *O.E.D.*, *a.*II.5.
  Shall's] shall we.

SC II]   ANTONIO AND MELLIDA   151

in thine ear—I was about to say—but I'll forbear.   40
[*Shouts offstage.*]
Balurdo. I come, I come! More than most honeysuckle-sweet
ladies, pine not for my presence. I'll return in pomp.
Well spoke, Sir Geoffrey Balurdo. As I am a true knight,
I feel honourable eloquence begin to grope me already.
Exeunt [BALURDO *and the* Page.]
Piero. Faith, mad niece, I wonder when thou wilt marry?   45
Rosaline. Faith, kind uncle, when men abandon jealousy, for-
sake taking of tobacco, and cease to wear their beards so
rudely long. O, to have a husband with a mouth continually smoking, with a bush of furze on the ridge of his
chin, ready still to slop into his foaming chaps! Ah, 'tis   50
more than most intolerable.
Piero. Nay, faith, sweet niece, I was mighty strong in thought
we should have shut up night with an old comedy: The
Prince of Milan shall have Mellida, and thou shouldst
have—   55
Rosaline. Nobody, good sweet uncle. I tell you, sir, I have
thirty-nine servants, and my monkey—that makes the
fortieth. Now, I love all of them lightly for something,

40. thine] *Dilke*; mine *Q.*   40.1. S.D.] *Hunter subst.*   44.1 *Exeunt*] *This
ed.; Exit Q.*

39–40. *Shall's . . . forbear*] These two lines could be rearranged as a couplet,
i.e., 'Shall's . . . ear / I . . . forbear', but in this play Marston's dialogue often
hovers between prose and verse (e.g., v.ii.81–94); sometimes prose is versified
and, at times, verse is unevenly metrical, e.g., Mellida's speech at IV.i.207–13.
41–2. *More . . . ladies*] you ladies who are more sweet than the sweetest
honeysuckle.
44. *grope me*] taking hold of my thoughts, *O.E.D.*, *v.*4.b.
47. *tobacco*] Rosaline has already declared her detestation for the tobacco
habit, I.i.126–8: 'A great tobacco taker too—that's flat, / For his eyes look as
if they had been hung / In the smoke of his nose.'
48–51. *O . . . intolerable*] Cf. *M. Ado*, II.i.27–9, 'Lord! I could not endure a
husband with a beard on his face; I had rather lie in the woollen.'
49. *a bush of furze*] a spiny evergreen shrub, with yellow flowers.
50. *slop . . . chaps*] i.e., drool until his lips and beard are foamy.
chaps] jaws.
54. *Milan*] Galeazzo is the son of the Duke of Florence. The error may, in
fact, derive from Marston's use of his historical sources, for Galeazzo Maria
was the son of Francesco Sforza, Duke of Milan; see 'Sources', p. 17.
56–8.] Cf. Rosaline's remark to Mellida, 'By my nine-and-thirtieth servant,
sweet, / Thou art in love', I.i.114–15.

but affect none of them seriously for anything. One's a
passionate fool, and he flatters me above belief; the   60
second's a testy ape, and he rails at me beyond reason;
the third's as grave as some censor, and he strokes up his
mustachios three times, and makes six plots of set faces
before he speaks one wise word; the fourth's as dry as
the bur of an artichoke; the fifth paints, and hath always   65
a good colour for what he speaks; the sixth—
Piero. Stay, stay, sweet niece, what makes you thus suspect
young gallants' worth?
Rosaline. O, when I see one wear a periwig, I dread his hair;
another wallow in a great slop, I mistrust the proportion   70
of his thigh; and wears a ruffled boot, I fear the fashion
of his leg. Thus something in each thing, one trick in
everything makes me mistrust imperfection in all parts;
and there's the full point of my addiction.

> *The cornets sound a sennet. Enter* GALEAZZO, MAZZAGENTE,
> *and* BALURDO *in masquery.*

Piero. The room's too scant. Boys, stand in there, close.   75
Mellida. [*To Galeazzo*] In faith, fair sir, I am too sad to dance.
Piero. How's that, how's that? Too sad? By heaven, dance,
    And grace him, too, or—go to, I say no more.

---

62. *censor*] hostile critic.
63. *makes . . . faces*] i.e., like an actor rehearsing a part, he creates (plots) a
variety of poses (sets or fixes his face). Cf. III.ii.118.5–6.
65. *bur*] dry husk.
65–6. *paints . . . colour*] i.e., uses make-up and varies it, and his argument,
according to what impression he wishes to make. The metaphor is extended by
the deliberate ambiguity in the word 'paints', which means 'to use cosmetics',
'to depict in words', and 'to flatter'.
70. *great slop*] very large and wide baggy breeches, *O.E.D.*, *sb.*¹4.*pl.*
71. *ruffled boot*] wide, leather boot with fringed or scalloped top, usually
turned down to display embroidered stockings.
74. *full point*] complete catalogue.
addiction] inclination, liking.
74.2. in masquery] i.e., masked and costumed for the masque. Cf. *A.R.*,
V.v.0.2, '*Enter* ANTONIO, PANDULPHO, *and* ALBERTO *in maskery.*'
75. *scant*] small, limited. Complaints about the restricted size of the Paul's
stage are not uncommon; cf. *What You Will*, A3, 'for, good faith, the stage is so
very little', and *Jack Drum*, v.i.(H), (after a galliard), 'Good Boy, i'faith, I
would thou had'st more room.'

Mellida. [*Examining Galeazzo's device*]
    A burning glass, the word, *Splendente Phoebo*.
    'Tis too curious; I conceit it not.   80
Galeazzo. Faith, I'll tell thee. I'll no longer burn than you'll
    shine and smile upon my love. For look ye, fairest, by
    your pure sweets,
    I do not dote upon your excellence,
    And, faith, unless you shed your brightest beams   85
    Of sunny valour and acceptive grace
    Upon my tender love, I do not burn.
    Marry, but shine, and I'll reflect your beams
    With fervent ardour.
    Faith, I would be loath to flatter thee, fair soul, because 90
    I love, not dote; court like thy husband, which thy
    father swears tomorrow morn I must be. This is all, and
    now from henceforth, trust me, Mellida, I'll not speak
    one wise word to thee more.
Mellida. I trust ye.   95
Galeazzo. By my troth, I'll speak pure fool to thee now.
Mellida. You will speak the liker yourself.
Galeazzo. Good faith, I'll accept of the coxcomb, so you will
    not refuse the bauble.
Mellida. Nay, good sweet, keep them both; I am enamoured of 100
    neither.
Galeazzo. Go to, I must take you down for this. Lend me your
    ear.   [*They step aside.*]

79. Splendente Phoebo] 'While the Sun God shines.' Phoebus is a poetic
appellation for Apollo, but the word is simply Greek for 'the radiant'.
    80. *curious*] obscure, intricate.
    conceit] understand.
    91. *court like thy husband*] i.e., pay court, like one who aspires to be your
husband.
    96. *fool*] (lover's) nonsense.
    98. *coxcomb*] fool's cap.
    99. *bauble*] the fantastically carved stick, surmounted by ass's ears, carried
by the Court Jester as a badge of office. Two other implications are also
intended—firstly, Galeazzo is insisting that Mellida agree to accept him as a
lover (not refusing his 'bauble') and, secondly, with the Q reading 'bable', he is
asking her to listen to his lover's confidences ('speak pure fool'). Cf. *R&J*, 'this
drivelling love is like a great natural that runs lolling up and down to hide his
bauble in a hole', II.iv.89–91.
    102. *take you down*] Both 'take you to task' and 'take you to bed'.
    102–3. *Lend . . . ear*] Proverbial, Dent E18.

Rosaline. [*Examining Mazzagente's device*]
A glow-worm, the word *Splendescit tantum tenebris.*
Mazzagente. O lady, the glow-worm figurates my valour,   105
which shineth brightest in most dark, dismal, and
horrid achievements.
Rosaline. Or, rather, your glow-worm represents your wit,
which only seems to have fire in it, though indeed 'tis
but an *ignis fatuus* and shines only in the dark dead night   110
of fools' admiration.
Mazzagente. Lady, my wit hath spurs, if it were disposed to
ride you.
Rosaline. Faith, sir, your wit's spurs have but walking rowels
—dull, blunt, they will not draw blood. The gentlemen   115
ushers may admit them the presence for any wrong they
can do to ladies.   [*They step aside.*]
Balurdo. Truly, I have strained a note above E la for a device.
Look you, 'tis a fair ruled singing book; the word, *Perfect, if it were pricked.*   120
Flavia. Though you are masked, I can guess who you are by

104. Splendescit . . . tenebris] 'It shines only in the dark.'
105. *figurates*] is an emblem of.
110. ignis fatuus] will o' the wisp.
112–13. *to ride you*] i.e., both 'to challenge you' and 'to make love to you'.
Rosaline's reply suggests that Mazzagente is (physically) an incapable lover,
for his 'spur' is blunt.
114. *walking rowels*] blunt, short wheels on spurs for walking as opposed to
riding.
115–16. *gentlemen ushers*] i.e., the servants who were responsible for
admitting people to the court.
116. *admit them the presence*] admit them to the presence (chamber), i.e.,
allow spurs to be worn in the presence of the Duke.
118. *above E la*] 'E' sung to the note 'la', i.e., above the highest note in the
Hexachord, or old musical scale, which began at G (Wood). Cf. *Blurt, Master
Constable*, E4, 'It shall be your first and finest praise, to sing the note of every
new fashion at first sight and, if you can, to stretch that note above E la.'
119–20. *the word . . . pricked*] Balurdo is unconsciously making a bawdy
joke and further boasting about his singing. 'Word' may mean both 'motto'
and 'the text of a song' (*O.E.D.*, sb.I.I.e.*spec.*), and 'pricked' means notes
written down as opposed to music learnt by heart. He claims, then, to have
sung the song perfectly by heart, without the benefit of the written music, and
the motto of the song book confirms this. His language also suggests that
perfection (a circle) is only completed if it is 'pricked' or entered.
120. pricked] (of the music) 'written down' and 'thrust at' (as a lover).

SC II]   ANTONIO AND MELLIDA   155

your wit. You are not the exquisite Balurdo, the most
rarely shaped Balurdo?
Balurdo. Who, I? No, I am not Sir Geoffrey Balurdo. I am not
as well known by my wit as an alehouse by a red lattice. I   125
am not worthy to love and be beloved of Flavia.
Flavia. I will not scorn to favour such good parts as are applauded in your rarest self.
Balurdo. Truly, you speak wisely and like a gentlewoman of
fourteen years of age. You know the stone called *lapis*;   130
the nearer it comes to the fire the hotter it is. And the
bird which the geometricians call *avis*, the farther it is
from the earth, the nearer it is to the heaven. And love,
the nigher it is to the flame, the more remote—there's a
word, 'remote'—the more remote it is from the frost.   135
Your wit is quick; a little thing pleaseth a young lady,
and a small favour contenteth an old courtier. And so,
sweet mistress, I truss my codpiece point.

[*A flourish sounds;*] *enter* FELICE.

122. *exquisite*] excellent, accomplished, but also 'precious' or affected.
125. *lattice*] window. A red painted window was a common sign for an inn or
alehouse; cf. George Wilkins' *The Miseries of Enforced Marriage*, 1607, D4, 'Be
mild in a tavern; 'tis treason to the red lattice, enemy to their sign post, and
slave to humour.'
127–8.] Flavia's speech is deliberately ambiguous, for it can mean both 'I
am not ashamed to applaud your fine qualities' and 'I will not deign to favour
the parts that are so rare [i.e., seldom found] in you.'
130. *fourteen*] The suggestion that Flavia is actually about fourteen may well
be literally true. Cf. II.i.2 and see *Paul's*, p. 83.
lapis] Latin for 'stone', used generically to refer to a variety of minerals.
This whole passage (129–38) is essentially a parody of Euphuism.
132. *geometricians*] Both 'students of geometry' and 'land surveyors'.
Balurdo is responding ironically with this nonsense to Flavia's disparagement
of his wit (121–3).
avis] Latin for 'bird'.
135. *remote*] removed, set apart. Balurdo once again savours a word of which
he is particularly proud. Cf. 'limn', and 'proclivity', v.i.7, 15.
136. *Your wit is quick*] i.e., you are quick-witted enough to savour my
compliment (and thus please me).
thing] Both 'wit' and 'male member'. Cf. Dent T188, 'Little things are
pretty', and T189, 'Little things catch light minds (please fools)', and also
Volpone, III.iii.9–10, 'your dwarf, he's little and witty, / And every thing, as it
is little, is pretty.'
138. *truss . . . point*] lace up the top of my codpiece (the bagged appendage
on the front of the breeches).

Piero. What might import this flourish? Bring us word.
Felice. Stand away. Here's such company of flyboats hulling   140
about this galleas of greatness that there's no boarding
him. [*To Piero*] Do you hear, yon thing called Duke?
Piero. How now, blunt Felice, what's the news?
Felice. Yonder's a knight hath brought Andrugio's head,
And craves admittance to your chair of state.   145

Cornets sound a sennet; enter ANDRUGIO *in armour.*

Piero. Conduct him with attendance sumptuous;
Sound all the pleasing instruments of joy;
Make triumph, stand on tiptoe whilst we meet.
O sight most gracious, O revenge most sweet!
Andrugio. [*Reading Piero's proclamation*] 'We vow, by the   150
honour of our birth, to recompense any man that bringeth
Andrugio's head with twenty thousand double pistolets and
the endearing to our choicest love.'
Piero. We still with most unmoved resolve confirm
Our large munificence, and here breathe   155
A sad and solemn protestation:
When I recall this vow, O, let our house
Be even commanded, stained, and trampled on,
As worthless rubbish of nobility.
Andrugio. Then, here, Piero, is Andrugio's head,   160
[*Raising his visor*]
Royally casquèd in a helm of steel.

---

154. resolve] *Dilke*; resolu'd *Q.*   160.1. S.D.] *Bullen subst.*

140. *flyboats*] small fast sailing vessels.
hulling] drifting with sails furled.
141. *galleas*] galleon.
boarding] i.e., both 'going on board' (a galleon) and 'making him pay
attention'.
144. *Andrugio's head*] This device, as Hunter suggests, may be derived from
the *Arcadia* where, in the story of the Paphlagonian unkind King, Plexirtus
'having gotten a passport for one that pretended he would put Plexirtus alive
into his hands with the king his brother, he himself (though much
against the minds of the valiant brothers, who rather wished to die in brave
defence) with a rope about his neck barefooted, came to offer himself to the
discretion of Leonatus' (Feuillerat, I:213).
156. *sad*] serious.

Give me thy love, and take it. My dauntless soul
Hath that unbounded vigour in his spirits
That it can bear more rank indignity
With less impatience than thy cankered hate   165
Can sting and venom his untainted worth
With the most viperous sound of malice. Strike!
O, let no glimpse of honour light thy thoughts.
If there be any heat of royal breath
Creeping in thy veins, O, stifle it.   170
Be still thyself, bloody and treacherous!
Fame not thy house with an admirèd act
Of princely pity. Piero, I am come
To soil thy house with an eternal blot
Of savage cruelty. Strike, or bid me strike!   175
I pray my death, that thy ne'er-dying shame
Might live immortal to posterity.
Come, be a princely hangman; stop my breath.
O, dread thou shame no more than I dread death.
Piero. We are amazed, our royal spirits numbed   180
In stiff astonished wonder at thy prowess,
Most mighty, valiant, and high-tow'ring heart.
We blush and turn our hate upon ourselves
For hating such an unpeered excellence.
I joy my state, him whom I loathed before   185
That now I honour, love, nay more, adore.

The still flutes sound a mournful sennet. Enter [LUCIO *with*]
a coffin.

But stay. What tragic spectacle appears?

186.1. LUCIO *with*] *Hunter; not in Q.*

---

162. *it*] (my) head.
172. *Fame*] make famous, or, 'defame'.
184. *unpeered*] unequalled, unrivalled. Cf. *A.R.*, I.i.10, 'unpeered mischief'.
185–6. *I joy ... honour*] I rejoice in my state that I now honour him (Andrugio) whom I previously loathed.
186.1. still flutes] probably recorders, instruments with a soft tone. Marston is fond of simulated, surprise recoveries from apparent death. Cf. *Jack Drum*, D2, '*Mammon.* Dead, Kate. Dead, Kate. Dead is the boy [Pasquil], / That kept rich Mammon from his joy. *Mammon sings, 'Lantara, etc.' Pasquil riseth and striketh him.*' See also 223 below.

Whose body bear you in that mournful hearse?
Lucio. The breathless trunk of young Antonio.
Mellida. Antonio! Ay me, my lord, my love, my—   190
Andrugio. Sweet precious issue of most honoured blood,
    Rich hope, ripe virtue, O untimely loss!
    [*To Lucio*] Come hither, friend. Prithee, do not weep.
    Why, I am glad he's dead. He shall not see
    His father's vanquished by his enemy,   195
    Even in princely honour. Nay, prithee, speak.
    How died the wretched boy?
Lucio. My lord—
Andrugio. I hope he died yet like my son, i'faith.
Lucio. Alas, my lord—   200
Andrugio. He died unforced, I trust, and valiantly.
Lucio. Poor gentleman, being—
Andrugio. Did his hand shake or his eye look dull,
    His thoughts reel, fearful when he struck the stroke?
    An if they did, I'll rend them out the hearse,   205
    Rip up his cerecloth, mangle his bleak face,
    That when he comes to heaven the powers divine
    Shall ne'er take notice that he was my son.
    I'll quite disclaim his birth. Nay, prithee, speak.
    An 'twere not hooped with steel, my breast would break.   210
Mellida. O, that my spirit in a sigh could mount
    Into the sphere where thy sweet soul doth rest!
Piero. O, that my tears, bedewing thy wan cheek,
    Could make new spirit sprout in thy cold blood!

194–5. Why ... dead. He ... see / His father's vanquished] *Hunter subst.*;
Why, ... deade, he ... see / His fathers vanquisht, *Q.*

---

189. *breathless*] with no breath of life.
201. *unforced*] i.e., Andrugio is anxious to determine that Antonio died the death of a Stoic, a noble suicide.
205. *An if*] if.
206. *cerecloth*] shroud.
mangle his bleak face] Andrugio vows to physically disfigure Antonio, if Antonio has disgraced (disfigured) the reputation of his blood-line by commiting suicide in a cowardly manner.
210. *hooped with steel*] Andrugio is still in armour.
212. *sphere*] Mellida is presumably referring to the Primum Mobile or highest sphere of heaven, where God and the saints resided.

Balurdo. Verily, he looks as pitifully as a poor John. As I am a   215
    true knight, I could weep like a stoned horse.
Andrugio. [*To Piero*] Villain, 'tis thou hast murderèd my son.
    Thy unrelenting spirit, thou black dog,
    That took'st no passion of his fatal love,
    Hath forced him give his life untimely end.   220
Piero. O, that my life, her love, my dearest blood
    Would but redeem one minute of his breath!
Antonio. [*Arising from the coffin*]
    I seize that breath. Stand not amazed, great states;
    I rise from death, that never lived till now.
    Piero, keep thy vow, and I enjoy   225
    More unexpressèd height of happiness
    Than power of thought can reach. If not, lo, here
    There stands my tomb and here a pleasing stage.
    Most wished spectators of my tragedy,
    To this end have I feigned, that her fair eye,   230
    For whom I lived, might bless me ere I die.
Mellida. Can breath depaint my unconceivèd thoughts?
    Can words describe my infinite delight
    Of seeing thee, my lord Antonio?
    O, no! Conceit, breath, passion, words be dumb,   235
    Whilst I instil the dew of my sweet bliss
    In the soft pressure of a melting kiss.
                                            [*She embraces him.*]

222.1. S.D.] *Bullen subst.*

215. *poor John*] salted or dried hake. Cf. *Blurt, Master Constable*, B3v, 'What
meat eats the Spaniard? / Dried pilchards and poor John.'
216. *stoned*] gelded. The horse weeps for its lost manhood. Cf. *A.R.*,
I.iii.32–3, 'I'll carry for my device my grandfather's great stone-horse flinging
up his head and jerking out his left leg; the word, *Wighy Purt*', but here the
horse is not yet gelded.
219. *passion of*] compassion on.
223. *I ... breath*] i.e., I attest your words.
states] kings, rulers (i.e., Piero and Andrugio).
224. *never lived*] i.e., Antonio has never been fully alive until now (when he
is reunited with Mellida and Andrugio, and reconciled with Piero).
226. *unexpressèd*] inexpressible.
232. *depaint*] portray in words.
235. *Conceit*] thought.
236. *I instil ... bliss*] i.e., an extravagant way of saying that, with the
moisture of her lips, she will seal their reunion in a kiss.

Sic, sic iuvat ire sub umbras.
Piero. Fair son—now I'll be proud to call thee son—
　Enjoy me thus. [*He embraces him.*] My very breast is
　　thine;   240
　Possess me freely, I am wholly thine.
Antonio. Dear father!
Andrugio. Sweet son, sweet son—I can speak no more—
　My joy's passion flows above the shore
　And chokes the current of my speech.   245
Piero. [*To Galeazzo*] Young Florence' prince, to you my lips
　　must beg
　For a remittance of your interest.
Galeazzo. In your fair daughter? With all my thought.
　So help me, faith, the naked truth I'll unfold:
　He that was ne'er hot will soon be cold.   250
Piero. No man else makes claim unto her?
Mazzagente. The valiant speak truth in brief: no.
Balurdo. Truly, for Sir Geoffrey Balurdo, he disclaims to have
　had anything in her.
Piero. Then here I give her to Antonio.   255
　[*To Andrugio*] Royal, valiant, most respected prince,
　Let's clip our hands. I'll thus observe my vow.
　I promised twenty thousand double pistolets,
　With the endearing to my dearest love,
　To him that brought thy head. Thine be the gold   260
　To solemnise our houses' unity.
　My love be thine, the all I have be thine.
　Fill us fresh wine. The form we'll take by this:

238. Sic ... umbras] 'Thus, thus it is my joy to descend to the shades beneath' (or, as Loeb has it, 'I go gladly into the dark'), Virgil, *Aeneid*, IV.660. The same line is cited by Hieronimo in *The Spanish Tragedy*, II.v.78.
239. *son*] son-in-law.
247. *For ... interest*] i.e., for giving up the claim to which you have a legal right.
250. *hot ... cold*] The phrase 'hot love is soon cold' is proverbial, Dent L483.
254. *anything in her*] i.e., Balurdo disclaims any legal right to Mellida, and (perhaps unwittingly) denies that he has had any physical relationship with her (anything in her).
257. *clip*] clasp.
263. *form*] formal ratification (of the unity of their houses).

We'll drink a health while they two sip a kiss.
[*A health is drunk*; *Antonio and Mellida embrace.*]
Now there remains no discord that can sound   265
Harsh accents to the ear of our accord;
So please you, niece, to match?
Rosaline. Troth, uncle, when my sweet-faced coz hath told me
how she likes the thing called wedlock, maybe I'll take a
survey of the check-roll of my servants, and he that hath   270
the best parts of, I'll prick him down for my husband.
Balurdo. [*To Piero*] For passion of love now, remember me to
my mistress, Lady Rosaline, when she is pricking down
the good parts of her servants. As I am a true knight, I
grow stiff. I shall carry it.   275
Piero. I will.
Sound Lydian wires! Once make a pleasing note
On nectar streams of your sweet airs to float.
Antonio. Here ends the comic crosses of true love.
O, may the passage most successful prove!   280
                                              [*Exeunt.*]

[*THE END.*]

267. you] *Dilke*; your *Q*.   280.2 *THE END*] *FINIS Q*.
───
264. *sip a kiss*] Cf. *Jack Drum*, C4v, 'I did but softly sip / The roseal juice of
your reviving breath.' The phrase 'sip a kiss' is probably derived from the
Latin tag 'oscula libare'.
270. *check-roll*] list. Halliwell cites the Additions to the Ordinances made at
Eltham in the reign of Henry VIII: 'Item, the said clerks-comptrollers shall
make for every quarter in the year, a roll of parchment that shall be called the
check-roll, which shall contain the names of all them which shall be of the
ordinary and within the check of the household.'
271. *prick*] mark (with double entendre). This double entendre is
anticipated by 'best parts' (271). It is continued (perhaps unwares) by Balurdo
with 'pricking' (273), 'good parts' (274), and 'grow stiff' (275).
277. *Sound Lydian wires*] Play soft and gentle music.
Once] once and for all.
277–8. *Once . . . float*] i.e., As soon as you commence the music by striking
the right note to please us, your music will float on streams of nectar.
280. *the passage*] the exchange of vows, the marriage, and the course of
events (the reconciliation), *O.E.D.*, *sb*.III.13 and b.

[Enter] Epilogue [ANDRUGIO].

Gentlemen, though I remain an armed epilogue, I stand not as a
peremptory challenger of desert, either for him that composed
the comedy or for us that acted it, but a most submissive sup-
pliant for both. What imperfection you have seen in us, leave
with us and we'll amend it; what hath pleased you, take with   5
you and cherish it. You shall not be more ready to embrace anything commendable than we will endeavour to amend all things
reprovable. What we are is by your favour. What we shall be
rests all in your applausive encouragements.

                                                    Exit.

0.1. Epilogue] Epilogus *Q.*

1. *armed*] It is probably Andrugio who delivers the Epilogue, since he is
fully 'casquèd in a helm of steel' (v.ii.161). In *Poetaster*, Jonson's Prologue is
armed, probably thus mocking Marston's armed Epilogue. Shakespeare, in
turn, has an armed Prologue, 'but not in confidence / Of author's pen or
actor's voice' (23–4), for *Troilus and Cressida*; it has been suggested that this is
an ironic comment on Jonson's usage.

8. *What we are*] such success as we have attained at the present.

9. *your applausive encouragements*] the encouragement that you give us by
applauding. Cf. II.i.111, 'applausive elocuty'.

Glossarial Index to the Commentary

An asterisk before a word or phrase indicates that Marston was, according to the information available to the *O.E.D.*, the first to use this word or phrase in a formal, printed context. Where the commentary lemma is a line(s) reference, the annotation is indexed under a key word(s) from the text.

Marston, Plays of, ed. H H Wood, Vol III. Histriomastic
(Edinburgh, 1939)